Walter Savage Landor, Charles G. (Charles George) Crump

Poems, Dialogues in Verse, and Epigrams

Vol. I

Walter Savage Landor, Charles G. (Charles George) Crump

Poems, Dialogues in Verse, and Epigrams
Vol. I

ISBN/EAN: 9783337158149

Printed in Europe, USA, Canada, Australia, Japan

Cover: Foto ©ninafisch / pixelio.de

More available books at **www.hansebooks.com**

POEMS DIALOGUES IN VERSE AND EPIGRAMS BY WALTER SAVAGE LANDOR EDITED WITH NOTES BY CHARLES G. CRUMP

IN TWO VOLUMES

FIRST VOLUME

DRAMATIC SCENES

LONDON: PRINTED FOR J. M. DENT & CO., AND PUBLISHED BY THEM AT ALDINE HOUSE, 69 GREAT EASTERN STREET. MDCCCXCII.

TABLE OF CONTENTS.

INTRODUCTION.

In his prose writings Walter Savage Landor seems to
have soon found the manner best suited to his thoughts.
The Commentary on Trotter's " Life of Fox " is written
in the same language as that used by him in later life.
" It contains," says Mr Colvin, " his views on men,
books, and governments, set forth in the manner that
was most natural to him, that is, miscellaneously and
without sequence, in a prose, which . . . is at once
condensed and lucid, weighty without emphasis, and
stately without effort or inflation." This is a descrip-
tion of his prose style in the year 1812, and the
words might apply to all the prose that he wrote
during his life. Where he fails in prose, he fails
not in style, but in temper and in discretion; some-
times harping on one topic until the reader is driven
to believe in Canning's perfection from weariness
of abuse, sometimes displaying an absence of any
critical power, startling in a man who had made
criticism part of the business of life. But whatever
the defects of matter and treatment may be, the
language bears the same stamp. It would be easier

to recognise as Landor's a detached passage of his prose, than to do the same for any other modern author, setting aside those cases where style has become a mere mannerism.

But with his verse the case is different. Lines there are in his poems, and even long passages, written with a pen cut from an eagle's feather. But in too many cases the ink has flowed from a humbler quill. He never attained that mastery over verse, which would have made it an instrument fit to express all his thoughts and fancies; for the aptest utterance of his graver and more majestic thoughts the reader must turn to Landor's prose. He was not unaware of this himself. In his prose works there are many passages which show the pride he took in his command of language. Many men have said with Horace, *exegi monumentum aere perennius*. Few have expressed that conviction as majestically as Landor. "What I write," he says in one place, "is not written on slate; and no finger, not that of Time himself, who dips it in the mist of years, can efface it." But of his verse he never speaks so confidently. He ranked himself as the best of living prose writers, but in poetry he felt that there were men living who were his masters. He speaks with indifference of men who borrowed from his prose; he bitterly resented what he believed to be a theft from Gebir, committed by Wordsworth. In a man of Landor's temper this is no small indication that in his inmost heart he mistrusted his success as a poet.

And yet, when this is said, there is more to be added. Landor, though not in the first rank, stands above the second.   Indeed, in his most successful moments he stands alone.   There has never been an English poet capable of the perfection and grace possessed by his shorter poems ; and only one poet since Milton has written blank verse of so majestic and harmonious a sound.   The only modern poem that can be placed beside Gebir in this respect is Hyperion ; Count Julian stands alone.   Could Landor have gone on writing in this vein, he would have won a high station as a poet.

But splendid as these two achievements are, each shows clearly that it is a solitary effort.   In Gebir there are often passages of terrible obscurity ; what is worse, there are instances of what look like perverse disregard of poetic dignity.   The poem is pitched in a majestic vein of thought.   But here and there are fatal touches of burlesque.   When Tamar tells Gebir that the Nymph's feet—

> " resembled those long shells explored
> By him who to befriend his steed's dim sight
> Would blow the pungent powder in his eye,"

the reader can only marvel with De Quincey.   Landor himself cut out the amazing lines which ran—

> " Tamar, who listened still amidst amaze
> Held never thought on progeny."

But he did so because the passage contained a panegyric on Napoleon, and not because he saw the badness of them.   Other passages of a like kind might be quoted.   But these are enough to show that though no lover of poetry can read Gebir without delight, none can avoid the conclusion that there are faults in it which spring not from inexperience but from a false conception of poetic art.

In the present volumes is included another poem in the same style as Gebir, called "From the Phocæans," which has never been reprinted since its first publication. It shows even more clearly than Gebir that Landor had chosen a method of writing in which it was impossible that success should be attained. In spite of many incidental beauties, "The Phocæans" is involved in style and narrative, always obscure and frequently unnatural. The author felt this himself; he never finished the poem, never reprinted it, and never made another attempt of the kind. "Chrysaor," which he wrote during the same period, is a success, but a success which surprises the reader.

While making these attempts at Epic style, Landor was in fact discovering his real powers as a poet. The thoughts natural to a man's mind may be too turbulent and rugged to provide him with fit material for verse; and yet he may be a poet. In this case he mus do as Landor did, trust to external events for his subjects and write occasional verse. Any incident, even the slightest, may in this way result in a poem. If the incident and the poet are fortunate, that poem may be a stanza four lines long clinging to the memory with a charming persistency. Of such brief poems Landor has written a larger number than any English poet. Such verses as many of those among the first LXVI. of the Poems and Epigrams in these volumes cannot be matched elsewhere in English. They all have one source, Landor's love for Ianthe, the most enduring feeling of his life. And yet the reader will not find among them all one line to tell him what Landor thought in himself; on the other hand, in every poem it is easy to guess what kind of occasion provoked it.

This kind of verse has its triumphs; it has also its failures. A trivial incident, an unpoetic moment, may together produce a weak and pointless poem. The number of such poems produced by Landor, especially in his later life, is terribly large. It is surprising that he should have cared to collect the album verses, the poetic tributes to young ladies, the mere scraps scrawled down by an idle pen, which make so large a show in his works, and obscure so much his real successes. To reprint this mass of verse is to prolong the injury Landor did to his own fame. I have preferred to run the risk of making a selection from Landor's poems, hoping that if by so doing I fall into some errors, I at least avoid the guilt of reprinting what Landor in his wiser moments never would have published.

There is, however, one group of Landor's poems to which these criticisms do not apply. He had all his life spent much time and trouble on writing Latin verses, and had attained a rare excellence in that kind of composition. It is not necessary here to give any detailed criticism of his Latin poems. Many of them are epigrams like those of Martial and Catullus, occasional verse, with the merits and faults of the English poems already mentioned. But the group of narrative poems, which, in their English form, Landor named

the Hellenics, stand on a different footing. In
treatment they sometimes recall the writings of Ovid,
but they are far more direct and less artificial. In the
collected works of 1846 a large number appear for the
first time in English, translated from the Latin originals.
Here and there the verse has the failings likely to be
found in translations; but in spite of this the Hellenics
are good reading. The Hamadryad, in particular, is as
graceful a setting of a graceful story as any poet could
have devised. There is not a needless word in it, and
yet not an opportunity for a fine touch is missed. The
remaining poems do not quite reach this level, but in
all there is an even excellence of treatment rarely to be
found in Landor's work, either in prose or verse.
There are not the splendid, though accidental, successes
of the shorter poems; but there is, what is better, a
sustained mastery and careful workmanship.

In every criticism the critic must take account of his
own prejudices. I should not have thought it needful
to say so much in dispraise of Landor's poems, were
there not a disposition among critics to overpraise them
at the expense of his prose. It is not hard to see the
reason of this. Much of Landor's prose it is difficult
to read with patience; the matter is full of offence, now
to one side, now to the other. Every reader has a
group of dogmas, social, political, and religious, which
have crystallised in his mind under the various influences
of training and character. Whatever these dogmas
may be, Landor, in his prose works, is sure to outrage
some of them before many pages have been turned, and
to outrage them in a manner which might suit a grand
inquisitor with a turn for practical joking. In his

poems there are fewer of these stumbling-blocks; and the reader, who is disposed to admire Landor, but is annoyed by the vigorous freakishness of his prose, has a natural temptation to overestimate his poems.

So far I have only spoken of the narrative and occasional poems. There remain two other classes—the odes and poems akin to them in spirit and form—and the dramatic scenes. Of the first of these classes it is not needful to say much. The best work that Landor ever did in that style is to be found in the volume called "The Italics," printed in the year 1848. The poem addressed to St Charles Borromeo, and that on the death of the Brothers Bandieri, are spirited and swift in their motion, as all odes should be; nor do they fall much below the level on which they start. With these may be placed the poem addressed to Tyrannicide. But there are exceptions; when Landor borrows Pindar's wings, he meets too often the fate of Icarus, sets his name to a tedious exercise in verse. Even the Ode to Southey is hardly redeemed by its glorious last stanza: the reader skips most of the prefatory verses to reach the lines—

> " Not were that submarine
> Gem-lighted city mine,
> Wherein my name engraven by thy hand
> Above the royal gleam of blazonry shall stand ;
> Not, were all Syracuse
> Pour'd forth before my Muse,
> With Hiero's cars and steeds, and Pindar's lyre
> Brightening the path with more than solar fire,
> Could I, as would beseem, requite the praise
> Showered upon my low head from thy most lofty lays."

The Ode to Wordsworth is in another vein. The earlier stanzas curiously recall the rhythm of Wordsworth's own Ode to Lycoris, and the conclusion of the poem slips into the easy metre Landor uses so skilfully in many of his lighter poems. The Ode to Wordsworth is the pleasantest reading of all Landor's odes, but it is the least like an ode.

Landor's earliest attempt at Dramatic writing is, without any doubt, his most successful one. Just as Gebir reads like the first work of an Epic poet, Count Julian seems to promise the world a great tragedian. If Landor's later dramatic works had been more successful, criticism would have had to take a different view of Count Julian,—to pass lightly over the defects and praise the merits. It is true, one might have said, that the plot is not well explained to the reader, and that the characters are not clearly expressed. Practice will remedy that. But the mastery of verse and language, and the tragic force of expression, these will remain. It is unfortunately true that it was the evil qualities which remained. Landor's conception of the position of a reader of plays is a curious one. He treats him as though he were a stranger suddenly placed among a group of unknown people moved by unknown passions. He allows him to witness chance episodes in the conflict that is going on, and expects him to construct a theory of the characters and to discover their past and present history. It is a task few readers care to undertake. Few dramas can be more perplexing to the uninstructed reader than the trilogy dealing with the fate of Giovanna of Naples. It is true, that if the reader has the patience to find out for himself the history of Giovanna, before he attacks Landor's trilogy, he will find something in it to enjoy, something to admire. But if he first read Count Julian, and then turn to any other of Landor's plays, he will feel that he has passed from the high piercing air of the hills to a lower region not free from thorny entanglements. No one but a great dramatic poet could have written Count Julian ; a less man than Landor might have written the remainder of his dramas. Ippolito di Este and the Siege of Ancona are better than the others, but even these show few signs of the exceptional qualities of Count Julian.

To the sect of Landorians—for there are Landorians just as there are Wordsworthians—these criticisms may seem irreverent. The writer of them is not far removed from being of that opinion. It is difficult to refuse any wreath to an author whose pages have grown familiar to the eye. Every word that comes from his pen is fresh material for the study of his literary character. In his most trivial writings may lurk the secret of his greatest works. Thus to the student study makes his subject dear, and with the growth of this affection criticism flies. For Landorians, then, these criticisms *are* irreverent. Even for others they are incomplete, like all criticism. For criticism can but explain why the critic dislikes a piece of literature ; it cannot explain the charm that is possessed by lines like these—

> Child of a day, thou knowest not
> The tears that overflow thine urn,
> The gushing eyes that read thy lot,
> Nor, if thou knewest, couldst return !

> And why the wish! the pure and blest
>   Watch, like thy mother, o'er thy sleep.
> O peaceful night! O envied rest!
>   Thou wilt not ever see her weep.

Or again,

> Death stands above me, whispering low
>   I know not what into my ear:
> Of his strange language all I know
>   Is, there is not a word of fear.

And so does every great poet refute at the last those who comment on his faults.

[In order to save space in the textual notes in these volumes, I have indicated the various sources from which poems have been taken, by letters. The following general bibliography of Landor's poetical works will furnish a key to the letters:—

A. The Poems of Walter Savage Landor. London, 1795.
   A Moral Epistle; respectfully dedicated to Earl Stanhope. London, 1795.
B. Gebir, a poem in seven books. London, 1798.
C. Poems from the Arabic and Persian. Warwick and London, 1800.
D. Poetry by the author of Gebir. London, 1802.
E. Gebir, a poem in seven books. Oxford, 1803.
F. Simonidea. Bath and London, 1806.
G. Count Julian, a tragedy. London, 1812.
H. Gebir, Count Julian, and other poems. London, 1831.
I. Pericles and Aspasia. London, 1836.
J. The Pentameron and Pentalogia. London, 1837.

K. Ablett's Literary Hours.   1837.
    A Satire on Satirists, and Admonition to Detractors.
        London, 1837.
L. Andrea of Hungary and Giovanna of Naples.   London,
        1839.
M. Fra Rupert.   London, 1841.
N. The Works of Walter Savage Landor.   London, 1846.
O. The Hellenics, enlarged and completed.   London, 1847.
P. The Italics of Walter Savage Landor.   London, 1848.
Q. The Last Fruit off an Old Tree.   London, 1853.
R. Anthony and Octavius, Scenes for the Study.   London,
        1856.
S. Dry Sticks, Fagotted by Walter Savage Landor.   Edin-
        burgh, 1858.
T. The Hellenics of Walter Savage Landor, &c.   Edin-
        burgh, 1859.
U. Heroic Idylls, with additional poems.   1863.
V. Collected Works.   London, 1876.

To the above must be added, " Terry Hogan, an Idyll :
Bath, 1837 ; " and (perhaps) " The Bath Subscription Ball."
" Guy's Porridge Pot," a satire on Dr Parr, which has been
sometimes attributed to Walter Savage Landor, should, in all
probability, be ascribed to his brother, Robert Eyres Landor.]

DRAMATIC SCENES.

DRAMATIC SCENES.

———✳———

COUNT JULIAN.

None of these poems of a dramatic form were offered to the stage, being no better than *Imaginary Conversations* in metre.—W. S. L.

CHARACTERS.

Count Julian. Roderigo, *King of Spain.* Opas, *Metropolitan of Seville.* Sisabert, *betrothed to* Covilla. Muza, *Prince of Mauritania.* Abdalazis, *son of* Muza. Tarik, *Moorish Chieftain.* Covilla,* *daughter of* Julian. Egilona, *wife of* Roderigo. Hernando, Osma, Ramiro, &c., *Officers.*

FIRST ACT : FIRST SCENE.

Camp of Julian.

Opas. Julian.

Opas.   See her, Count Julian : if thou lovest God,
See thy lost child.
   Julian.   I have avenged me, Opas,
More than enough : I only sought to hurl

---

* The daughter of Count Julian is usually called Florinda. The city of Covilla, it is reported, was named after her. Here is no improbability : there would be a gross one in deriving the word, as is also pretended, from La Cava. Cities, in adopting a name, bear it usually as a testimony of victories or as an augury of virtues. Small and obscure places occasionally receive what their neighbours throw against them ; as *Puerto de la mala muger* in Murcia : but a generous people would affix no stigma to innocence and misfortune. It is remarkable that the most important era in Spanish history should be the most obscure. This is propitious to the poet, and above all to the tragedian. Few characters of such an era can be glaringly misrepresented, few facts offensively perverted.

The brand of war on one detested head,
And die upon his ruin.   O my country!
O lost to honour, to thyself, to me,
Why on barbarian hands devolves thy cause,
Spoilers, blasphemers!
  Opas.   Is it thus, Don Julian,   10
When thy own offspring, that beloved child
For whom alone these very acts were done
By them and thee, when thy Covilla stands
An outcast and a suppliant at thy gate,
Why that still stubborn agony of soul,
Those struggles with the bars thyself imposed?
Is she not thine? not dear to thee as ever?
  Julian.   Father of mercies! show me none, whene'er
The wrongs she suffers cease to wring my heart,
Or I seek solace ever, but in death.   20
  Opas.   What wilt thou do then, too unhappy man?
  Julian.   What have I done already?   All my peace
Has vanisht; my fair fame in aftertime
Will wear an alien and uncomely form,
Seen o'er the cities I have laid in dust,
Countrymen slaughtered, friends abjured!
  Opas.   And faith?
  Julian.   Alone now left me, filling up in part
The narrow and waste interval of grief:
It promises that I shall see again   30
My own lost child.
  Opas.   Yes, at this very hour.
  Julian.   Till I have met the tyrant face to face,
And gain'd a conquest greater than the last,
Till he no longer rules one rood of Spain,
And not one Spaniard, not one enemy,
The least relenting, flags upon his flight,
Till we are equal in the eyes of men,
The humblest and most wretched of our kind,
No peace for me, no comfort, no . . no child!   40
  Opas.   No pity for the thousands fatherless,
The thousands childless like thyself, nay more,
The thousands friendless, helpless, comfortless . .

Such thou wilt make them, little thinking so,
Who now perhaps, round their first winter fire,
Banish, to talk of thee, the tales of old,
Shedding true honest tears for thee unknown :
Precious be these and sacred in thy sight,
Mingle them not with blood from hearts thus kind.
If only warlike spirits were evoked   50
By the war-demon; I would not complain,
Or dissolute and discontented men ;
But wherefore hurry down into the square
The neighbourly, saluting, warm-clad race,
Who would not injure us, and can not serve ;
Who, from their short and measured slumber risen,
In the faint sunshine of their balconies,
With a half-legend of a martyrdom
And some weak wine and withered grapes before them,
Note by their foot the wheel of melody   60
That catches and rolls on the Sabbath dance.
To drag the steady prop from failing age,
Break the young stem that fondness twines around,
Widen the solitude of lonely sighs,
And scatter to the broad bleak wastes of day
The ruins and the phantoms that replied,
Ne'er be it thine.
    Julian.   Arise, and save me, Spain !

FIRST ACT : SECOND SCENE.

Muza *enters.*

    Muza.   Infidel chief, thou tarriest here too long,
And art perhaps repining at the days
Of nine continued victories o'er men
Dear to thy soul, tho' reprobate and base.
Away !   [*He retires.*
    Julian.   I follow.   Could my bitterest foes
Hear this ! ye Spaniards, this ! which I foreknew

And yet encounter'd ; could they see your Julian
Receiving orders from and answering
These desperate and heaven-abandoned slaves,　　　　10
They might perceive some few external pangs,
Some glimpses of the hell wherein I move,
Who never have been fathers.
 Opas.   These are they
To whom brave Spaniards must refer their wrongs !
 Julian. Muza, that cruel and suspicious chief,
Distrusts his friends more than his enemies,
Me more than either ; fraud he loves and fears,
And watches her still footfall day and night.
 Opas. O Julian ! such a refuge ! such a race !　　　20
 Julian. . . Calamities like mine alone implore.
No virtues have redeem'd them from their bonds ;
Wily ferocity, keen idleness,
And the close cringes of ill-whispering want,
Educate them to plunder and obey :
Active to serve him best whom most they fear,
They show no mercy to the merciful,
And racks alone remind them of the name.
 Opas. O everlasting curse for Spain and thee !
 Julian. Spain should have vindicated then her wrongs　30
In mine, a Spaniard's and a soldier's wrongs.
 Opas. Julian, are thine the only wrongs on earth ?
And shall each Spaniard rather vindicate
Thine than his own ? is there no Judge of all ?
Shall mortal hand seize with impunity
The sword of vengeance from the armoury
Of the Most High ? easy to wield, and starred
With glory it appears ; but all the host
Of the archangels, should they strive at once,
Would never close again its widening blade.　　　　40
 Julian. He who provokes it hath so much to rue.
Where'er he turn, whether to earth or heaven,
He finds an enemy, or raises one.
 Opas. I never yet have seen where long success
Hath followed him who warred upon his king.
 Julian. Because the virtue that inflicts the stroke

Dies with him, and the rank ignoble heads
Of plundering faction soon unite again,
And prince-protected share the spoil at rest.

FIRST ACT: THIRD SCENE.

Guard announces a Herald. OPAS *departs.*

Guard. A messenger of peace is at the gate,
My lord, safe access, private audience,
And free return, he claims.
Julian. Conduct him in.

RODERIGO *enters as a herald.*

A messenger of peace! audacious man!
In what attire appearest thou? a herald's?
Under no garb can such a wretch be safe.
Roderigo. Thy violence and fancied wrongs I know,
And what thy sacrilegious hands would do,
O traitor and apostate!   10
Julian. What they would
They can not: thee of kingdom and of life
'Tis easy to despoil, thyself the traitor,
Thyself the violator of allegiance.
O would all-righteous Heaven they could restore
The joy of innocence, the calm of age,
The probity of manhood, pride of arms,
And confidence of honour! the august
And holy laws trampled beneath thy feet,
And Spain! O parent, I have lost thee too!   20
Yes, thou wilt curse me in thy latter days,
Me, thine avenger. I have fought her foe,
Roderigo, I have gloried in her sons,
Sublime in hardihood and piety:
Her strength was mine: I, sailing by her cliffs,
By promontory after promontory,
Opening like flags along some castle-tower,
Have sworn before the cross upon our mast
Ne'er shall invader wave his standard there.

Roderigo.   Yet there thou plantest it, false man, thyself.   30
Julian.   Accursed he who makes me this reproach,
And made it just!   Had I been happy still,
I had been blameless: I had died with glory
Upon the walls of Ceuta.
Roderigo.   Which thy treason
Surrendered to the Infidel.
Julian.   'Tis hard
And base to live beneath a conqueror;
Yet, amid all this grief and infamy,
'Twere something to have rusht upon the ranks   40
In their advance; 'twere something to have stood
Defeat, discomfiture, and, when around
No beacon blazes, no far axle groans
Thro' the wide plain, no sound of sustenance
Or succour soothes the still-believing ear,
To fight upon the last dismantled tower,
And yield to valour, if we yield at all.
But rather should my neck lie trampled down
By every Saracen and Moor on earth,
Than my own country see her laws o'erturn'd   50
By those who should protect them.   Sir, no prince
Shall ruin Spain, and, least of all, her own.
Is any just or glorious act in view,
Your oaths forbid it: is your avarice,
Or, if there be such, any viler passion
To have its giddy range and to be gorged,
It rises over all your sacraments,
A hooded mystery, holier than they all.
Roderigo.   Hear me, Don Julian; I have heard thy wrath
Who am thy king, nor heard man's wrath before.   60
Julian.   Thou shalt hear mine, for thou art not my king.
Roderigo.   Knowest thou not the altered face of war?
Xeres is ours; from every region round
True loyal Spaniards throng into our camp:
Nay, thy own friends and thy own family,
From the remotest provinces, advance
To crush rebellion: Sisabert is come,
Disclaiming thee and thine; the Asturian hills

Oppose to him their icy chains in vain ;
But never wilt thou see him, never more,   70
Unless in adverse war and deadly hate.
 Julian. So lost to me ! so generous, so deceived ! I
  grieve to hear it.
 Roderigo.   Come, I offer grace,
Honour, dominion : send away these slaves,
Or leave them to our sword, and all beyond
The distant Ebro to the towns of France
Shall bless thy name and bend before thy throne.
I will myself accompany thee, I,
The king, will hail thee brother.
 Julian.   Ne'er shalt thou   80
Henceforth be king : the nation in thy name
May issue edicts, champions may command
The vassal multitudes of marshal'd war,
And the fierce charger shrink before the shouts,
Lower'd as if earth had open'd at his feet,
While thy mail'd semblance rises tow'rd the ranks,
But God alone sees thee.
 Roderigo.   What hopest thou ?
To conquer Spain, and rule a ravaged land ?
To compass me around ? to murder me ?   90
 Julian. No, Don Roderigo : swear thou, in the fight
That thou wilt meet me, hand to hand, alone,
That, if I ever save thee from a foe . .
 Roderigo. I swear what honour asks. First, to Covilla
Do thou present my crown and dignity.
 Julian. Darest thou offer any price for shame ?
 Roderigo. Love and repentance.
 Julian.   Egilona lives ;
And were she buried with her ancestors,
Covilla should not be the gaze of men,   100
Should not, despoil'd of honour, rule the free.
 Roderigo. Stern man ! her virtues well deserve the throne.
 Julian. And Egilona, what hath she deserv'd,
The good, the lovely ?
 Roderigo.   But the realm in vain
Hoped a succession.

Julian.   Thou hast torn away
The roots of royalty.
    Roderigo.   For her, for thee.
    Julian.   Blind insolence! base insincerity!   110
Power and renown no mortal ever shared
Who could retain or grasp them to himself:
And, for Covilla? patience! peace! for her?
She call upon her God, and outrage him
At his own altar! *she* repeat the vows
She violates in repeating! who abhors
Thee and thy crimes, and wants no crown of thine.
Force may compel the abhorrent soul, or want
Lash and pursue it to the public ways;
Virtue looks back and weeps, and may return   120
To these, but never near the abandon'd one
Who drags religion to adultery's feet,
And rears the altar higher for her sake.
    Roderigo.   Have then the Saracens possest thee quite?
And wilt thou never yield me thy consent?
    Julian.   Never.
    Roderigo.   So deep in guilt, in treachery!
Forced to acknowledge it! forced to avow
The traitor!
    Julian.   Not to thee, who reignest not,   130
But to a country ever dear to me,
And dearer now than ever! What we love
Is loveliest in departure! One I thought,
As every father thinks, the best of all,
Graceful and mild and sensible and chaste:
Now all these qualities of form and soul
Fade from before me, nor on any one
Can I repose, or be consoled by any.
And yet in this torn heart I love her more
Than I could love her when I dwelt on each,   140
Or claspt them all united, and thankt God,
Without a wish beyond. Away, thou fiend!
O ignominy, last and worst of all!
I weep before thee . . like a child . . like mine . .
And tell my woes, fount of them all! to thee!

FIRST ACT: FOURTH SCENE.

ABDALAZIS *enters.*

Abdalazis.   Julian, to thee, the terror of the faithless,
I bring my father's order to prepare
For the bright day that crowns thy brave exploits.
Our enemy is at the very gate,
And art thou here, with women in thy train,
Crouching to gain admittance to their lord,
And mourning the unkindness of delay!
    Julian (agitated, goes toward the door, and returns).   I am
        prepared: Prince, judge not hastily.
    Abdalazis.   Whether I should not promise all they ask,
I too could hesitate, though earlier taught   10
The duty to obey, and should rejoice
To shelter in the universal storm
A frame so delicate, so full of fears,
So little used to outrage and to arms,
As one of these, so humble, so uncheer'd
At the gay pomp that smooths the track of war.
When she beheld me from afar dismount,
And heard my trumpet, she alone drew back,
And, as though doubtful of the help she seeks,
Shudder'd to see the jewels on my brow,   20
And turn'd her eyes away, and wept aloud.
The other stood awhile, and then advanced:
I would have spoken; but she waved her hand
And said, " Proceed, protect us, and avenge,
And be thou worthier of the crown thou wearest."
Hopeful and happy is indeed our cause,
When the most timid of the lovely hail
Stranger and foe.
    Roderigo (unnoticed by Abdalazis).   And shrink but to
        advance.
    Abdalazis.   Thou tremblest? whence, O Julian! whence
        this change?   30

Thou lovest still thy country.
   Julian.   Abdalazis !
All men with human feelings love their country.
Not the highborn or wealthy man alone,
Who looks upon his children, each one led
By its gay handmaid from the high alcove,
And hears them once a-day ; not only he
Who hath forgotten, when his guest inquires
The name of some far village all his own ;
Whose rivers bound the province, and whose hills   40
Touch the last cloud upon the level sky :
No ; better men still better love their country.
'Tis the old mansion of their earliest friends,
The chapel of their first and best devotions.
When violence or perfidy invades,
Or when unworthy lords hold wassail there,
And wiser heads are drooping round its moats,
At last they fix their steady and stiff eye
There, there alone, stand while the trumpet blows
And view the hostile flames above its towers   50
Spire, with a bitter and severe delight.
   Abdalazis (taking his hand).   Thou feelest what thou
       speakest, and thy Spain
Will ne'er be shelter'd from her fate by thee.
We, whom the Prophet sends o'er many lands,
Love none above another ; Heaven assigns
Their fields and harvests to our valiant swords,
And 'tis enough : we love while we enjoy.
Whence is the man in that fantastic guise ?
Suppliant ? or herald ? he who stalks about,
And once was even seated while we spoke :   60
For never came he with us o'er the sea.
   Julian.   He comes as herald.
   Roderigo.   Thou shalt know full soon,
Insulting Moor !
   Abdalazis.   He ill endures the grief
His country suffers : I will pardon him.
He lost his courage first, and then his mind ;
His courage rushes back, his mind yet wanders.

The guest of heaven was piteous to these men,
And princes stoop to feed them in their courts.   70

FIRST ACT: FIFTH SCENE.

RODERIGO *is going:* MUZA *enters with* EGILONA :
RODERIGO *starts back.*

Muza (sternly to EGILONA).   Enter, since 'tis the custom
  in this land.
Egilona (passing MUZA, *points to* ABDALAZIS).   Is this our
  future monarch, or art thou?
Julian.   'Tis Abdalazis, son of Muza, prince
Commanding Africa, from Abyla
To where Tunisian pilots bend the eye
O'er ruin'd temples in the glassy wave.
Till quiet times and ancient laws return
He comes to govern here.
  Roderigo.   To-morrow's dawn
Proves that.   10
  Muza.   What art thou?
  Roderigo (drawing his sword).   King.
  Abdalazis.   Amazement!
  Muza.   Treason!
  Egilona.   O horror!
  Muza.   Seize him.
  Egilona.   Spare him! fly to me!
  Julian.   Urge me not to protect a guest, a herald,
The blasts of war roar over him unfelt.
  Egilona.   Ah fly, unhappy!   20
  Roderigo.   Fly! no, Egilona!
Dost thou forgive me? dost thou love me? still?
  Egilona.   I hate, abominate, abhor thee . . go,
Or my own vengeance . .
  RODERIGO (*takes* JULIAN'S *hand ; invites him to attack* MUZA
    and ABDALAZIS.)   Julian!
  Julian.   Hence, or die.

SECOND ACT: FIRST SCENE.

Camp of JULIAN.

JULIAN *and* COVILLA.

Julian.   Obdurate?   I am not as I appear.
Weep, my beloved child ! Covilla, weep
Into my bosom ; every drop be mine
Of this most bitter soul-empoisoning cup :
Into no other bosom than thy father's
Canst thou or wouldst thou pour it.
    Covilla.   Cease, my lord,
My father, angel of my youth, when all
Was innocence and peace.
    Julian.   Arise, my love,   10
Look up to heaven . . where else are souls like thine !
Mingle in sweet communion with its children,
Trust in its providence, its retribution,
And I will cease to mourn ; for, O my child,
These tears corrode, but thine assuage, the heart.
    Covilla.   And never shall I see my mother too,
My own, my blessed mother ?
    Julian.   Thou shalt see
Her and thy brothers.
    Covilla.   No ! I can not look   20
On them, I can not meet their lovely eyes,
I can not lift mine up from under theirs.
We all were children when they went away ;
They now have fought hard battles, and are men,
And camps and kings they know, and woes and crimes.
Sir, will they never venture from the walls
Into the plain ?   Remember, they are young,
Hardy and emulous and hazardous,
And who is left to guard them in the town ?
    Julian.   Peace is throughout the land : the various tribes   30
Of that vast region sink at once to rest,

Like one wide wood when every wind lies husht.
  Covilla.   And war, in all its fury, roams o'er Spain !
  Julian.   Alas ! and will for ages : crimes are loose
At which ensanguined War stands shuddering,
And calls for vengeance from the powers above,
Impatient of inflicting it himself.
Nature in these new horrors is aghast
At her own progeny, and knows them not.
I am the minister of wrath ; the hands   40
That tremble at me, shall applaud me too,
And seal their condemnation.
  Covilla.   O kind father,
Pursue the guilty, but remember Spain.
  Julian.   Child, thou wert in thy nursery short time since,
And latterly hast past the vacant hour
Where the familiar voice of history
Is hardly known, however nigh, attuned
In softer accents to the sickened ear ;
But thou hast heard, for nurses tell these tales,   50
Whether I drew my sword for Witiza
Abandoned by the people he betrayed,
Tho' brother to the woman who of all
Was ever dearest to this broken heart,
Till thou, my daughter, wert a prey to grief,
And a brave country brookt the wrongs I bore.
For I had seen Rusilla guide the steps
Of her Theodofred, when burning brass
Plunged its fierce fang into the fount of light,
And Witiza's the guilt ! when, bent with age,   60
He knew the voice again, and told the name
Of those whose proffer'd fortunes had been laid
Before his throne, while happiness was there,
And strain'd the sightless nerve tow'rd where they stood,
At the forced memory of the very oaths
He heard renew'd from each, but heard afar,
For they were loud, and him the throng spurn'd off.
  Covilla.   Who were all these ?
  Julian.   All who are seen to-day
On prancing steeds richly caparisoned   70

In loyal acclamation round Roderigo ;
Their sons beside them, loving one another
Unfeignedly, thro' joy, while they themselves
In mutual homage mutual scorn suppress.
Their very walls and roofs are welcoming
The king's approach, their storied tapestry
Swells its rich arch for him triumphantly
At every clarion blowing from below.
   Covilla.   Such wicked men will never leave his side.
   Julian.   For they are insects which see nought beyond 80
Where they now crawl ; whose changes are complete,
Unless of habitation.
   Covilla.   Whither go
Creatures unfit for better or for worse ?
   Julian.   Some to the grave, where peace be with them ! some
Across the Pyrenean mountains far,
Into the plains of France ; suspicion there
Will hang on every step from rich and poor,
Grey quickly-glancing eyes will wrinkle round
And courtesy will watch them, day and night.   90
Shameless they are, yet will they blush amid
A nation that ne 'er blushes : some will drag
The captive 's chain, repair the shatter'd bark,
Or heave it from a quicksand to the shore
Among the marbles of the Lybian coast,
Teach patience to the lion in his cage,
And, by the order of a higher slave,
Hold to the elephant their scanty fare
To please the children while the parent sleeps.
   Covilla.   Spaniards ? Must they, dear father, lead such
     lives ?   100
   Julian.   All are not Spaniards who draw breath in Spain,
Those are, who live for her, who die for her,
Who love her glory, and lament her fall.
O may I too . .
   Covilla.   But peacefully, and late,
Live and die here !
   Julian.   I have, alas ! myself
Laid waste the hopes where my fond fancy stray'd,

And view their ruins with unalter'd eyes.
  Covilla. My mother will at last return to you. 110
Might I once more, but . . could I now? behold her
Tell her . . ah me! what was my rash desire?
No, never tell her these inhuman things,
For they would waste her tender heart away
As they waste mine; or tell when I have died,
Only to show her that her every care
Could not have saved, could not have comforted;
That she herself, clasping me once again
To her sad breast, had said, Covilla! go,
Go, hide them in the bosom of thy God! 120
Sweet mother! that far-distant voice I hear,
And, passing out of youth and out of life,
I would not turn at last, and disobey.

SECOND ACT: SECOND SCENE.

Sisabert *enters.*

  Sisabert. Uncle, and is it true, say, can it be,
That thou art leader of these faithless Moors?
That thou impeachest thy own daughter's fame
Thro' the whole land, to seize upon the throne
By the permission of these recreant slaves?
What shall I call thee? art thou, speak Count Julian,
A father, or a soldier, or a man?
  Julian. All, or this day had never seen me here.
  Sisabert. O falsehood! worse than woman's!
  Covilla.   Once, my cousin, 10
Far gentler words were utter'd from your lips.
If you loved me, you loved my father first,
More justly and more steadily, ere love
Was passion and illusion and deceit.
  Sisabert. I boast not that I never was deceived,
Covilla, which beyond all boasts were base,
Nor that I never loved; let this be thine.

Illusions ! just to stop us, not delay,
Amuse, not occupy ! Too true ! when love
Scatters its brilliant foam, and passes on   20
To some fresh object in its natural course,
Widely and openly and wanderingly,
'Tis better : narrow it, and it pours its gloom
In one fierce cataract that stuns the soul.
Ye hate the wretch ye make so, while ye choose
Whoever knows you best and shuns you most.
      Covilla.   Shun *me* then : be beloved more and more.
Honour the hand that show'd you honour first,
Love . . O my father ! speak, proceed, persuade,
Your voice alone can utter it . . another.   30
      Sisabert.   Ah lost Covilla ! can a thirst of power
Alter thy heart thus to abandon mine,
And change my very nature at one blow ?
      Covilla.   I told you, dearest Sisabert, 'twas vain
To urge me more, to question or confute.
      Sisabert.   I know it, for another wears the crown
Of Witiza my father ; who succeeds
To king Roderigo will succeed to me.
Yet thy cold perfidy still calls me dear,
And o'er my aching temples breathes one gale   40
Of days departed to return no more.
      Julian.   Young man, avenge our cause.
      Sisabert.   What cause avenge ?
      Covilla.   If I was ever dear to you, hear me,
Not vengeance ; heaven will give that signal soon.
O Sisabert, the pangs I have endured
On your long absence . .
      Sisabert.   Will be now consoled.
Thy father comes to mount my father's throne ;
But though I would not a usurper king,   50
I prize his valour and defend his crown :
No stranger and no traitor rules o'er me,
Or unchastised inveigles humble Spain.
Covilla, gavest thou no promises ?
Nor thou, Don Julian ? Seek not to reply.
Too well I know, too justly I despise,

Thy false excuse, thy coward effrontery;
Yes, when thou gavest them across the sea,
An enemy wert thou to Mahomet,
And no appellant to his faith or leagues.   60
    Julian.   'Tis well: a soldier hears throughout in silence.
I urge no answer: to those words, I fear,
Thy heart with sharp compunction will reply.
    Sisabert (to Covilla).   Then I demand of thee, before thou
        reign,
Answer me . . while I fought against the Frank
Who dared to sue thee? blazon'd in the court,
Not trailed thro' darkness, were our nuptial bands;
No; Egilona joined our hands herself,
The peers applauded and the king approved.
    Julian.   Hast thou yet seen that king since thy return? 70
    Covilla.   Father! O Father!
    Sisabert.   I will not implore
Of him or thee what I have lost for ever.
These were not, when we parted, thy alarms;
Far other, and far worthier of thy heart
Were they, which Sisabert could banish then.
Fear me not now, Covilla! thou hast changed,
I am changed too.   I lived but where thou livedst,
My very life was portion'd off from thine:
Upon the surface of thy happiness   80
Day after day I gazed, I doted, there
Was all I had, was all I coveted;
So pure, serene, and boundless it appear'd:
Yet, for we told each other every thought,
Thou knowest well, if thou rememberest,
At times I fear'd; as tho' some demon sent
Suspicion without form into the world,
To whisper unimaginary things.
Then thy fond arguing banisht all but hope,
Each wish and every feeling was with thine,   90
Till I partook thy nature, and became
Credulous and incredulous like thee.
We, who have met so alter'd, meet no more.
Mountains and seas! ye are not separation:

Death ! thou dividest, but unitest too
In everlasting peace and faith sincere.
Confiding love ! where is thy resting-place ?
Where is thy truth, Covilla ? where ? . . Go, go . .
I should believe thee and adore thee still.　　　[*Goes.*
　　Covilla.　O Heaven ! support me, or desert me quite,　100
And leave me lifeless this too trying hour !
He thinks me faithless.
　　Julian.　　　　　　He must think thee so.
　　Covilla.　O tell him, tell him all, when I am dead . .
He will die too, and we shall meet again.
He will know all when these sad eyes are closed.
Ah can not he before ? must I appear
The vilest . . O just Heaven ! can it be thus ?
I am . . all earth resounds it . . lost, despised,
Anguish and shame unutterable seize me.　　　　　110
'Tis palpable, no phantom, no delusion,
No dream that wakens with o'erwhelming horror ;
Spaniard and Moor fight on this ground alone,
And tear the arrow from my bleeding breast
To pierce my father's, for alike they fear.
　　Julian.　Invulnerable, unassailable
Are we, alone perhaps of human kind,
Nor life allures us more nor death alarms.
　　Covilla.　Fallen, unpitied, unbelieved, unheard !
I should have died long earlier.　Gracious God !　　120
Desert me to my sufferings, but sustain
My faith in thee !　O hide me from the world,
And from yourself, my father, from your fondness,
That opened in this wilderness of woe
A source of tears . . it else had burst my heart,
Setting me free for ever : then perhaps
A cruel war had not divided Spain,
Had not o'erturn'd her cities and her altars,
Had not endanger'd you ! O haste afar
Ere the last dreadful conflict that decides　　　　130
Whether we live beneath a foreign sway . .
　　Julian.　Or under him whose tyranny brought down
The curse upon his people.　O child ! child !

Urge me no further, talk not of the war,
Remember not our country.
   Covilla.   Not remember !
What have the wretched else for consolation ?
What else have they who pining feed their woe ?
Can I, or should I, drive from memory
All that was dear and sacred ? all the joys   140
Of innocence and peace ?   When no debate
Was in the convent, but what hymn, whose voice,
To whom among the blessed it arose,
Swelling so sweet ; when rang the vesper-bell
And every finger ceast from the guitar,
And every tongue was silent through our land ;
When, from remotest earth, friends met again,
Hung on each other's neck, and but embraced,
So sacred, still, and peaceful was the hour.
Now, in what climate of the wasted world,   150
Not unmolested long by the profane,
Can I pour forth in secrecy to God
My prayers and my repentance ? where beside
Is the last solace of the parting soul ?
Friends, brethren, parents, dear indeed, too dear
Are they, but somewhat yet the heart requires,
That it may leave them lighter and more blest.
   Julian.   Wide are the regions of our far-famed land :
Thou shalt arrive at her remotest bounds,
See her best people, choose some holiest house ;   160
Whether where Castro from surrounding vines
Hears the hoarse ocean roar among his caves,
And, thro' the fissure in the green churchyard,
The wind wail loud the calmest summer day ;
Or where Santona leans against the hill,
Hidden from sea and land by groves and bowers.
   Covilla.   O ! for one moment in those pleasant scenes
Thou placest me, and lighter air I breathe :
Why could I not have rested, and heard on !
My voice dissolves the vision quite away,   170
Outcast from virtue, and from nature too !
   Julian.   Nature and virtue ! they shall perish first.

God destined them for thee, and thee for them,
Inseparably and eternally !
The wisest and the best will prize thee most,
And solitudes and cities will contend
Which shall receive thee kindliest.   Sigh not so :
Violence and fraud will never penetrate
Where piety and poverty retire,
Intractable to them and valueless,   180
And lookt at idly like the face of heaven.
If strength be wanted for security,
Mountains the guard, forbidding all approach
With iron-pointed and uplifted gates,
Thou wilt be welcome too in Aguilar,
Impenetrable, marble-turreted,
Surveying from aloft the limpid ford,
The massive fane, the sylvan avenue ;
Whose hospitality I proved myself,
A willing leader in no impious war   190
When fame and freedom urged me ; or mayst dwell
In Reynosa's dry and thriftless dale,
Unharvested beneath October moons,
Among those frank and cordial villagers.
They never saw us, and, poor simple souls !
So little know they whom they call the great,
Would pity one another less than us,
In injury, disaster, or distress.
    Covilla.   But they would ask each other whence our grief,
That they might pity.   200
    Julian.   Rest then just beyond,
In the secluded scenes where Ebro springs
And drives not from his fount the fallen leaf,
So motionless and tranquil its repose.
    Covilla.   Thither let us depart, and speedily.
    Julian.   I can not go : I live not in the land
I have reduced beneath such wretchedness :
And who could leave the brave whose lives and fortunes
Hang on his sword ?
    Covilla.   Me hou canst leave, my father ;   210
Ah yes, for it is past ; too well thou seest

My life and fortunes rest not upon thee.
Long, happily . . could it be gloriously!
Still mayst thou live, and save thy country still!
 Julian.   Unconquerable land! unrival'd race!
Whose bravery, too enduring, rues alike
The power and weakness of accursed kings,
How cruelly hast thou neglected me!
Forcing me from thee, never to return,
Nor in thy pangs and struggles to partake!   220
I hear a voice! 'tis Egilona: come,
Recall thy courage, dear unhappy girl,
Let us away.

SECOND ACT: THIRD SCENE.

Egilona *enters.*

 Egilona.   Remain; I order thee.
Attend, and do thy duty: I am queen,
Unbent to degradation.
 Covilla.   I attend
Ever most humbly and most gratefully,
My too kind sovran, cousin now no more.
Could I perform but half the services
I owe her, I were happy for a time,
Or dared I show her half my love, 'twere bliss.
 Egilona.   Oh! I sink under gentleness like thine.   10
Thy sight is death to me; and yet 'tis dear.
The gaudy trappings of assumptive state
Drop at the voice of nature to the earth,
Before thy feet.   I can not force myself
To hate thee, to renounce thee; yet . . Covilla!
Yet . . O distracting thought! 'tis hard to see,
Hard to converse with, to admire, to love,
As from my soul I do, and must do, thee,
One who hath robb'd me of all pride and joy,
All dignity, all fondness.   I adored   20
Roderigo.   He was brave, and in discourse
Most voluble; the masses of his mind

Were vast, but varied ; now absorb'd in gloom,
Majestic, not austere ; now their extent
Opening and waving in bright levity . .
   Julian.   Depart, my daughter.   'Twere as well to bear
His presence as his praise.   Go ; she will dream
This phantasm out, nor notice thee depart.
[Covilla goes.

   Egilona.   What pliancy ! what tenderness ! what life !
O for the smiles of those who smile so seldom,   30
The love of those who know no other love !
Such he was, Egilona, who was thine.
   Julian.   While he was worthy of the realm and thee.
   Egilona.   Can it be true then, Julian, that thy aim
Is sovranty ? not virtue nor revenge ?
   Julian.   I swear to heaven, nor I nor child of mine
Ever shall mount to this polluted throne.
   Egilona.   Then am I yet a queen.   The savage Moor
Who could not conquer Ceuta from thy sword
In his own country, not with every wile   40
Of his whole race, not with his myriad crests
Of cavalry, seen from the Calpian highths
Like locusts on the parcht and gleamy coast,
Will never conquer Spain.
   Julian.   Spain then was conquer'd
When fell her laws before the traitor king.

SECOND ACT : FOURTH SCENE.

Officer announces Opas.

O queen, the metropolitan attends
On matter of high import to the state,
And wishes to confer in privacy.
   Egilona (to *Julian*).   Adieu then ; and whate'er betide
     the country,
Sustain at least the honours of our house.
[Julian goes before Opas enters.
   Opas.   I can not but commend, O Egilona,
Such resignation and such dignity.

Indeed he is unworthy ; yet a queen
Rather to look for peace, and live remote
From cities, and from courts, and from her lord,   10
I hardly could expect in one so young,
So early, widely, wondrously, admired.
   Egilona.   I am resolv'd : religious men, good Opas,
In this resemble the vain libertine ;
They find in woman no consistency,
No virtue but devotion, such as comes
To infancy or age or fear or love,
Seeking a place of rest, and finding none
Until it soar to heaven.
   Opas.   A spring of mind   20
That rises when all pressure is removed,
Firmness in pious and in chaste resolves,
But weakness in much fondness ; these, O queen,
I did expect, I own.
   Egilona.   The better part
Be mine ; the worse hath been, and is no more.
   Opas.   But if Roderigo have at length prevail'd
That Egilona willingly resigns
All claim to royalty, and casts away,
Indifferent or estranged, the marriage-bond   30
His perjury tore asunder, still the church
Hardly can sanction his new nuptial rites.
   Egilona.   What art thou saying ? what new nuptial rites ?
   Opas.   Thou knowest not ?
   Egilona.   Am I a wife ? a queen ?
Abandon it ! my claim to royalty !
Whose hand was on my head when I arose
Queen of this land ? whose benediction sealed
My marriage-vow ? who broke it ? was it I ?
And wouldst thou, virtuous Opas, wouldst thou dim   40
The glorious light of thy declining days ?
Wouldst thou administer the sacred vows
And sanction them, and bless them, for another,
And bid her live in peace while I am living ?
Go then ? I execrate and banish him
For ever from my sight : we were not born

For happiness together; none on earth
Were ever so dissimilar as we.
He is not worth a tear, a wish, a thought;
Never was I deceived in him; I found   50
No tenderness, no fondness, from the first.
A love of power, a love of perfidy,
Such is the love that is return'd for mine.
Ungrateful man! 'twas not the pageantry
Of regal state, the clarions, nor the guard,
Nor loyal valour, nor submissive beauty,
Silence at my approach, awe at my voice,
Happiness at my smile, that led my youth
Toward Roderigo. I had lived obscure,
In humbleness, in poverty, in want,   60
Blest, O supremely blest, with him alone;
And he abandons me, rejects me, scorns me,
Insensible! inhuman! for another!
Thou shalt repent thy wretched choice, false man!
Crimes such as thine call loudly for perdition;
Heaven will inflict it, and not I; but I
Neither will fall alone nor live despised.
         [A trumpet sounds.

 Opas. Peace, Egilona! he arrives: compose
Thy turbid thoughts, meet him with dignity.
 Egilona. He! in the camp of Julian! trust me, sir, 70
He comes not hither, dares no longer use
The signs of state, and flies from every foe.
        [Retires some distance.

SECOND ACT: FIFTH SCENE.

Enter Muza *and* Abdalazis.

 Muza to *Abdalazis.* I saw him but an instant, and
  disguised,
Yet this is not the traitor; on his brow
Observe the calm of wisdom and of years.
 Opas. Whom seekest thou?
 Muza.   Him who was king I seek.

He came array'd as herald to this tent.
　Abdalazis.　Thy daughter! was she nigh? perhaps for her
Was this disguise.
　Muza.　　　　　　Here, Abdalazis, kings
Disguise from other causes; they obtain　　　　10
Beauty by violence, and power by fraud.
Treason was his intent: we must admit
Whoever come; our numbers are too small
For question or selection, and the blood
Of Spaniards shall win Spain for us to-day.
　Abdalazis.　The wicked can not move from underneath
Thy ruling eye.
　Muza.　　　　　Right! Julian and Roderigo
Are leagued against us, on these terms alone,
That Julian's daughter weds the Christian king.　　20
　Egilona (rushing forward).　'Tis true . . and I proclaim it.
　Abdalazis.　　　　　　　　Heaven and earth!
Was it not thou, most lovely, most high-souled,
Who wishedst us success, and me a crown?
　　　　　　　　　　　　　　[OPAS *goes abruptly.*
　Egilona.　I give it . . I am Egilona, queen
Of that detested man.
　Abdalazis.　　　　　　　I touch the hand
That chains down fortune to the throne of fate,
And will avenge thee; for 'twas thy command,
'Tis Heaven's.　My father! what retards our bliss?　　30
Why art thou silent?
　Muza.　　　　　　Inexperienced years
Rather would rest on the soft lap, I see,
Of pleasure, after the fierce gusts of war.
O destiny! that callest me alone,
Hapless, to keep the toilsome watch of state,
Painful to age, unnatural to youth,
Adverse to all society of friends,
Equality, and liberty, and ease,
The welcome cheer of the unbidden feast,　　　40
The gay reply, light, sudden, like the leap
Of the young forester's unbended bow,
But, above all, to tenderness at home,

And sweet security of kind concern
Even from those who seem most truly ours.
Who would resign all this, to be approacht,
Like a sick infant by a canting nurse,
To spread his arms in darkness, and to find
One universal hollowness around?
Forego a little while that bane of peace: 50
Love may be cherisht.
  Abdalazis.   'Tis enough; I ask
No other boon.
  Muza.   Not victory?
  Abdalazis.   Farewell,
O queen! I will deserve thee; why do tears
Silently drop, and slowly, down thy veil?
I shall return to worship thee, and soon;
Why this affliction? O, that I alone
Could raise or could repress it!   60
  Egilona.   We depart,
Nor interrupt your counsels, nor impede;
O may they prosper, whatsoe'er they be,
And perfidy soon meet its just reward!
The infirm and peaceful Opas . . whither gone?
  Muza. Stay, daughter; not for counsel are we met,
But to secure our arms from treachery,
O'erthrow and stifle base conspiracies,
Involve in his own toils our false ally . .
  Egilona. Author of every woe I have endured!   70
Ah sacrilegious man! he vowed to heaven
None of his blood should ever mount the throne.
  Muza. Herein his vow indeed is ratified;
Yet faithful ears have heard this offer made,
And weighty was the conference that ensued,
And long, not dubious; for what mortal e'er
Refused alliance with illustrious power,
Though some have given its enjoyments up,
Tired and enfeebled by satiety?
His friends and partisans, 'twas his pretence,   80
Should pass uninterrupted; hence his camp
Is open every day to enemies.

You look around, O queen, as though you fear'd
Their entrance.   Julian I pursue no more;
You conquer him.   Return we.   I bequeath
Ruin, extermination, not reproach.
How we may best attain your peace and will
We must consider in some other place,
Not, lady, in the midst of snares and wiles
How to supplant your charms and seize your crown.   90
I rescue it; fear not.   Yes, we retire.
Whatever is your wish becomes my own,
Nor is there in this land but who obeys.

        [He leads her away.

THIRD ACT: FIRST SCENE.

Palace in Xeres.

RODERIGO *and* OPAS.

Roderigo.   Impossible! she could not thus resign
Me, for a miscreant of Barbary,
A mere adventurer; but that citron face
Shall bleach and shrivel the whole winter long,
There on yon cork-tree by the sallyport.
She shall return.
    Opas.   To fondness and to faith?
Dost thou retain them, if she could return?
    Roderigo.   Retain them? she has forfeited by this
All right to fondness, all to royalty.   10
    Opas.   Consider and speak calmly: she deserves
Some pity, some reproof.
    Roderigo.   To speak then calmly,
Since thine eyes open and can see her guilt . .
Infamous and atrocious! let her go . .
Chains . .
    Opas.   What! in Muza's camp?
    Roderigo.   My scorn supreme!
    Opas.   Say pity.
    Roderigo.   Ay, ay, pity: that suits best.   20
I loved her, but *had* loved her; three whole years

Of pleasure, and of varied pleasure too,
Had worn the soft impression half away.
What I once felt, I would recall ; the faint
Responsive voice grew fainter each reply :
Imagination sank amid the scenes
It labour'd to create : the vivid joy
Of fleeting youth I follow'd and possest.
'Tis the first moment of the tenderest hour,
'Tis the first mien on entering new delights,   30
We give our peace, our power, our souls, for these.
  Opas. Thou hast ; and what remains ?
  Roderigo.   Roderigo : one
Whom hatred can not reach nor love cast down.[1]
  Opas. Nor gratitude nor pity nor remorse
Call back, nor vows nor earth nor heaven controul.
But art thou free and happy ? art thou safe ?
By shrewd contempt the humblest may chastise
Whom scarlet and its ermine can not scare,
And the sword skulks for everywhere in vain.   40
Thee the poor victim of thy outrages,
Woman, with all her weakness, may despise.
  Roderigo. But first let quiet age have intervened.
  Opas. Ne'er will the peace or apathy of age
Be thine, or twilight steal upon thy day.
The violent choose, but cannot change, their end ;
Violence, by man or nature, must be theirs ;
Thine it must be ; and who to pity thee ?
  Roderigo. Behold my solace ! none. I want no pity.
  Opas. Proclaim we those the happiest of mankind 50
Who never knew a want ? O what a curse
To thee this utter ignorance of thine !
Julian, whom all the good commiserate,
Sees thee below him far in happiness.
A state indeed of no quick restlessness,
No glancing agitation, one vast swell
Of melancholy, deep, impassable,

[1 G. reads:
 Roderigo.   Myself—Roderigo,
Whom hatred cannot reach nor love cast down.]

Interminable, where his spirit alone
Broods and o'ershadows all, bears him from earth,
And purifies his chasten'd soul for heaven.   60
Both heaven and earth shall from thy grasp recede.
Whether on death or life thou arguest,
Untutor'd savage or corrupted heathen
Avows no sentiment so vile as thine.
   Roderigo.   Nor feels?
   Opas.   O human nature ! I have heard
The secrets of the soul, and pitied thee.
Bad and accursed things have men confess'd
Before me, but have left them unarrayed,
Naked, and shivering with deformity.   70
The troubled dreams and deafening gush of youth
Fling o'er the fancy, struggling to be free,
Discordant and impracticable things :
If the good shudder at their past escapes,
Shall not the wicked shudder at their crimes?
They shall : and I denounce upon thy head
God's vengeance : thou shalt rule this land no more.
   Roderigo.   What ! my own kindred leave me and renounce
      me !
   Opas.   Kindred? and is there any in our world
So near us as those sources of all joy,   80
Those on whose bosom every gale of life
Blows softly, who reflect our images
In loveliness through sorrows and through age,
And bear them onward far beyond the grave?
   Roderigo.   Methinks, most reverend Opas, not inapt
Are these fair views; arise they from Seville ?
   Opas.   He who can scoff at them, may scoff at me.
Such are we, that the Giver of all Good
Shall, in the heart he purifies, possess
The latest love ; the earliest, no, not there !   90
I've known the firm and faithful : even from them
Life's eddying spring shed the first bloom on earth.
I pity them, but ask their pity too :
I love the happiness of men, and praise
And sanctify the blessings I renounce.

Roderigo.   Yet would thy baleful influence undermine
The heaven-appointed throne.
Opas.   The throne of guilt
Obdurate, without plea, without remorse.
Roderigo.   What power hast thou ? perhaps thou soon
    wilt want   100
A place of refuge.
Opas.   Rather say, perhaps
My place of refuge will receive me soon.
Could I extend it even to thy crimes,
It should be open ; but the wrath of heaven
Turns them against thee and subverts thy sway :
It leaves thee not, what wickedness and woe
Oft in their drear communion taste together,
Hope and repentance.
Roderigo.   But it leaves me arms,   110
Vigour of soul and body, and a race
Subject by law and dutiful by choice,
Whose hand is never to be holden fast
Within the closing cleft of gnarled creeds ;
No easy prey for these vile mitred Moors.
I, who received thy homage, may retort
Thy threats, vain prelate, and abase thy pride.
Opas.   Low must be those whom mortal can sink lower,
Nor high are they whom human power may raise.
Roderigo.   Judge now : for hear the signal.   120
Opas.   And derides
Thy buoyant heart the dubious gulphs of war ?
Trumpets may sound, and not to victory.
Roderigo.   The traitor and his daughter feel my power.
Opas.   Just God ! avert it !
Roderigo.   Seize this rebel priest.
I will alone subdue my enemies.   [*Goes out.*

THIRD ACT : SECOND SCENE.

Ramiro *and* Osma *enter from opposite sides.*

Ramiro.   Where is the king ? his car is at the gate,
His ministers attend him, but his foes

Are yet more prompt, nor will await delay.
   Osma.   Nor need they, for he meets them as I speak.
   Ramiro.   With all his forces ? or our cause is lost.
Julian and Sisabert surround the walls.
   Osma.   Surround, sayst thou ? enter they not the gates ?
   Ramiro.   Perhaps ere now they enter.
   Osma.   Sisabert
Brings him our prisoner.   10
   Ramiro.   They are friends ! they held
A parley ; and the soldiers, when they saw
Count Julian, lower'd their arms and hail'd him king.
   Osma.   How ? and he leads them in the name of king ?
   Ramiro.   He leads them ; but amid that acclamation
He turn'd away his head, and call'd for vengeance.
   Osma.   In Sisabert, and in the cavalry
He led, were all our hopes.
   Opas.   Woe, woe is theirs
Who have no other.   20
   Osma.   What are thine ? obey
The just commands of our offended king :
Conduct him to the tower . . off . . instantly.
                [Guard *hesitates :* Opas *goes.*
Ramiro, let us haste to reinforce . .
   Ramiro.   Hark ! is the king defeated ? hark !
   Osma.   I hear
Such acclamation as from victory
Arises not, but rather from revolt,
Reiterated, interrupted, lost.
Favour like this his genius will retrieve   30
By time or promises or chastisement,
Whiche'er he choose ; the speediest is the best.
His danger and his glory let us share ;
'Tis ours to serve him.
   Ramiro.   While he rules 'tis ours.
What chariot-wheels are thundering o'er the bridge ?
   Osma.   Roderigo's ; I well know them.
   Ramiro.   Now, the burst
Of acclamation ! now ! again, again.
   Osma.   I know the voices ; they are for Roderigo.   40

Ramiro.   Stay, I entreat thee.   One hath now prevail'd.
So far is certain.
    Osma.   Ay, the right prevails.
    Ramiro.   Transient and vain their joyance who rejoice
Precipitately and intemperately,
And bitter thoughts grow up where'er it fell.
    Osma.   Nor vain and transient theirs who idly float
Down popularity's unfertile stream,
And fancy all their own that rises round.
    Ramiro.   If thou yet lovest, as I know thou dost,   50
Thy king . .
    Osma.   I love him ; for he owes me much,
Brave soul ! and can not, though he would, repay.
Service and faith, pure faith and service hard,
Throughout his reign, if these things be desert,
These have I borne toward him, and still bear.
    Ramiro.   Come, from thy solitary eyrie come,
And share the prey, so plenteous and profuse,
Which a less valorous brood will else consume.
Much fruit is shaken down in civil storms :   60
And shall not orderly and loyal hands
Gather it up ? (*Loud Shouts.*)   Again ! and yet refuse ?
How different are those citizens without
From thee ! from thy serenity ! thy arch,
Thy firmament, of intrepidity !
For their new lord, whom they have never served,
Afraid were they to shout, and only struck
The pavement with their ferrels and their feet :
Now they are certain of the great event
Voices and hands they raise, and all contend   70
Who shall be bravest in applauding most.
Knowest thou these ?
    Osma.   Their voices I know well . .
And can they shout for him they would have slain ?
A prince untried they welcome ; soon their doubts
Are blown afar.
    Ramiro.   Yes, brighter scenes arise.
The disunited he alone unites,
The weak with hope he strengthens, and the strong

With justice.   80
   Osma.   Wait : praise him when time hath given
A soundness and consistency to praise :
He shares it amply who bestows it right.
   Ramiro.   Doubtest thou ?
   Osma.   Be it so : let us away ;
New courtiers come.
   Ramiro.   And why not join the new ?
Let us attend him and congratulate ;
Come on ; they enter.
   Osma.   This is now my post   90
No longer : I could face them in the field,
I can not here.
   Ramiro.   To-morrow all may change ;
Be comforted.
   Osma.   I want nor change nor comfort.
   Ramiro.   The prisoner's voice !
   Osma.   The metropolitan's ?
Triumph he may . . not over me forgiven.
This way, and thro' the chapel : none are there.
                            [*Goes out.*

THIRD ACT: THIRD SCENE.

Opas *and* Sisabert.

   Opas.   The royal threat still sounds along these halls :
Hardly his foot hath past them, and he flees
From his own treachery ; all his pride, his hopes,
Are scatter'd at a breath ; even courage fails
Now falsehood sinks from under him.   Behold,
Again art thou where reign'd thy ancestors ;
Behold the chapel of thy earliest prayers,
Where I, whose chains are sunder'd at thy sight.
Ere they could close around these aged limbs,
Received and blest thee, when thy mother's arm   10
Was doubtful if it loost thee ! with delight
Have I observed the promises we made
Deeply impressed and manfully perform'd.

Now, to thyself beneficent, O prince,
Never henceforth renew those weak complaints
Against Covilla's vows and Julian's faith,
His honour broken, and her heart estranged.
O, if thou holdest peace or glory dear,
Away with jealousy ; brave Sisabert,
Smite from thy bosom, smite that scorpion down :   20
It swells and hardens amid mildew'd hopes,
O'erspreads and blackens whate'er most delights,
And renders us, haters of loveliness,
The lowest of the fiends ; ambition led
The higher on, furious to dispossess,
From admiration sprung and frenzied love.
This disengenuous soul-debasing passion,
Rising from abject and most sordid fear,
Consumes the vitals, pines, and never dies.
For Julian's truth have I not pledged my own ? [1]   30
Have I not sworn Covilla weds no other ?
   Sisabert.   Her persecutor have not I chastised ?
Have not I fought for Julian, won the town,
And liberated thee ?
   Opas.   But left for him
The dangers of pursuit, of ambuscade,
Of absence from thy high and splendid name.
   Sisabert.   Do probity and truth want such supports?
   Opas.   Gryphens and eagles, ivory and gold,
Can add no clearness to the lamp above,   40

[1 G. reads here :
      Rising from abject and most sordid fear
      Stings her own breast with bitter self-reproof.
      Consumes the vitals, pines, and never dies.
      Love, honour, justice, numberless the forms,
      Glorious and high the stature she assumes ;
      But watch the wandering, changeful mischief well,
      And thou shalt see her, with low, lurid light,
      Search where the souls most valued treasure lies,
      Or, more embodied to our vision, stand
      With evil eye, and sorcery hers alone
      Looking away her helpless progeny,
      And drawing poison from its very smiles.
      For Julian's truth have I not pledged my own ?]

But many look for them in palaces
Who have them not, and want them not, at home.
Virtue and valour and experience
Are never trusted by themselves alone
Further than infancy and idiocy :
The men around him, not the man himself,
Are lookt at, and by these is he preferr'd.
'Tis the green mantle of the warrener
And his loud whistle that alone attract
The lofty gazes of the noble herd :   50
And thus, without thy countenance and help
Feeble and faint is yet our confidence,
Brief perhaps our success.
    Sisabert.   Should I resign
To Abdalazis her I once adored ?
He truly, he must wed a Spanish queen !
He rule in Spain ! ah ! whom could any land
Obey so gladly as the meek, the humble,
The friend of all who have no friend beside,
Covilla ! could he choose or could he find   60
Another who might so confirm his power ?
And now indeed from long domestic wars
Who else survives of all our ancient house ?
    Opas.   But Egilona.
    Sisabert.   Vainly she upbraids
Roderigo.
    Opas.   She divorces him, abjures,
And carries vengeance to that hideous highth
Which piety and chastity would shrink
To look from, on the world or on themselves.   70
    Sisabert.   She may forgive him yet.
    Opas.   Ah, Sisabert !
Wretched are those a woman has forgiven :
With her forgiveness ne'er hath love return'd.
Ye know not till too late the filmy tie
That holds heaven's precious boon eternally
To such as fondly cherish her ; once go
Driven by mad passion, strike but at her peace,
And, though she step aside from broad reproach,

Yet every softer virtue dies away.   80
Beaming with virtue inaccessible
Stood Egilona; for her lord she lived,
And for the heavens that raised her sphere so high :
All thoughts were on her, all, beside her own.
Negligent as the blossoms of the field,
Array'd in candour and simplicity,
Before her path she heard the streams of joy
Murmur her name in all their cadences,
Saw them in every scene, in light, in shade,
Reflect her image, but acknowledged them   90
Hers most complete when flowing from her most.
All things in want of her, herself of none,
Pomp and dominion lay beneath her feet
Unfelt and unregarded.   Now behold
The earthly passions war against the heavenly !
Pride against love, ambition and revenge
Against devotion and compliancy :
Her glorious beams adversity hath blunted ;
And coming nearer to our quiet view,
The original clay of coarse mortality   100
Hardens and flaws around her.
     Sisabert.   Every germ
Of virtue perishes when love recedes
From those hot shifting sands, the female heart.
     Opas.   His was the fault ; be his the punishment.
'Tis not their own crimes only, men commit,
They harrow them into another's breast,
And they shall reap the bitter growth with pain.
     Sisabert.   Yes, blooming royalty will first attract
These creatures of the desert.   Now I breathe   110
More freely.   She is theirs if I pursue
The fugitive again.   He well deserves
The death he flies from.   Stay !   Don Julian twice
Call'd him aloud, and he, methinks, replied.
Could not I have remain'd a moment more
And seen the end ? although with hurried voice
He bade me intercept the scattered foes,
And hold the city barr'd to their return.

May Egilona be another's wife
Whether he die or live! but oh! Covilla!   120
She never can be mine! yet she may be
Still happy . . no, Covilla, no . . not happy,
But more deserving happiness without it.
Mine never! nor another's.   'Tis enough.
The tears I shed no rival can deride ;
In the fond intercourse a name once cherisht
Will never be defended by faint smiles,
Nor given up with vows of alter'd love.
And is the passion of my soul at last
Reduced to this? is this my happiness?   130
This my sole comfort? this the close of all
Those promises, those tears, those last adieus,
And those long vigils for the morrow's dawn?
    Opas.   Arouse thee! be thyself.   O Sisabert,
Awake to glory from these feverish dreams :
The enemy is in our land ; two enemies ;
We must quell both : shame on us if we fail.
    Sisabert.   Incredible ! a nation be subdued
Peopled as ours.
    Opas.   Corruption may subvert   140
What force could never.
    Sisabert.   Traitors may.
    Opas.   Alas !
If traitors can, the basis is but frail.
I mean such traitors as the vacant world
Echoes most stunningly : not fur-robed knaves
Whose whispers raise the dreaming bloodhound's ear
Against benighted famisht wanderers,
While with remorseless guilt they undermine
Palace and shed, their very father's house.   150
O blind ! their own, their children's heritage,
To leave more ample space for fearful wealth.
Plunder in some most harmless guise they swathe,
Call it some very meek and hallow'd name,
Some known and borne by their good forefathers,
And own and vaunt it thus redeem'd from sin.
These are the plagues heaven sends o'er every land

Before it sink . . the portents of the street,
Not of the air . . lest nations should complain
Of distance or of dimness in the signs,   160
Flaring from far to Wisdom's eye alone :
These are the last : these, when the sun rides high
In the forenoon of doomsday, revelling,
Make men abhor the earth, arraign the skies.
Ye who behold them spoil field after field,
Despising them in individual strength,
Not with one torrent sweeping them away
Into the ocean of eternity,
Arise ! despatch ! no renovating gale,
No second spring awaits you : up, begone,   170
If you have force and courage even for flight.
The blast of dissolution is behind.
  Sisabert. How terrible ! how true ! what voice like thine
Can rouse and warn the nation ! If she rise,
Say, whither go, where stop we ?
  Opas.   God will guide.
Let us pursue the oppressor to destruction ;
The rest is heaven's : must we move no step
Because we can not see the boundaries
Of our long way, and every stone between ?   180
  Sisabert. Is not thy vengeance for the late affront,
For threats and outrage and imprisonment ?
  Opas. For outrage, yes ; imprisonment and threats
I pardon him, and whatsoever ill
He could do *me.*
  Sisabert.   To hold Covilla from me !
To urge her into vows against her faith,
Against her beauty, youth, and inclination,
Without her mother's blessing, nay, without
Her father's knowledge and authority,   190
So that she never will behold me more,
Flying afar for refuge and for help
Where never friend but God will comfort her !
  Opas. These and more barbarous deeds were perpetrated.
  Sisabert. Yet her proud father deign'd not to inform
Me, whom he loved and taught, in peace and war,

Me, whom he called his son before I hoped
To merit it by marriage or by arms.
He offer'd no excuse, no plea ; exprest
No sorrow ; but with firm unfaltering voice   200
Commanded me . . I trembled as he spoke . .
To follow where he led, redress his wrongs,
And vindicate the honour of his child.
He call'd on God, the witness of his cause,
On Spain the partner of his victories ;
And yet amid these animating words
Roll'd the huge tear down his unvisor'd face ;
A general swell of indignation rose
Thro' the long line, sobs burst from every breast,
Hardly one voice succeeded ; you might hear   210
The impatient hoof strike the soft sandy plain.
But when the gates flew open, and the king
In his high car came forth triumphantly,
Then was Count Julian's stature more elate ;
Tremendous was the smile that smote the eyes
Of all he past.   ' *Fathers, and sons, and brothers,*'
He cried, ' *I fight your battles, follow me !*
Soldiers we know no danger but disgrace ! '
' *Father, and general, and king,*' they shout,
And would proclaim him : back he cast his face,   220
Pallid with grief, and one loud groan burst forth ;
It kindled vengeance thro' the Asturian ranks,
And they soon scatter'd, as the blasts of heaven
Scatter the leaves and dust, the astonisht foe.
    Opas.   And doubtest thou his truth ?
    Sisabert.   I love . . and doubt . .
Fight . . and believe : Roderigo spoke untruths ;
In him I place no trust ; but Julian holds
Truths in reserve : how should I quite confide !
    Opas.   By sorrows thou beholdest him opprest ;   230
Doubt the more prosperous.   March, Sisabert,
Once more against his enemy and ours :
Much hath been done, but much there yet remains.

FOURTH ACT: FIRST SCENE.

Tent of JULIAN.

RODERIGO *and* JULIAN.

Julian.　　The people had deserted thee, and throng'd [1]
My standard, had I raised it, at the first;
But once subsiding, and no voice of mine
Calling by name each grievance to each man,
They, silent and submissive by degrees,
Bore thy hard yoke, and hadst thou but opprest,
Would still have borne it: thou hast now deceived;
Thou hast done all a foreign foe could do
And more against them; with ingratitude
Not hell itself could arm the foreign foe;　　　　10
'Tis forged at home and kills not from afar.
Amid whate'er vain glories fell upon
Thy rainbow span of power, which I dissolve,
Boast not how thou conferredst wealth and rank,
How thou preservedst me, my family,
All my distinctions, all my offices,
When Witiza was murder'd; that I stand
Count Julian at this hour by special grace.
The sword of Julian saved the walls of Ceuta,
And not the shadow that attends his name:　　　　20
It was no badge, no title, that o'erthrew
Soldier and steed and engine.　Don Roderigo!
The truly and the falsely great here differ:
These by dull wealth or daring fraud advance;
Him the Almighty calls amid his people
To sway the wills and passions of mankind.
The weak of heart and intellect beheld

---

[1] [G. begins this act.
　　　Julian.　To stop perhaps at any wickedness
　　　　　　　Appears a merit now, and at the time
　　　　　　　Prudence or policy it often is
　　　　　　　Which afterwards seems magnanimity.
　　　　　　　The people had deserted thee, &c.]

Thy splendour, and adored thee lord of Spain :
I rose .. Roderigo lords o'er Spain no more.
   Roderigo.   Now to a traitor's add a boaster's name.   30
   Julian.   Shameless and arrogant, dost thou believe
I boast for pride or pastime ? forced to boast,
Truth cost me more than falsehood e'er cost thee.
Divested of that purple of the soul,
That potency, that palm of wise ambition,
Cast headlong by thy madness from that high,
That only eminence 'twixt earth and heaven,
Virtue, which some desert, but none despise,
Whether thou art beheld again on earth,
Whether a captive or a fugitive,   40
Miner or galley-slave, depends on me ;
But he alone who made me what I am
Can make me greater or can make me less.
   Roderigo.   Chance, and chance only, threw me in thy
      power ;
Give me my sword again and try my strength.
   Julian.   I tried it in the front of thousands.
   Roderigo.   Death
At least vouchsafe me from a soldier's hand.
   Julian.   I love to hear thee ask it : now my own
Would not be bitter ; no, nor immature.   50
   Roderigo.   Defy it, say thou rather.
   Julian.   Death itself
Shall not be granted thee, unless from God ;
A dole from his and from no other hand.
Thou shalt now hear and own thine infamy.
   Roderigo.   Chains, dungeons, tortures .. but I hear no
      more.
   Julian.   Silence, thou wretch ! live on .. ay, live ..
      abhorr'd.
Thou shalt have tortures, dungeons, chains enough ;
They naturally rise and grow around
Monsters like thee, everywhere, and for ever.   60
   Roderigo.   Insulter of the fallen ! must I endure
Commands as well as threats ? my vassal's too ?
Nor breathe from underneath his trampling feet ?

Julian.   Could I speak patiently who speak to thee,
I would say more : part of thy punishment
It should be, to be taught.
  Roderigo.   Reserve thy wisdom
Until thy patience come, its best ally :
I learn no lore, of peace or war, from thee.
  Julian.   No, thou shalt study soon another tongue,   70
And suns more ardent shall mature thy mind.
Either the cross thou bearest, and thy knees
Among the silent caves of Palestine
Wear the sharp flints away with midnight prayer,
Or thou shalt keep the fasts of Barbary,
Shalt wait amid the crowds that throng the well
From sultry noon till the skies fade again,
To draw up water and to bring it home
In the crackt gourd of some vile testy knave,
Who spurns thee back with bastinaded foot   80
For ignorance or delay of his command.
  Roderigo.   Rather the poison or the bowstring.
  Julian.   Slaves
To other's passions die such deaths as those :
Slaves to their own should die . .
  Roderigo.   What worse ?
  Julian.   Their own.
  Roderigo.   Is this thy counsel, renegade ?
  Julian.   Not mine :
I point a better path, nay, force thee on.   90
I shelter thee from every brave man's sword
While I am near thee : I bestow on thee
Life : if thou die, 'tis when thou sojournest
Protected by this arm and voice no more :
'Tis slavishly, 'tis ignominiously,
'Tis by a villian's knife.
  Roderigo.   By whose ?
  Julian.   Roderigo's.
  Roderigo.   O powers of vengeance ! must I hear ? . .
     endure ? . .
Live ?   100
  Julian.   Call thy vassals : no ? then wipe the drops

Of froward childhood from thy shameless eyes.
So! thou canst weep for passion; not for pity.
   Roderigo.   One hour ago I ruled all Spain! a camp
Not larger than a sheepfold stood alone
Against me: now, no friend throughout the world
Follows my steps or hearkens to my call.
Behold the turns of fortune, and expect
No better: of all faithless men the Moors
Are the most faithless: from thy own experience   110
Thou canst not value nor rely on them.
   Julian.   I value not the mass that makes my sword,
Yet while I use it I rely on it.
   Roderigo.   Julian, thy gloomy soul still meditates . .
Plainly I see it . . death to me . . pursue
The dictates of thy leaders, let revenge
Have its full sway, let Barbary prevail,
And the pure creed her elders have embraced:
Those placid sages hold assassination
A most compendious supplement to law.   120
   Julian.   Thou knowest not the one, nor I the other.
Torn hast thou from me all my soul held dear,
Her form, her voice, all, hast thou banisht from me,
Nor dare I, wretched as I am! recall
Those solaces of every grief erewhile.
I stand abased before insulting crime,
I falter like a criminal myself;
The hand that hurl'd thy chariot o'er its wheels,
That held thy steeds erect and motionless
As molten statues on some palace-gate,   130
Shakes as with palsied age before thee now.
Gone is the treasure of my heart for ever,
Without a father, mother, friend, or name.
Daughter of Julian . . Such was her delight . .
Such was mine too! what pride more innocent,
What surely less deserving pangs like these,
Than springs from filial and parental love!
Debarr'd from every hope that issues forth
To meet the balmy breath of early life,
Her sadden'd days, all cold and colourless,   140

Will stretch before her their whole weary length
Amid the sameness of obscurity.
She wanted not seclusion to unveil
Her thoughts to heaven, cloister, nor midnight bell ;
She found it in all places, at all hours :
While to assuage my labours she indulged
A playfulness that shunn'd a mother's eye,
Still to avert my perils there arose
A piety that even from *me* retired.
  Roderigo.   Such was she ! what am I ! those are the arms
That are triumphant when the battle fails.   [150
O Julian ! Julian ! all thy former words
Struck but the imbecile plumes of vanity,
These thro' its steely coverings pierce the heart.
I ask not life nor death ; but, if I live,
Send my most bitter enemy to watch
My secret paths, send poverty, send pain . .
I will add more . . wise as thou art, thou knowest
No foe more furious than forgiven kings.
I ask not then what thou would'st never grant :   160
May heaven, O Julian, from thy hand receive
A pardon'd man, a chasten'd criminal.
  Julian.   This further curse hast thou inflicted ; wretch !
I can not pardon thee.
  Roderigo.   Thy tone, thy mien,
Refute those words.
  Julian.   No . . I can *not* forgive.
  Roderigo.   Upon my knee, my conqueror, I implore !
Upon the earth, before thy feet . . hard heart !
  Julian.   Audacious ! hast thou never heard that prayer 170
And scorn'd it ? 'tis the last thou shouldst repeat.
Upon the earth ! upon her knees, O God ?
  Roderigo.   Resemble not a wretch so lost as I :
Be better ; O ! be happier ; and pronounce it.
  Julian.   I swerve not from my purpose : thou art mine,
Conquered ; and I have sworn to dedicate,
Like a torn banner on my chapel's roof,
Thee to that power from whom thou hast rebell'd.
Expiate thy crimes by prayer, by penances.

Roderigo.   Hasten the hour of trial, speak of peace.   180
Pardon me not then, but with purer lips
Implore of God, who *would* hear *thee*, to pardon.
  Julian.   Hope it I may . . pronounce it . . O Roderigo!
Ask it of him who can ; I too will ask,
And, in my own transgressions, pray for thine.
  Roderigo.   One name I dare not . .
  Julian.   Go ; abstain from that ;
I do conjure thee, raise not in my soul
Again the tempest that has wreckt my fame ;
Thou shalt not breathe in the same clime with her.   190
Far o'er the unebbing sea thou shalt adore
The eastern star, and may thy end be peace.

FOURTH ACT : SECOND SCENE.

Roderigo *goes :* Hernando *enters.*

Hernando.   From the prince Tarik I am sent, my lord.
  Julian.   A welcome messenger, my brave Hernando.
How fares it with the gallant soul of Tarik ?
  Hernando.   Most joyfully ; he scarcely had pronounced
Your glorious name, and bid me urge your speed,
Than, with a voice as though it answer'd heaven,
' *He shall confound them in their dark designs,*'
Cried he, and turn'd away, with that swift stride
Wherewith he meets and quells his enemies.
  Julian.   Alas ! I can not bear felicitation,   10
Who shunn'd it even in felicity.
  Hernando.   Often we hardly think ourselves the happy
Unless we hear it said by those around.
O my lord Julian, how your praises cheer'd
Our poor endeavours ! sure, all hearts are open,
Lofty and low, wise and unwise, to praise.
Even the departed spirit hovers round
Our blessings and our prayers : the corse itself
Hath shined with other light than the still stars
Shed on its rest, or the dim taper nigh.   20
My father, old men say who saw him dead,

And heard your lips pronounce him good and happy,
Smiled faintly through the quiet gloom that eve,
And the shroud throbb'd upon his grateful breast.
Howe'er it be, many who tell the tale
Are good and happy from that voice of praise.
His guidance and example were denied
My youth and childhood : what I am I owe . .
    Julian.   Hernando, look not back : a narrow path
And arduous lies before thee : if thou stop   30
Thou fallest ; go right onward, nor observe
Closely and rigidly another's way,
But, free and active, follow up thy own.
    Hernando.   The voice that urges now my manly step
Onward in life, recalls me to the past,
And from that fount I freshen for the goal.
Early in youth, among us villagers
Converse and ripen'd council you bestow'd.
O happy days of (far departed !) peace,
Days when the mighty Julian stoopt his brow   40
Entering our cottage-door ; another air
Breath'd through the house, tired age and lightsome youth
Beheld him with intensest gaze ; these felt
More chasten'd joy ; they more profound repose.
Yes, my best lord, when labour sent them home
And midday suns, when from the social meal
The wicker window held the summer heat,
Prais'd have those been who, going unperceived,
Open'd it wide that all might see you well :
Nor were the children blamed, hurrying to watch   50
Upon the mat what rush would last arise
From your foot's pressure, ere the door was closed,
And not yet wondering how they dared to love.
Your counsels are more precious now than ever,
But are they . . pardon if I err . . the same ?
Tarik is gallant, kind, the friend of Julian,
Can he be more ? or ought he to be less ?
Alas ! his faith !
    Julian.   In peace or war ? Hernando.
    Hernando.   O, neither ; far above it ; faith in God.   60

Julian. 'Tis God's, not thine: embrace it not, nor hate it.
Precious or vile, how dare we seize that offering,
Scatter it, spurn it, in its way to heaven,
Because we know it not? the sovran lord
Accepts his tribute, myrrh and frankincense
From some, from others penitence and prayer:
Why intercept them from his gracious hand?
Why dash them down? why smite the supplicant?
    Hernando. 'Tis what they do.
    Julian.   Avoid it thou the more. 70
If time were left me, I could hear well-pleased
How Tarik fought up Calpe's fabled cliff,
While I pursued the friends of Don Roderigo
Across the plain, and drew fresh force from mine.
O! had some other land, some other cause,
Invited him and me, I then could dwell
On this hard battle with unmixt delight.
    Hernando.   Eternal is its glory, if the deed
Be not forgotten till it be surpast:
Much praise by land, by sea much more, he won,   80
For then a Julian was not at his side,
Nor led the van, nor awed the best before;
The whole, a mighty whole, was his alone.
There might be seen how far he shone above
All others of the day: old Muza watcht
From his own shore the richly laden fleet,
Ill-arm'd and scatter'd, and pursued the rear
Beyond those rocks that bear St Vincent's name,
Cutting the treasure, not the strength, away;
Valiant, where any prey lies undevour'd   90
In hostile creek or too confiding isle.
Tarik, with his small barks, but with such love
As never chief from rugged sailor won,
Smote their high masts and swelling rampires down,
And Cadiz wept in fear o'er Trafalgar.
Who that beheld our sails from off the highths,
Like the white birds, nor larger, tempt the gale
In sunshine and in shade, now almost touch
The solitary shore, glance, turn, retire,

Would think these lovely playmates could portend   100
Such mischief to the world, such blood, such woe ;
Could draw to them from far the peaceful hinds,
Cull the gay flower of cities, and divide
Friends, children, every bond of human life ;
Could dissipate whole families, could sink
Whole states in ruin, at one hour, one blow.
     Julian.   Go, good Hernando ? who *would* think these things ?
Say to the valiant Tarik I depart
Forthwith : he knows not from what heaviness
Of soul I linger here ; I could endure   110
No converse, no compassion, no approach,
Other than thine, whom the same cares improved
Beneath my father's roof, my foster-brother,
To brighter days and happier end, I hope ;
In whose fidelity my own resides
With Tarik and with his compeers and chief.
I cannot share the gladness I excite,
Yet shall our Tarik's generous heart rejoice.

FOURTH ACT : THIRD SCENE.

Egilona *enters :* Hernando *goes.*

     Egilona.   O fly me not because I am unhappy,
Because I am deserted fly me not ;
It was not so before, and can it be
Ever from Julian ?
     Julian.   What would Egilona
That Julian's power with her new lords can do ?
Surely her own must there preponderate.
     Egilona.   I hold no suit to them.   Restore, restore
Roderigo.
     Julian.   He no longer is my prisoner.   10
     Egilona.   Escapes he then ?
     Julian.   Escapes he, dost thou say ?
O Egilona ! what unworthy passion . .
     Egilona.   Unworthy, when I loved him, was my passion ;

The passion that now swells my heart is just.
  Julian.   What fresh reproaches hath he merited?
  Egilona.   Deep-rooted hatred shelters no reproach.
But whither is he gone?
  Julian.   Far from the walls.
  Egilona.   And I knew nothing?   20
  Julian.   His offence was known
To thee at least.
  Egilona.   Will it be expiated?
  Julian.   I trust it will.
  Egilona.   This withering calm consumes me.
He marries then Covilla! 'twas for this
His people were excited to rebell,
His sceptre was thrown by, his vows were scorn'd,
And I . . and I . .
  Julian.   Cease, Egilona!   30
  Egilona.   Cease?
Sooner shalt thou to live than I to reign.

FIFTH ACT: FIRST SCENE.

Tent of MUZA.

MUZA.   TARIK.   ABDALAZIS.

  Muza.   To have first landed on these shores appears
Transcendant glory to the applauded Tarik.
  Tarik.   Glory, but not transcendant, it appears,
What might in any other.
  Muza.   Of thyself
All this vain boast?
  Tarik.   Not of myself: 'twas Julian.
Against his shield the refluent surges roll'd,
While the sea-breezes threw the arrows wide,
And fainter cheers urged the reluctant steeds.   10
  Muza.   That Julian, of whose treason I have proofs,
That Julian, who rejected my commands
Twice, when our mortal foe besieged the camp,
And forced my princely presence to his tent.

Tarik.   Say rather, who without one exhortation,
One precious drop from true believer's vein,
Marcht, and discomfited our enemies.
I found in him no treachery.   Hernando,
Who, little versed in moody wiles, is gone
To lead him hither, was by him assign'd   20
My guide, and twice in doubtful fight his arm
Protected me : once on the highths of Calpe,
Once on the plain, when courtly jealousies
Tore from the bravest and the best his due,
And gave the dotard and the coward command :
Then came Roderigo forth : the front of war
Grew darker : him, equal in chivalry,
Julian alone could with success oppose.
    Abdalazis.   I doubt their worth who praise their enemies.
    Tarik.   And theirs doubt I who persecute their friends.   30
    Muza.   Thou art in league with him.
    Tarik.   Thou wert, by oaths ;
I am without them ; for his heart is brave.
    Muza.   Am I to bear all this ?
    Tarik.   All this and more :
Soon wilt thou see the man whom thou hast wrong'd,
And the keen hatred in thy breast conceal'd
Find its right way, and sting thee to the core.
    Muza.   Hath he not foil'd us in the field ? not held
Our wisdom to reproach ?   40
    Tarik.   Shall we abandon
All he hath left us in the eyes of men ?
Shall we again make him our adversary
Whom we have proved so, long and fatally ?
If he subdue for us our enemies,
Shall we raise others, or, for want of them,
Convert him into one against his will ?

FIFTH ACT : SECOND SCENE.

Hᴇʀɴᴀɴᴅᴏ *enters.* Tᴀʀɪᴋ *continues.*

Here comes Hernando from that prince himself.
    Muza.   Who scorns, himself, to come.

Hernando.   The queen detains him.
Abdalazis.   How ! Egilona ?
Muza.   'Twas my will.
Tarik.   At last
He must be happy ; for delicious calm
Follows the fierce enjoyment of revenge.
  Hernando.   That calm was never his, no other will be.
Thou knowest not, and mayest thou never know,   10
How bitter is the tear that fiery shame
Scourges and tortures from the soldier's eye.
Whichever of these bad reports be true,
He hides it from all hearts to wring his own,
And drags the heavy secret to the grave.
Not victory that o'ershadows him sees he ;
No airy and light passion stirs abroad
To ruffle or to soothe him ; all are quell'd
Beneath a mightier, sterner stress of mind :
Wakeful he sits, and lonely, and unmoved,   20
Beyond.the arrows, views, or shouts of men ;
As oftentimes an eagle, ere the sun
Throws o'er the varying earth his early ray,
Stands solitary, stands immovable
Upon some highest cliff, and rolls his eye,
Clear, constant, unobservant, unabased,
In the cold light above the dews of morn.
He now assumes that quietness of soul
Which never but in danger have I seen
On his staid breast.   30
  Tarik.   Danger is past ; he conquers ;
No enemy is left him to subdue.
  Hernando.   He sank not, while there was, into himself.
Now plainly see I from his alter'd tone,
He can not live much longer.   Thanks to God !
  Tarik.   What ! wishest thou thy once kind master dead ?
Was he not kind to thee, ungrateful slave !
  Hernando.   The gentlest, as the bravest, of mankind.
Therefore shall memory dwell more tranquilly
With Julian once at rest, than friendship could,   40
Knowing him yearn for death with speechless love.

For his own sake I could endure his loss,
Pray for it, and thank God; yet mourn I must
Him above all, so great, so bountiful,
So blessed once! bitterly must I mourn.
'Tis not my solace that 'tis his desire;
Of all who pass us in life's drear descent
We grieve the most for those that wisht to die.
A father to us all, he merited,
Unhappy man! all a good father's joy   50
In his own house, where seldom he hath been,
But, ever mindful of its dear delights,
He form'd one family around him ever.
  Tarik.   Yes, we have seen and known him.   Let his fame
Refresh his friends, but let it stream afar,
Nor in the twilight of home-scenes be lost.
He chose the best, and cherisht them; he left
To self-reproof the mutinies of vice;
Avarice, that dwarfs Ambition's tone and mien;
Envy, sick nursling of the court; and Pride   60
That can not bear his semblance nor himself;
And Malice, with blear visage half-descried
Amid the shadows of her hiding-place.
  Hernando.   What could I not endure, O gallant man,
To hear him spoken of as thou hast spoken!
O! I would almost be a slave to him
Who calls me one.
  Muza.   What! art thou not? begone.
  Tarik.   Reply not, brave Hernando, but retire.
All can revile, few only can reward.   70
Behold the meed our mighty chief bestows!
Accept it, for thy services, and mine.
More, my bold Spaniard, hath obedience won
Than anger, even in the ranks of war.
  Hernando.   The soldier, not the Spaniard, shall obey. [*Goes.*
  Muza (to *Tarik*).   Into our very council bringest thou
Children of reprobation and perdition?
Darkness thy deeds and emptiness thy speech,
Such images thou raisest as buffoons
Carry in merriment on festivals;   80

Nor worthiness nor wisdom would display
To public notice their deformities,
Nor cherish them nor fear them ; why shouldst thou ?
   Tarik.   I fear not them nor thee.

FIFTH ACT :   THIRD SCENE.

EGILONA *enters.*

Abdalazis.   Advance, O queen.
Now let the turbulence of faction cease.
   Muza.   Whate'er thy purpose, speak, and be composed.
   Egilona.   He goes ; he is afar ; he follows her ;
He leads her to the altar, to the throne ;
For, calm in vengeance, wise in wickedness,
The traitor hath prevail'd, o'er him, o'er me,
O'er you, the slaves, the dupes, the scorn of Julian.
What have I heard ! what have I seen !
   Muza.   Proceed.   10
   Abdalazis.   And I swear vengeance on his guilty head
Who intercepts from thee the golden rays
Of sovranty, who dares rescind thy rights,
Who steals upon thy rest, and breathes around
Empoison'd damps o'er that serenity
Which leaves the world, and faintly lingers here.
   Muza.   Who shuns thee . .
   Abdalazis.   Whose desertion interdicts
Homage, authority, precedency . .
   Muza.   Till war shall rescue them . .   20
   Abdalazis.   And love restored.
   Egilona.   O generous Abdalazis ! never ! never !
My enemies . . Julian alone remains . .
The worst in safety, far beyond my reach,
Breathe freely on the summit of their hopes,
Because they never stopt, because they sprang
From crime to crime, and trampled down remorse.
Oh ! if her heart knew tenderness like mine !
Grant vengeance on the guilty ; grant but that,
I ask no more ; my hand, my crown is thine.   30

Fulfill the justice of offended heaven,
,Assert the sacred rights of royalty,
Come not in vain, crush the rebellious crew,
Crush, I implore, the indifferent and supine.
  Muza. Roderigo thus escaped from Julian's tent?
  Egilona. No, not escaped, escorted, like a king.
The base Covilla first pursued her way
On foot; but after her the royal car,
Which bore me from San Pablo's to the throne,
Empty indeed, yet ready at her voice,   40
Roll'd o'er the plain amid the carcases
Of those who fell in battle or in flight:
She, a deceiver still, to whate'er speed
The moment might incite her, often stopt
To mingle prayers with the departing breath,
Improvident! and those with heavy wounds
Groan'd bitterly beneath her tottering knee.
  Tarik. Now, by the clement and the merciful!
The girl did well. When I breathe out my soul,
Oh! if compassion give one pang the more,   50
That pang be mine; here be it, in this land:
Such women are they in this land alone.
  Egilona. Insulting man!
  Muza.   We shall confound him yet.
Say, and speak quickly, whither went the king?
Thou knewest where was Julian.
  Abdalazis.   I will tell
Without his answer: yes, my friends! yes, Tarik,
Now will I speak, nor thou for once reply.
There is, I hear, a poor half-ruined cell   60
In Xeres, whither few indeed resort,
Green are the walls within, green is the floor
And slippery from disuse; for Christian feet
Avoid it, as half-holy, half-accurst.
Still in its dark recess fanatic Sin
Abases to the ground his tangled hair,
And servile scourges and reluctant groans
Roll o'er the vault uninterruptedly,
Till (such the natural stillness of the place)

The very tear upon the damps below   70
Drops audible, and the heart's throb replies.
There is the idol maid of Christian creed,
And taller images whose history
I know not nor inquired.   A scene of blood,
Of resignation amid mortal pangs,
And other things exceeding all belief.
Hither the aged Opas of Seville
Walkt slowly, and behind him was a man
Barefooted, bruised, dejected, comfortless,
In sackcloth ; the white ashes on his head   80
Dropt as he smote his breast ; he gather'd up,
Replaced them all, groan'd deeply, lookt to heaven,
And held them like a treasure with claspt hands.
    Egilona.   O ! was Roderigo so abased ?
    Muza.   'Twas he.
Now, Egilona, judge between your friends
And enemies : behold what wretches brought
The king, thy lord, Roderigo, to disgrace.
    Egilona.   He merited . . but not from them . . from me
This, and much worse : had I inflicted it,   90
I had rejoiced . . at what I ill endure.
    Muza.   For thee, for thee alone, we wisht him here,
But other hands releast him.
    Abdalazis.   With what aim
Will soon appear to those discerning eyes.
    Egilona.   I pray thee, tell what past until that hour.
    Abdalazis.   Few words, and indistinct : repentant sobs
Fill'd the whole space ; the taper in his hand,
Lighting two small dim lamps before the altar,
He gave to Opas ; at the idol's feet   100
He laid his crown, and wiped his tears away.
The crown reverts not, but the tears return.
    Egilona.   Yes, Abdalazis ! soon, abundantly.
If he had only call'd upon my name,
Seeking my pardon e'er he lookt to heaven's,
I could have . . no ! he thought not once on me !
Never shall he find peace or confidence ;
I will rely on fortune and on thee,

Nor fear my future lot: sure, Abdalazis,
A fall so great can never happen twice,   110
Nor man again be faithless, like Roderigo.
  Abdalazis.   Faithless he may be still, never so faithless.
Fainter must be the charms, remote the days,
When memory and dread example die,
When love and terror thrill the heart no more,
And Egilona is herself forgotten.

FIFTH ACT : FOURTH SCENE.

JULIAN *enters.*

  Tarik.   Turn, and behold him! who is now confounded?
Ye who awaited him, where are ye? speak.
Is some close comet blazing o'er your tents?
Muza! Abdalazis! princes! conquerors!
Summon, interrogate, command, condemn.
  Muza.   Justly, Don Julian . . but respect for rank
Allays resentment, nor interrogates
Without due form . . justly may we accuse
This absence from our councils, from our camp;
This loneliness in which we still remain   10
Who came invited to redress your wrongs.
Where is the king?
  Julian.   The people must decide.
  Muza.   Imperfectly, I hope, I understand
Those words, unworthy of thy birth and age.
  Julian.   O chieftain, such have been our Gothic laws.
  Muza.   Who then amid such turbulence is safe?
  Julian.   He who observes them: 'tis no turbulence,
It violates no peace: 'tis surely worth
A voice, a breath of air, thus to create   20
By their high will the man, form'd after them
In their own image, vested with their power,
To whom they trust their freedom and their lives.
  Muza.   They trust! the people! God assigns the charge,
Kings open but the book of destiny
And read their names; all that remains for them

The mystic hand from time to time reveals.
Worst of idolaters! idolater
Of that refractory and craving beast
Whose den is in the city, at thy hand   30
I claim our common enemy, the king.
   Julian.   Sacred from justice then; but not from malice!
   Tarik.   Surrender him, my friend: be sure his pains
Will not be soften'd.
   Julian.   'Tis beyond my power.
   Tarik.   To-morrow . . if in any distant fort
He lies to-night: send after him.
   Julian.   My faith
Is plighted, and he lives . . no prisoner.
   Egilona.   I knew the truth.   40
   Abdalazis (to JULIAN).   Now, Tarik, hear and judge.
Was he not in thy camp? and in disguise?
   Tarik.   No: I will answer thee.
   Muza.   Audacious man!
Had not the Kalif Walid placed thee here,
Chains and a traitor's death should be thy doom.
Speak, Abdalazis! Egilona, speak.
Were ye not present? was not I myself?
And aided not this Julian his escape?
   Julian.   'Tis true.   50
   Tarik.   Away then friendship! to thy fate
I leave thee: thou hast render'd Muza just,
Me hostile to thee.   Who is safe? a man
Arm'd with such power, and with such perfidy!
   Julian.   Stay, Tarik! hear me; for to thee alone
Would I reply.
   Tarik.   Thou hast replied already.   [*Goes.*
   Muza.   We, who were enemies, would not inquire
Too narrowly what reasons urged thy wrath
Against thy sovran lord: beneath his flag   60
The Christians first assail'd us from these shores,
And we seiz'd gladly the first aid we found
To quell a wealthy and a warlike king.
We never held to thee the vain pretence
That 'twas thy quarrel our brave youth espoused,

Thine, who hast wrought us much disgrace and woe.
From perils and from losses here we rest
And drink of the fresh fountain at our feet,
Not madly following such illusive streams
As overspread the dizzy wilderness,   70
And vanish from the thirst they have seduced.
Ours was the enterprise, the land is ours.
What gain we by our toils, if he escape
Whom we came hither solely to subdue?
    Julian.   Is there no gain to live in amity?
    Muza.   The gain of traffickers and idle men;
Courage and zeal expire upon such calms.
Further, what amity can Moors expect
When you have joined your forces?
    Julian.   From the hour   80
That he was vanquisht, I have laid aside
All power, all arms.
    Muza.   How can we trust thee, once
Deceived, and oftener than this once despised?
Thou camest hither with no other aim
Than to deprive Roderigo of his crown
For thy own brow.
    Egilona.   Julian, base man, 'tis true.
He comes a prince, no warrior, at this hour.
    Muza.   His sword, O queen, would not avail him
    now.   90
    Abdalazis.   Julian, I feel less anger than regret.
No violence of speech, no obloquy,
No accusation shall escape my lips:
Need there is none, nor reason, to avoid
My questions: if thou value truth, reply.
Hath not Roderigo left the town and camp?
Hath not thy daughter?
    Egilona.   Past the little brook
Towards the Betis. From a tower I saw
The fugitives, far on their way; they went   100
Over one bridge, each with arm'd men . . not half
A league of road between them . . and had join'd,
But that the olive-groves along the path

Conceal'd them from each other, not from me :
Beneath me the whole level I survey'd,
And, when my eyes no longer could discern
Which track they took, I knew it from the storks
Rising in clouds above the reedy plain.
    Muza.   Deny it, if thou canst.
    Julian.   I order'd it.   110
    Abdalazis.   None could beside. Lo! things in such a
      mass
Falling together on observant minds,
Create suspicion and establish proof :
Wanted there fresh . . why not employ our arms ?
Why go alone ?
    Muza.   To parley, to conspire,
To reunite the Spaniards, which we saw,
To give up treaties, close up enmities,
And ratify the deed with Moorish blood.
    Julian. Gladly would Spain procure your safe return, 120
Gladly would pay large treasures for the aid
You brought against oppression.
    Muza.   Pay she shall
The treasures of her soil, her ports, her youth :
If she resist, if she tumultuously
Call forth her brigands and we lose a man,
Dreadful shall be our justice ; war shall rage
Through every city, hamlet, house, and field,
And, universal o'er the gasping land,
Depopulation.   130
    Julian.   They shall rue the day
Who dare these things.
    Muza.   Let order then prevail.
In vain thou sendest far away thy child,
Thy counsellor the metropolitan,
And Sisabert : prudence is mine no less.
Divide with us our conquests, but the king
Must be deliver'd up.
    Julian.   Never by me.
    Muza. False then were thy reproaches, false thy grief. 140
    Julian. O Egilona ! were thine also feign'd ?

Abdalazis.   Say, lovely queen, neglectful of thy charms
Turn'd he his eyes toward the young Covilla?
Did he pursue her to the mad excess
Of breaking off her vows to Sisabert,
And marrying her, against the Christian law?
  Muza.   Did he prefer so?
  Abdalazis.   Could he prefer
To Egilona . .
  Egilona.   Her! the child Covilla?   150
Eternal hider of a foolish face,
Incapable of any thing but shame,
To me? old man! to me? O Abdalazis!
No: he but follow'd with slow pace my hate.
And can not pride check these unseemly tears?   [*Goes.*
  Muza.   The most offended, an offended woman,
A wife, a queen, is silent on the deed.
  Abdalazis.   Thou disingenuous and ignoble man,
Spreading these rumours! sending into exile
All those their blighting influence injured most: 160
And whom? thy daughter and adopted son,
The chieftains of thy laws and of thy faith.
Call any witnesses, proclaim the truth,
And set at last thy heart, thy fame, at rest.
  Julian.   Not, if I purposed or desired to live,
My own dishonour would I e'er proclaim
Amid vindictive and reviling foes.
  Muza.   Calling us foes, avows he not his guilt?
Condemns he not the action we condemn,
Owning it his, and owning it dishonour?   170
'Tis well my cares prest forward, and struck home.
  Julian.   Why smilest thou?   I never saw that smile
But it portended an atrocious deed.
  Muza.   After our manifold and stern assaults,
With every tower and battlement destroy'd,
The walls of Ceuta still were strong enough . .
  Julian.   For what? who boasted now her brave defence,
Or who forbade your entrance after peace?
  Muza.   None: for who could? their engines now arose
To throw thy sons into the arms of death.   180

For this erect they their proud crests again.
Mark him at last turn pale before a Moor.
   Julian.   Imprudent have they been, their youth shall plead.
   Abdalazis. O father! could they not have been detain'd?
   Muza. Son, thou art safe, and wert not, while they lived.
   Abdalazis. I fear'd them not.
   Muza.   And therefore wert not safe:
Under their star the blooming Egilona
Would watch for thee the nuptial lamp in vain.
   Julian. Never, oh never, hast thou workt a wile   190
So barren of all good! Speak out at once,
What hopest thou by striking this alarm?
It shocks my reason, not my fears or fondness.
   Muza. Be happy then as ignorance can be;
Soon wilt thou hear it shouted from our ranks.
Those who once hurl'd defiance o'er our heads,
Scorning our arms, and scoffing at our faith,
The nightly wolf hath visited, unscared,
And loathed them as her prey; for famine first,
Achieving in few days the boast of years,   200
Sank their young eyes and open'd us the gates:
Ceuta, her port, her citadel, is ours.
   Julian. Blest boys! inhuman as thou art, what guilt
Was theirs?
   Muza.   Their father's.
   Julian. O support me, Heaven!
Against this blow! all others I have borne.
Ermenegild! thou mightest, sure, have lived!
A father's name awoke no dread of thee!
Only thy mother's early bloom was thine!   210
There dwelt on Julian's brow . . thine was serene . .
The brightened clouds of elevated souls,
·Fear'd by the most below: those who lookt up
Saw at their season in clear signs advance
Rapturous valour, calm solicitude,
All that impatient youth would press from age,
Or sparing age sigh and detract from youth:
Hence was his fall! my hope! myself! my Julian
Alas! I boasted . . but I thought on him,

Inheritor of all . . all what ? my wrongs . .   220
Follower of me . . and whither ? to the grave . .
Ah no : it should have been so years far hence !
Him at this moment I could pity most,
But I most prided in him ; now I know
I loved a name, I doated on a shade.
Sons ! I approach the mansions of the just,
And my arms clasp you in the same embrace,
Where none shall sever you . . and do I weep !
And do they triumph o'er my tenderness !
I had forgotten my inveterate foes   230
Everywhere nigh me, I had half forgotten
Your very murderers, while I thought on you :
For, O my children, ye fill all the space
My soul would wander o'er . . O bounteous heaven !
There is a presence, if the well-beloved
Be torn from us by human violence,
More intimate, pervading, and complete,
Than when they lived and spoke like other men ;
And their pale images are our support
When reason sinks, or threatens to desert us.   240
I weep no more . . pity and exultation
Sway and console me : are they . . no ! . . both dead ?
    Muza.   Ay, and unsepulchred.
    Julian.   Nor wept nor seen
By any kindred and far-following eye ?
    Muza.   Their mother saw them, if not dead, expire.
    Julian.   O cruelty . . to them indeed the least !
My children, ye are happy . . ye have lived
Of heart unconquer'd, honour unimpair'd,
And died, true Spaniards, loyal to the last.   250
    Muza.   Away with him.
    Julian.   Slaves ! not before I lift
My voice to heaven and man : though enemies
Surround me, and none else, yet other men
And other times shall hear : the agony
Of an opprest and of a bursting heart
No violence can silence ; at its voice
The trumpet is o'erpower'd, and glory mute,

And peace and war hide all their charms alike.
Surely the guests and ministers of heaven   260
Scatter it forth through all the elements,
So suddenly, so widely, it extends,
So fearfully men breathe it, shuddering
To ask or fancy how it first arose.
  Muza.   Yes, they shall shudder : but will that, henceforth,
Molest my privacy, or shake my power ?
  Julian.   Guilt hath pavilions, but no privacy.
The very engine of his hatred checks
The torturer in his transport of revenge,
Which, while it swells his bosom, shakes his power,   270
And raises friends to his worst enemy.
  Muza.   Where now are thine ? will they not curse the day
That gave thee birth, and hiss thy funeral !
Thou hast left none who could have pitied thee.
  Julian.   Many, nor those alone of tenderer mould,
For me will weep ; many, alas, through me !
Already I behold my funeral ;
The turbid cities wave and swell with it,
And wrongs are lost in that day's pageantry :
Opprest and desolate, the countryman   280
Receives it like a gift ; he hastens home,
Shows where the hoof of Moorish horse laid waste
His narrow croft and winter garden-plot,
Sweetens with fallen pride his children's lore,
And points their hatred, but applauds their tears.
Justice, who came not up to us through life,
Loves to survey our likeness on our tombs,
When rivalry, malevolence, and wrath,
And every passion that once storm'd around,
Is calm alike without them as within.   290
Our very chains make the whole world our own,
Bind those to us who else had past us by,
Those at whose call, brought down to us, the light
Of future ages lives upon our name.
  Muza.   I may accelerate that meteor's fall,
And quench that idle ineffectual light,
Without the knowledge of thy distant world.

Julian.   My world and thine are not that distant one.
Is age less wise, less merciful, than grief,
To keep this secret from thee, poor old man !   300
Thou canst not lessen, canst not aggravate
My sufferings, canst not shorten or extend
Half a sword's length between my God and me.
I thank thee for that better thought than fame,
Which none however, who deserve, despise,
Nor lose from view till all things else are lost.
    Abdalazis.   Julian, respect his age, regard his power.
Many who fear'd not death, have dragg'd along
A piteous life in darkness and in chains.
Never was man so full of wretchedness   310
But something may be suffered after all,
Perhaps in what clings round his breast and helps
To keep the ruin up, which he amid
His agony and frenzy overlooks,
But droops upon at last, and clasps and dies.
    Julian.   Although a Muza send far underground,
Into the quarry whence the palace rose,
His mangled prey, climes alien and remote
Mark and record the pang.   While overhead
Perhaps he passes on his favourite steed,   320
Less heedful of the misery he inflicts
Than of the expiring sparkle from a stone,
Yet we, alive or dead, have fellow-men
If ever we have served them, who collect
From prisons and from dungeons our remains,
And bear them in their bosom to their sons.
Man's only relics are his benefits ;
These, be there ages, be there worlds, between,
Retain him in communion with his kind :
Hence is our solace, our security,   330
Our sustenance, till heavenly truth descends,
Covering with brightness and beatitude
The frail foundations of these humbler hopes,
And, like an angel guiding us, at once
Leaves the loose chain and iron gate behind.
    Muza.   Take thou my justice first, then hope for theirs.

I, who can bend the living to my will,
Fear not the dead, and court not the unborn :
Their arm will never reach me, nor shall thine.
  Abdalazis. Pity, release him, pardon him, my father ! 340
Forget how much thou hatest perfidy.
Think of him, once so potent, still so brave,
So calm, so self-dependent in distress,
I marvel at him : hardly dare I blame
When I behold him fallen from so high,
And so exalted after such a fall.
Mighty must that man be, who can forgive
A man so mighty ; seize the hour to rise,
Another never comes : O say, my father !
Say, " Julian, be my enemy no more."   •350
He fills me with a greater awe than e'er
The field of battle, with himself the first,
When every flag that waved along our host
Droopt down the staff, as if the very winds
Hung in suspense before him.   Bid him go
And peace be with him, or let me depart.
Lo ! like a god, sole and inscrutable,
He stands above our pity.
  Julian.   For that wish . .
Vain as it is, 'tis virtuous . . O, for that,   360
However wrong thy censure and thy praise,
Kind Abdalazis ! mayst thou never feel
The rancour that consumes thy father's breast,
Nor want the pity thou hast sought for mine !
  Muza.   Now hast thou seal'd thy doom.
  Julian.   And thou thy crimes.
  Abdalazis.   O father ! heed him not : those evil words
Leave neither blight nor blemish : let him go.
  Muza.   A boy, a very boy art thou indeed !
One who in early day would sally out   370
To chase the lion, and would call it sport,
But, when more wary steps had closed him round,
Slink from the circle, drop the toils, and blanch
Like a lithe plant from under snow in spring.
  Abdalazis.   He who ne'er shrank from danger, might
    shrink now,

And ignominy would not follow here.
   Muza.   Peace, Abdalazis!   How is this? he bears
Nothing that warrants him invulnerable :
Shall I then shrink to smite him? shall my fears
Be greatest at the blow that ends them all?   380
Fears? no! 'tis justice, fair, immutable,
Whose measured step at times advancing nigh
Appals the majesty of kings themselves.
O were he dead! though then revenge were o'er!

FIFTH ACT : FIFTH SCENE.

Officer.   Thy wife, Count Julian !
Julian.   Speak !
Officer.   Is dead.
Julian.   Adieu
Earth! and the humblest of all earthly hopes,
To hear of comfort, though to find it vain.
Thou murderer of the helpless! shame of man!
Shame of thy own base nature! 'tis an act
He who could perpetrate could not avow,
Stain'd, as he boasts to be, with innocent blood,   10
Dead to reproach, and blind to retribution.
   Officer.   Julian! be just; 'twill make thee less unhappy.
Grief was her end: she held her younger boy
And wept upon his cheek; his naked breast
By recent death now hardening and inert,
Slipt from her knee; again with frantic grasp
She caught it, and it weigh'd her to the ground :
There lay the dead.
   Julian.   She ?
   Officer.   And the youth her son.   20
   Julian.   Receive them to thy peace, eternal God !
O soother of my hours, while I beheld
The light of day, and thine! adieu, adieu !
And, my Covilla! dost thou yet survive ?
Yes, my lost child, thou livest yet . . in shame !

O agony, past utterance ! past thought !
That throwest death, as some light idle thing,
With all its terrors, into dust and air,
I will endure thee ; I, whom heaven ordain'd
Thus to have serv'd beneath my enemies,   30
Their conqueror, thus to have revisited
My native land with vengeance and with woe.
Henceforward shall she recognise her sons,
Impatient of oppression or disgrace,
And rescue them, or perish ; let her hold
This compact, written with her blood and mine.
Now follow me: but tremble : years shall roll
And wars rage on, and Spain at last be free.

IPPOLITO DI ESTE.*

Ippolito.   Now all the people follow the procession
Here may I walk alone, and let my spirits
Enjoy the coolness of these quiet aisles.
Surely no air is stirring ; every step
Tires me ; the columns shake, the ceiling fleets,
The floor beneath me slopes, the altar rises.
Stay ! here she stept : what grace ! what harmony !
It seem'd that every accent, every note
Of all the choral music, breath'd from her :
From her celestial airiness of form   10
I could have fancied purer light descended.
Between the pillars, close and wearying,
I watcht her as she went : I had rusht on ;
It was too late ; yet, when I stopt, I thought
I stopt full soon : I cried, *Is she not there ?*
She *had* been : I had seen her shadow burst
The sunbeam as she parted : a strange sound,
A sound that stupified and not aroused me,
Fill'd all my senses : such was never felt
Save when the sword-girt Angel struck the gate,   20
And Paradise wail'd loud and closed for ever.
She should return ; the hour is past away.
How can I bear to see her (yet I will)
Springing, she fondly thinks, to meet the man
I most abhor, my father's base-born son,
Ferrante !

* Ferrante and Giulio were brothers, by the father's side, to the
Duke Alfonso and the Cardinal Ippolito di Este. The cardinal
deprived Ferrante of his eyes for loving the same object as his
Eminence, and because she had praised the beauty of them.

Rosalba (*entering*).   What! I called him? in my haste
To languish at his beauty, to weigh down
His eyelids with my lips for gazing on me:
Surely I spoke the name, and knew it not   30
Until it bounded back and smote me so!
    Ippolito.   Curses upon them both!
                              [*Advancing toward her.*
Welcome, sweet lady!
    Rosalba.   Lord Cardinal! you here? and unattended?
    Ippolito.   We wait the happy lover, do we not?
    Rosalba.   Ferrante then betrayed the secret to you!
And are you come to honour with your presence . .
    Ippolito.   Has the Duke sign'd the contract?
    Rosalba.   For what bride?
Ferrante writes *Ferrante* plain enough;   40
And I do think, altho' I once or twice
Have written it instead of mine, at last
I am grown steadier, and could write *Rosalba.*
    Ippolito.   Sport not with one your charms have cast too low.
    Rosalba.   Sport not with one your hand would raise too
        high.
    Ippolito.   Again that taunt! the time may come, Rosalba,
When I could sanctify the blissful state
I have aspired to.
    Rosalba.   Am not I mere ice?
Show not I girlish forwardness, the fears   50
Of infancy, the scruples of old age?
Have not you said so? and said more . . you hate them?
How could you bear me, or what wish from me?
    Ippolito.   That which another will not long retain.
    Rosalba.   You know him little and me less.
    Ippolito.   I know
Inconstancy in him.
    Rosalba.   And what in me?
    Ippolito.   Intolerance for his betters.
    Rosalba.   Ignorance,   60
But not intolerance of them, is my fault.
    Ippolito.   No?
    Rosalba.   Call it thus, and cast it on the rest.

Ippolito.   Some are there whose close vision sees but one
In the whole world, and would not see another
For the whole world, were that one out of it.
    Rosalba.   Are there some such?   O may they be my
        friends!
O how, before I know them, I do love them!
    Ippolito.   After no strife, no censure, no complaint,
Have not your tears been seen, when you have left him,   70
Thro' tediousness, distaste, dislike, and grief
(Ingenuous minds must feel it, and may own it)
That love, so rashly promist, would retire,
Hating exaction, circumvention, bonds?
    Rosalba.   Such grief is yet unknown to me.   I know
All tears are not for sorrow : many swell
In the warm depths of gratitude and bliss;
But precious over all are those that hang
And tremble at the tale of generous deeds.
These he relates when he might talk, as you do,   80
Of passion : but he sees my heart, he finds
What fragrance most refreshes it.
                              How high,
O Heaven! must that man be, who loves, and who
Would still raise others higher than himself
To interest his beloved!
                      All my soul
Is but one drop from his, and into his
Falls, as earth's dew falls into earth again.
    Ippolito.   Yet would it not be wise to trust a friend   90
Able to counsel in extremes and straits?
    Rosalba.   Is it not wise in darkness and in storm
To trust the wave that lashes us, and pray
Its guidance on the rocks whereto it tends?
I have my guide, Lord Cardinal! he alone
Is ship and pilot to me, sea and star :
Counsel from others, knowing him, would be
Like worship of false gods ; in me no less
Than profanation and apostacy.
    Ippolito.   We may retire ; he comes not here to-day.   100
    Rosalba.   Then will I not retire, but lay my head

Upon the feet of any pitying saint
Until he comes, altho' it be to-morrow.
　Ippolito.　To-morrow he may fail : the sovran will
By rescript has detained and must delay him.
　Rosalba.　Lead, lead me to Ferrante.
　Ippolito.　　　　　　　　　　Were I worthy.
　Rosalba.　Proud cruel man ! that bitter sneer bodes ill.
May not I see him ?
　Ippolito.　　　　　　He may not see *you*.　　　110
　Rosalba.　O let him ! well my memory can supply
His beauteous image ; I can live on love
Saturate, like bees with honey, long drear days ;
He must see *me*, or cannot rest ; I can.

SECOND PART.

IPPOLITO, FERRANTE, *and* GIULIO, *in prison.*

　Ippolito.　Reasons of state, I fear, have dictated
This something like severity ; God grant
Here be no heresy : do both avow it,
Staring in silence at discovery ?
　Giulio.　No order forced me hither ; I am come
To share my brother's fate, whate'er it be,
And mitigate his sufferings.
　Ippolito.　　　　　　　　May they cease !
　Giulio.　Those words would have dissolved them into air,
Spoken but twenty furlongs from these bars.　　　10
　Ippolito.　I would do much to serve you ; but my faith
And my allegiance have two other lords,
The duke my brother, and the pope my God.
Ferrante then says nothing ?
　Ferrante.　　　　　　　He well knows
Thy hatred and its cause.
　Ippolito.　　　　　　Why should I hate you, . . .
My father's son, they say ?
　Ferrante.　　　　　　*They say !*　His blood
Runs in these veins, pure, for pure blood was hers　　　20

Who loved the youthful lover, and who died
When falser vows estranged the matchless prince.
  Ippolito.   He saw his error.
  Ferrante.   All men do when age
Bends down their heads, or gold shines in their way.
  Ippolito.   Altho' I would have helpt you in distress,
And just removed you from the court awhile,
You call'd me tyrant.
  Ferrante.   Calléd thee tyrant? I?
By Heaven! in tyrant there is something great   30
That never was in thee.   I would be killed
Rather by any monster of the wild
Than choakt by weeds and quicksands, rather crusht
By maddest rage than clay-cold apathy.
Those who act well the tyrant, neither seek
Nor shun the name ; and yet I wonder not
That thou repeatest it, and wishest me ;
It sounds like power, like policy, like courage,
And none who calls thee tyrant can despise thee.
Go, issue orders for imprisonment,   40
Warrants for death : the gibbet and the wheel,
Lo! the grand boundaries of thy dominion !
O what a mighty office for a minister
(And such Alfonso's brother calls himself)
To be the scribe of hawkers ! Man of genius !
The lanes and allies echo with thy works.
  Giulio.   Ah! do not urge him ; he may ruin you ;
He may pursue you to the grave.
  Ferrante.   He dares not :
Look at his collar ! see the saint he wears !   50
The amber saint may ask too much for that.
  Ippolito.   Atheist ! thy scoffs encourage every crime,
And strip thee, like a pestilence, of friends :
Theirs is the guilt to march against the law,
They mount the scaffold, and the blow is thine.
  Ferrante.   How venom burnishes his adder's crest,
How eloquent on scaffolds and on laws !
If such a noisome weed as falsehood is
Give frothy vigour to a worm like thee,
Crawl, eat, drink, sleep upon it, and farewell.   60

Ippolito (*to* Giulio).   Take you the sentence, and God be
  with both !   [*Goes.*
Giulio.   What sentence have we here ?
Ferrante.   Unseal and read it.
Giulio (*reading*).   Of sight ! of sight ! of sight !
Ferrante.   Would you escape,
My gentle Giulio ?   Run not thus around
The wide light chamber, press not thus your brow
Against the walls, with your two palms above.
Seek you the door then ? you are uncondemned
To lose the sight of one who is the bloom   70
And breath of life to you : the bolts are drawn
On me alone.   You carry in your breast
Most carefully our brother's precious gift :
Well, take it anywhere, but do not hope
Too much from any one.   Time softens rocks,
And hardens men.
  Giulio.   Pray then our God for help.
  Ferrante.   O my true brother, Giulio ! why thus hang
Around my neck and pour forth prayers for me ?
Where there are priests and kinsmen such as ours,   80
God hears not, nor is heard.   I am prepared
For death.
  Giulio.   Ah ! worse than death may come upon you,
Unless Heaven interpose.
  Ferrante.   I know the worst,
And bear one comfort in my breast that fire
And steel can ne'er force from it : she I love
Will not be his, but die as she hath lived.
Doubt you ? that thus you shake the head and sigh.
  Giulio.   Far other doubt was mine : even this shall
  cease.   90
  Ferrante.   Speak it.
  Giulio.   I must : God pardon me !
  Ferrante.   Speak on.
  Giulio.   Have we not dwelt in friendship from our birth,
Told the same courtier the same tale of joy,
And pointed where life's earliest thorn had pierced
Amid the sports of boyhood, ere the heart

Hath aught of bitter or unsound within ?
   Ferrante.   We have indeed.
   Giulio.   Has my advice been ill ? 100
   Ferrante.   Too often ill-observed, but always good.
   Giulio.   Brother, my words are not what better men
Would speak to you ; and yet my love, I think,
Must be more warm than theirs can ever be.
   Ferrante.   Brother's, friend's, father's, when was it like
      yours ?
   Giulio.   Which of them ever said what I shall say ?
   Ferrante.   Speak ; my desires are kindled, my fears
      quencht.
   Giulio.   Do not delay to die, lest crueller
Than common death befal you.
   Ferrante.   Then the wheel   110
Is ordered in that schedule !   Must she too
Have her chaste limbs laid bare ?   Here lies the rack ;
Here she would suffer ere it touch the skin.
No, I will break it with the thread of life
Ere the sound reach her.   Talk no more of Heaven,
Of Providence, of Justice.   Look on her.
Why should she suffer ? what hath she from Heaven
Of comfort or protection ?
   Giulio.   Talk not so.
Pity comes down when Hope hath flown away.   120
   Ferrante.   Illusion !
   Giulio.   If it were, which it is not,
Why break with vehement words such sweet illusion ?
For were there not above but empty air,
Nought but the clear blue sky where birds delight,
Soaring o'er myriad worlds of living dust
That roll in columns round the noontide ray,
Your heart would faint amid such solitude,
Would shrink in such vacuity ; that heart
(Ferrante ! can you hide its wants from me ?)   130
Rises and looks around and calls aloud
For some kind Being, some consoling bosom,
Whereon to place its sorrows, and to rest.
   Ferrante.   Oh ! that was here . . I cannot look beyond.

Giulio.   Hark! hear you not the people? to the window!
They shout and clap their hands when they first meet you
After short absence; what shall they now do?
Up! seize the moment; show yourself.
  Ferrante.   Stay, Giulio!
Draw me not thither; speak not of my wrongs;   140
I would await but not arouse their vengeance,
And would deserve but court not their applause.
Little of good shall good men hope from them,
Nothing shall wiser.   [*Aside.*
                  O were he away!
But if I fail, he must die too, being here.
  Giulio.   Let me call out: they are below the grate:
They would deliver you: try this one chance.
Obdurate! would you hold me down? They're gone!
  Ferrante.   Giulio! for shame! weep not, or here I
      stay   150
And let vile hands deform me.
  Giulio.   They shall never.
  Ferrante.   What smoke arises? Are there torches under?
Surely the crowd has past: 'tis from the stairs.
  Giulio.   Anticipate the blow.
  Ferrante.   One more must grieve!
And will she grieve like you, too tender Giulio!
Turn not away the head, the hand. What hold you?
Give, give it me. 'Tis keen. They call you forth.
Tell her . . no, say not we shall meet again,   160
For tears flow always faster at those words . .
May the thought come, but gently, like a dream.

THE SHADES OF AGAMEMNON AND
IPHIGENEIA.

Iphigeneia.   Father! I now may lean upon your breast,
And you with unreverted eyes will grasp
Iphigeneia's hand.
                              We are not shades
Surely! for yours throb yet.
                              And did my blood
Win Troy for Greece?
                              Ah! 'twas ill done, to shrink;
But the sword gleam'd so sharp; and the good priest
Trembled, and Pallas frown'd above, severe.   10
    Agamemnon.   Daughter!
    Iphigeneia   Beloved father! is [1] the blade
Again to pierce my bosom? 'tis unfit
For sacrifice; no blood is in its veins,
No God requires it here; here are no wrongs
To vindicate, no realms to overthrow.
You standing as at Aulis in the fane,
With face averted, holding (as before)
My hand; but yours burns not, as then it burn'd;
This alone shews me we are with the Blest,   20
Nor subject to the sufferings we have borne.
I will win back past kindness.
                              Tell me then,
Tell how my mother fares who loved me so,
And griev'd, as 'twere for you, to see me part.

[1 l. reads: " Is the blade
            Again to pierce a bosom now unfit
            For sacrifice? "]

Frown not, but pardon me for tarrying
Amid too idle words, nor asking how
She prais'd us both (which most ?) for what we did.
　Agamemnon.   Ye Gods who govern here ! do human pangs
Reach the pure soul thus far below ? do tears   30
Spring in these meadows ?
　Iphigeneia.   No, sweet father, no . .
I could have answered that ; why ask the Gods ?
　Agamemnon.   Iphigeneia ! O my child ! the Earth
Has gendered crimes unheard of heretofore,
And Nature may have changed in her last depths,
Together with the Gods and all their laws.
　Iphigeneia.   Father ! we must not let you here condemn ;
Not, were the day less joyful : recollect
We have no wicked here ; no king to judge.   40
Poseidon, we have heard, with bitter rage
Lashes his foaming steeds against the skies,
And, laughing with loud yell at winged fire,
Innoxious to his fields and palaces
Affrights the eagle from the sceptred hand ;
While Pluto, gentlest brother of the three
And happiest in obedience, views sedate
His tranquil realm, nor envies theirs above.
No change have we, not even day for night
Nor spring for summer.   50
　　　　　　　　　　All things are serene,
Serene too be your spirit !   None on earth
Ever was half so kindly in his house,
And so compliant, even to a child.
Never was snatch'd your robe away from me,
Though going to the council.   The blind man
Knew his good king was leading him indoors,
Before he heard the voice that marshal'd Greece.
Therefore all prais'd you.
　　　　　　　　　　Proudest men themselves   60
In others praise humility, and most
Admire it in the sceptre and the sword.
What then can make you speak thus rapidly
And briefly ? in your step thus hesitate ?

Are you afraid to meet among the good
Incestuous Helen here?
   Agamemnon.   Oh! Gods of Hell!
   Iphigeneia.   She hath not past the river.
                               We may walk
With our hands link'd nor feel our house's shame.   70
   Agamemnon.   Never mayst thou, Iphigeneia, feel it!
Aulis had no sharp sword, thou would'st exclaim,
Greece no avenger . . I, her chief so late,
Through Erebus, through Elysium, writhe beneath it.
   Iphigeneia.   Come; I have better diadems than those
Of Argos and Mycenai . . come away,
And I will weave them for you on the bank.
You will not look so pale when you have walked
A little in the grove, and have told all
Those sweet fond words the widow sent her child.   80
   Agamemnon.   Oh Earth! I suffered less upon thy shores!
                                       [*Aside.*

The bath that bubbled with my blood, the blows
That spilt it (O worse torture!) must she know!
Ah! the first woman coming from Mycenai
Will pine to pour this poison in her ear,
Taunting sad Charon for his slow advance.
Iphigeneia!
   Iphigeneia.   Why thus turn away!
Calling me with such fondness! I am here,
Father! and where you are, will ever be.   90
   Agamemnon.   Thou art my child . . yes, yes, thou art my
     child.
All was not once what all now is! come on,
Idol of love and truth! my child! my child!   [*Alone.*
Fell woman! ever false! false was thy last
Denunciation, as thy bridal vow;
And yet even that found faith with me! The dirk
Which sever'd flesh from flesh, where this hand rests,
Severs not, as thou boastedst in thy scoffs,
Iphigeneia's love from Agamemnon:
The wife's a spark may light, a straw consume,   100
The daughter's not her heart's whole fount hath quench'd,

'Tis worthy of the Gods, and lives for ever.
   Iphigeneia.   What spake my father to the Gods above?
Unworthy am I then to join in prayer?
If, on the last, or any day before,
Of my brief course on earth, I did amiss,
Say it at once, and let me be unblest;
But, O my faultless father! why should you?
And shun so my embraces?
                      Am I wild   110
And wandering in my fondness?
                         We are shades!
Groan not thus deeply; blight not thus the season
Of full-orb'd gladness! Shades we are indeed,
But mingled, let us feel it, with the blest.
I knew it, but forgot it suddenly,
Altho' I felt it all at your approach.
Look on me; smile with me at my illusion . .
You are so like what you have ever been
(Except in sorrow!) I might well forget   120
I could not win you as I used to do.
It was the first embrace since my descent
I ever aim'd at: those who love me live,
Save one, who loves me most, and now would chide me.
   Agamemnon.   We want not, O Iphigeneia, we
Want not embrace, nor kiss that cools the heart
With purity, nor words that more and more
Teach what we know, from those we know, and sink
Often most deeply where they fall most light.
Time was when for the faintest breath of thine   130
Kingdom and life were little.
   Iphigeneia.   Value them
As little now.
   Agamemnon.   Were life and kingdom all!
   Iphigeneia.[3]   Ah! by our death many are sad who loved
   us.
The little fond Electra, and Orestes

    [3 l. reads: "Ah! by our death many are sad who loved us.
             They will be happy too."]

So childish and so bold ! O that mad boy !
They will be happy too.
                              Cheer ! king of men !
Cheer ! there are voices, songs . . Cheer ! arms advance. 140
   Agamemnon.   Come to me, soul of peace !   These, these alone,
These are not false embraces.
   Iphigeneia.   Both are happy !
   Agamemnon.   Freshness breathes round me from some breeze above.
What are ye, winged ones ! with golden urns ?

THE HOURS (*Descending.*)

The Hours . . To each an urn we bring.
              Earth's purest gold
              Alone can hold
The lymph of the Lethean spring.

We, son of Atreus, we divide   150
The dulcet from the bitter tide
        That runs athwart the paths of men.
No more our pinions shalt thou see.
Take comfort !   We have done with thee,
        And must away to earth again.   [*Ascending.*
              Where thou art, thou
              Of braided brow,
Thou cull'd too soon from Argive bow'rs,
Where thy sweet voice is heard among
The shades that thrill with choral song,   160
None can regret the parted Hours.

Chorus of Argives.

Maiden ! be thou the spirit that breathes
        Triumph and joy into our song !
Wear and bestow these amaranth-wreathes,
        Iphigeneia ! they belong
To none but thee and her who reigns
(Less chaunted) on our bosky plains.

Semi-chorus.

Iphigeneia ! 'tis to thee
Glory we owe and victory.
Clash, men of Argos, clash your arms,   170
To martial worth and virgin charms.

Other Semi-chorus.

Ye men of Argos ! it was sweet
To roll the fruits of conquest at the feet
Whose whispering sound made bravest hearts beat fast.
  This we have known at home ;
  But hither we are come
To crown the king who ruled us first and last.

Chorus.

Father of Argos ! king of men !
 We chaunt the hymn of praise to thee.
In serried ranks we stand again,   180
 Our glory safe, our country free.
Clash, clash the arms we bravely bore
Against Scamander's God-defended shore.

Semi-chorus.

Blessed art thou who hast repell'd
Battle's wild fury, Ocean's whelming foam ;
 Blessed o'er all, to have beheld
Wife, children, house avenged, and peaceful home !

Other Semi-chorus.

 We, too, thou seest, are now
Among the happy, though the aged brow
From sorrow for us we could not protect,   190
 Nor, on the polisht granite of the well
 Folding our arms, of spoils and perils tell,
Nor lift the vase on the lov'd head erect.

Semi-chorus.

What whirling wheels are those behind ?
What plumes come flaring through the wind,
 Nearer and nearer ?   From his car
He who defied the heaven-born Powers of war

Pelides springs !   Dust,[4] dust are we
To him, O king, who bends the knee,[5]
Proud only to be first in reverent praise of thee.   200

Other Semi-chorus.

Clash, clash the arms !   None other race
Shall see such heroes face to face.
We too have fought ; and they have seen
Nor sea-sand grey nor meadow green*
Where Dardans stood against their men . .
Clash ! Io Pæan ! clash again !
Repinings for lost days repress . .
The flames of Troy had cheer'd us less.

Chorus.

Hark ! from afar more war-steeds neigh,
Thousands o'er thousands rush this way.   210
Ajax is yonder ! ay, behold
The radiant arms of Lycian gold !
Arms from admiring valour won,
Tydeus ! and worthy of thy son.
'Tis Ajax wears them now ; for he
Rules over Adria's stormy sea.

He threw them to the friend who lost
(By the dim judgment of the host)
Those wet with tears which Thetis gave
The youth most beauteous of the brave.   220
In vain ! the insatiate soul would go
For comfort to his peers below.
Clash ! ere we leave them all the plain,
Clash ! Io Pæan ! once again !

[4 l. reads : " But dust."]
[5 l. reads : " mailed knee."]

THE DEATH OF CLYTEMNESTRA.

ORESTES *and* ELECTRA.

Electra.   Pass on, my brother ! she awaits the wretch,
Dishonorer, despoiler, murderer. . .
None other name shall name him. . . she awaits
As would a lover.
     Heavenly Gods. . . what poison
O'erflows my lips ! . . .
      Adultress ! husband-slayer.
Strike her, the tigress !
     Think upon our father. . .
Give the sword scope . . think what a man was he.   10
How fond of her ! how kind to all about,
That he might gladden and teach us . . how proud
Of thee, Orestes tossing thee above
His joyous head and calling thee his crown.
Ah ! boys remember not what melts our hearts
And marks them evermore !
     Bite not thy lip,
Nor tramp as an unsteady colt the ground,
Nor stare against the wall, but think again
How better than all fathers was our father.   20
Go. . .
 Orestes.   Loose me then ! for this white hand Electra
Hath fastened upon mine with fiercer grasp
Than mine can grasp the sword.
 Electra.   Go, sweet Orestes !
I knew not I was holding thee. . . Avenge him !
(*Alone.*)   How he sprang from me !
     . . Sure, he now has reacht
The room before the bath. . .
     The bath door creaks ! 30
. . It hath creakt thus since he . . since thou, O father !
Ever since thou didst loosen its strong valves
Either with all thy dying weight or strength

Agonised with her stabs. . .
                          What plunge was that?
Ah me!
                . . What groans are those?
  Orestes.   (*Returning.*)   They sound through hell,
Rejoicing the Eumenides.*
                          She slew   40
Our father: she made thee the scorn of slaves;
Me (son of him who ruled this land and more)
She made an outcast. .
                    Would I had been so
For ever! ere such vengeance. . .
  Electra.   O that Zeus
Had let thy arm fall sooner at thy side
Without those drops! list! they are audible,
For they are many . . from the sword's point falling
And down from the mid blade!   50
                    Too rash Orestes!
Couldst thou not then have spared our wretched mother?
  Orestes.   The Gods could not.
  Electra.   She was not theirs, Orestes.
  Orestes.   And didst not thou. . .
  Electra.   'Twas I, 'twas I, who did it;
Of our unhappiest house the most unhappy!
Under this roof, by every God accursed,
There is no grief, there is no guilt, but mine.
  Orestes.   Electra! no!   60
                    'Tis now my time to suffer. .
Mine be, with all its pangs, the righteous deed.

* An ancient scholiast has recorded that the name of Eumenides
was given to these Goddesses after the expiation of Orestes. But
Catullus (called the learned by his countrymen) represents Ariadne
invoking them by this appellation long before the Trojan war. The
verses are the most majestic in the Roman language.
            Eumenides! quarum anguineis redimita capillis
            Frons expirantes praeportat pectoris iras,
            Huc, huc adventate! &c.

THE MADNESS OF ORESTES.

Orestes *and* Electra.

Orestes.   Heavy and murderous dreams, O my Electra,
Have dragged me from myself.
                     Is this Mycenai?
Are we . . are all who should be in our house?
Living? unhurt? our father here? our mother?
Why that deep gasp? for 'twas not sigh nor groan.
She then . . . 'twas she who fell! when? How? Beware!
No, no, speak out at once, that my full heart
May meet it, and may share with thee in all . .
In all . . . but that one thing.   10
                      It was a dream.
We may share all.
               They live? both live?
O say it!
   Electra.   The Gods have placed them from us, and there
     rolls
Between us that dark river . . .
   Orestes.   Blood! blood! blood!
I seé it roll; I see the hand above it,
Imploring; I see her.
               Hiss me not back,   20
Ye snake-hair'd maids! I will look on; I will
Hear the words gurgle thro' that cursed stream,
And catch that hand . . that hand . . . which slew my
    father!
It can not be . . . . how could it slay my father?
Death to the slave who spoke it! . . . slay my father!
It tost me up to him to earn a smile,
And was a smile then such a precious boon,
And royal state and proud affection nothing?
Ay, and thee too, Electra, she once taught
To take the sceptre from him at the door . . .   30
Not the bath-door, not the bath-door, mind that! .
And place it in the vestibule, against

The spear of Pallas, where it used to stand.
Where is it now? methinks I missed it there.
How we have trembled to be seen to move it!
Both looking up, lest that stern face should frown
Which always gazed on Zeus right opposite.
O! could but one tear more fall from my eyes,
It would shake off these horrid visages,
And melt them into air.   40
                         I am not yours,
Fell Goddesses! A just and generous power,
A bright-hair'd God directed me.
                                    And thus
Abased is he whom such a God inspired!

                                    [*After a pause.*
Into whose kingdom went they? did they go
Together?
     Electra.   Oh! they were not long apart.
     Orestes.   I know why thou art pale; I know whose head
Thy flower-like hands have garlanded; I know   50
For whom thou hast unbraided all thy love.
He well deserves it . . He shall have it all.
Glory and love shall crown thee, my brave sister!
     Electra.   I am not she of Sparta.   Let me live
(If live I must, Orestes!) not unnamed
Nor named too often . . speak no more of love,
Ill-omened and opprobrious in this house . .
A mother should have had, a father had it,
O may a brother let it dwell with him,
Unchangeable, unquestioned, solitary,   60
Strengthened and hallowed in the depths of grief!
Gaze not so angrily . . I dare not see thee,
I dare not look where comfort should be found.
     Orestes.   I dare and do behold them all day long,
And, were that face away so like my mother's,
I would advance and question and compel them . .
They hear me and they know it.
     Electra.   Hear me too,
Ye mighty ones! To me invisible!
And spare him! spare him! for without the Gods   70

He wrought not what he wrought: And are not ye
Partakers of their counsels and their power?
O spare the son of him whom ye and they
Sent against Ilion, to perform your will
And bid the rulers of the earth be just.
  Orestes.   And dare they frighten thee too? frighten thee?
And bend thee into prayer?
                              Off, hateful eyes!
Look upon me, not her.
                              Ay, thus; 'tis well.   80
Cheer, cheer thee, my Electra.
                              I am strong,
Stronger than ever . . steel, fire, adamant . .
But cannot bear thy brow upon my neck.
Can not bear these wild writhings, these loud sobs.
By all the Gods! I think thou art half mad. . .
I must away . . follow me not . . stand there!

THE PRAYER OF ORESTES.

  Orestes.   O King Apollo! God Apollo! god
Powerful to smite and powerful to preserve!
If there is blood upon me, as there seems,   90
Purify that black stain (thou only canst)
With every rill that bubbles from these caves
Audibly; and come willing to the work.
No; 'tis not they; 'tis blood; 'tis blood again
That bubbles in my ear, that shakes the shades
Of thy dark groves, and lets in hateful gleams,
Bringing me . . What dread sight! What sound abhorr'd!
What screams!   They are my mother's: 'Tis her eye
That through the snakes of those three furies glares,
And makes them hold their peace that she may speak.   100
Has thy voice bidden them all forth? they slink,
Some that would hide away, but must turn back,
And others like blue lightnings bound along
From rock to rock; and many hiss at me
As they draw nearer.   Earth, fire, water, all

Abominate the deed of Gods commanded.
Alas! I came to pray, not to complain;
And lo! my speech is impious as my deed!

THE PRIESTESS OF APOLLO.

Take refuge here amid our Delphian shades,
   O troubled breast!   110
Here the most pious of Mycenai's maids
   Shall watch thy rest
And wave the cooling laurel o'er thy brow,
   Nor insects swarm
Shall ever break thy slumbers, nor shalt thou
   Start at the alarm
Of boys infesting (as they do) the street
   With mocking songs,
Stopping and importuning all they meet,
   And heaping wrongs   120
Upon thy diadem'd and sacred head,
   Worse than when base
Œgisthus (shudder not!) his toils outspread
   Around thy race.
Altho' even in this fane the fitful blast
   Thou may'st hear roar,
Thy name among our highest rocks shall last
   For ever more.
   Orestes.   A calm comes over me: life brings it not
With any of its tides: my end is near.   130
O Priestess of the purifying god
Receive her (*pointing to his sister*), and when she hath closed
    mine eyes,
Do thou (weep not, my father's child!) close hers.

WALTER TYRREL AND WILLIAM RUFUS.

Rufus.   Tyrrel, spur onward! we must not await
The laggard lords : when they have heard the dogs
I warrant they will follow fast enough,
Each for his haunch.   Thy roan is mettlesome ;
How the rogue sides up to me, and claims
Acquaintance with young Yorkshire! not afraid
Of wrinkling lip, nor ear laid down like grass
By summer thunder-shower on Windsor mead.
  Tyrrel.   Behold, my liege! hither they troop amain,
Over yon gap.   10
  Rufus.   Over my pales ? the dolts
Have broken down my pales!
  Tyrrel.   Please you, my liege,
Unless they had, they must have ridden round
Eleven miles.
  Rufus.   Why not have ridden round
Eleven miles ? or twenty, were there need.
By our Lady! they shall be our carpenters
And mend what they have marr'd.   At any time
I can make fifty lords ; but who can make   20
As many head of deer, if mine escape ?
And sure they will, unless they too are mad.
Call me that bishop . . him with hunting-cap
Surcharged with cross, and scarlet above knee.
  Tyrrel (galloping forward.)   Ho! my lord bishop!
  Bishop.   Who calls *me* ?
  Tyrrel.   Your slave.
  Bishop.   Well said, if toned as well and timed as well.
Who art thou ? citizen or hind ? what wantest ?
  Tyrrel.   My lord ; your presence ; but before the king ;   30

Where it may grow more placid at its leisure.
The morn is only streakt with red, my lord !
You beat her out and out : how prettily
You wear your stocking over head and ears !
Keep off the gorse and broom ! they soon catch fire !
 Bishop. The king shall hear of this : I recognise
Sir Walter Tyrrel.
 Tyrrel.   And Sir Walter Tyrrel
By the same token duly recognises
The Church's well-begotten son, well-fed,   40
Well-mounted, and all well, except well-spoken,
The spiritual lord of Winchester.
 Bishop. Ay, by God's grace ! pert losel !
 Tyrrel.   Prick along
Lord bishop ! quicker ! catch fresh air ! we want it ;
We have had foul enough till dinner-time.
 Bishop. Varlet ! I may chastise this insolence.
 Tyrrel. I like those feathers : but there crows no cock
Without an answer. Though the noisiest throat
Sings from the belfrey of snug Winchester,   50
Yet he from Westminster hath stouter spurs.
 Bishop. God's blood ! were I no bishop . .
 Tyrrel.   Then thy own
Were cooler.
 Bishop. Whip that hound aside ! O Christ !
The beast has paw'd my housings ! What a day
For dirt !
 Tyrrel. The scent lies well ; pity no more
The housings ; look, my lord ! here trots the king !
 Rufus. Which of you broke my palings down ? 60
 Bishop.   God knows,
Most gracious sir.
 Rufus.   No doubt he does ; but you,
Bishop ! could surely teach us what God knows.
Ride back and order some score handicrafts
To fix them in their places.
 Bishop.   The command
Of our most gracious king shall be obeyed. [*Riding off.*
Malisons on the atheist ! Who can tell

Where are my squires and other men ? confused   70
Among the servitors of temporal lords !
I must e'en turn again and hail that brute.
Sir Walter ! good Sir Walter ! one half-word !
                       [TYRREL *rides toward him.*
Sir Walter ! may I task your courtesy
To find me any of my followers ?
   Tyrrel.   Willingly.
   Rufus.   Stay with me ; I want thee, Tyrrel !
What does the bishop bogle at ?
   Tyrrel.   At nothing.
He seeks his people, to retrieve the damage.   80
   Rufus.   Where are the lords ?
   Tyrrel.   Gone past your grace, bare-headed,
And falling in the rear.
   Rufus.   Well, prick then on.
I care but little for the chase to-day,
Although the scent lies sweetly.   To knock down
My paling is vexatious.   We must see
Our great improvements in this forest ; what
Of roads blockt up, of hamlets swept away,
Of lurking dens called cottages, and cells,   90
And hermitages.   Tyrrel ! thou didst right
And dutifully, to remove the house
Of thy forefathers.   'Twas an odd request
To leave the dovecote for the sake of those
Flea-bitten blind old pigeons.   There it stands !
But, in God's name ! what mean these hives ? the bees
May sting my dogs.
   Tyrrel.   They hunt not in the summer.
   Rufus.   They may torment my fawns.
   Tyrrel.   Sir, not unless   100
Driven from their hives : they like the flowers much better.
   Rufus.   Flowers ! and leave flowers too !
   Tyrrel.   Only some half-wild,
In tangled knots ; balm, clary, marjoram.
   Rufus.   What lies beyond this close briar hedge, that smells
Through the thick dew upon it, pleasantly ?
   Tyrrel.   A poor low cottage : the dry marl-pit shields it,

And, frail and unsupported like itself,
Peace-breathing honeysuckles comfort it
In its misfortunes.   110
   Rufus.   I am fain to laugh
At thy rank minstrelsy.   A poor low cottage!
Only a poor low cottage! where, I ween,
A poor low maiden blesses Walter Tyrrel.
   Tyrrel.   It may be so.
   Rufus.   No ; it may not be so.
My orders were that all should be removed ;
And, out of special favour, special trust
In thee, Sir Walter, I consign'd the care
Into thy own hands, of razing thy own house   120
And those about it ; since thou hast another
Fairer and newer, and more lands around.
   Tyrrel.   Hall, chapel, chamber, cellar, turret, grange,
Are level with the grass.
   Rufus.   What negligence
To leave the work then incomplete, when little
Was there remaining !   Strip that roof, and start
Thy petty game from cover.
   Tyrrel.   O my liege !
Command not this !   130
   Rufus.   Make me no confidant
Of thy base loves.
   Tyrrel.   Nor you, my liege ! nor any :
None such hath Walter Tyrrel.
   Rufus.   Thou 'rt at bay ;
Thou hast forgotten thy avowal, man !
   Tyrrel.   My father's house is (like my father) gone :
But in that house, and from that father's heart
Mine grew into his likeness, and held thence
Its rich possessions . . God forgive my boast !   140
He bade me help the needy, raise the low . .
   Rufus.   And stand against thy king !
   Tyrrel.   How many yokes
Of oxen, from how many villages
For miles around, brought I, at my own charge,
To bear away the rafters and the beams

That were above my cradle at my birth,
And rang when I was christened, to the carouse
Of that glad father and his loyal friends!
   Rufus.   He kept good cheer, they tell me.   150
   Tyrrel.   Yonder thatch
Covers the worn-out woman at whose breast
I hung, an infant.
   Rufus.   Ay! and none beside?
   Tyrrel.   Four sons have fallen in the wars.
   Rufus.   Brave dogs!
   Tyrrel.   She hath none left.
   Rufus.   No daughter!
   Tyrrel.   One.
   Rufus.   I thought it.
Unkennel her.   161
   Tyrrel.   Grace! pity! mercy on her!
   Rufus.   I will not have hot scents about my chase.
   Tyrrel.   A virtuous daughter of a virtuous mother
Deserves not this, my liege!
   Rufus.   Am I to learn
What any subject at my hand deserves?
   Tyrrel.   Happy, who dares to teach it, and who can!
   Rufus.   And thou, forsooth!
   Tyrrel.   I have done my duty, sire!   170
   Rufus.   Not half: perform the rest, or bide my wrath.
   Tyrrel.   What, break athwart my knee the staff of age?
   Rufus.   Question me, villain!
   Tyrrel.   Villain I am none.
   Rufus.   Retort my words! By all the saints! thou diest,
False traitor!
   Tyrrel.   Sire, no private wrong, no word
Spoken in angriness, no threat against
My life or honour, urge me . .
   Rufus.   Urge to what?   180
Dismountest?
   Tyrrel.   On my knees, as best beseems,
I ask . . not pardon, sire! but spare, oh spare
The child devoted, the deserted mother!
   Rufus.   Take her; take both.

Tyrrel.   She loves her home ; her limbs
Fail her ; her husband sleeps in that churchyard ;
Her youngest child, born many years the last,
Lies (not half-length) along the father's coffin.
Such separate love grows stronger in the stem   190
(I have heard say) than others close together,
And that, where pass these funerals, all life's spring
Vanishes from behind them, all the fruits
Of riper age are shrivel'd, every sheaf
Husky ; no gleaning left.   She would die here,
Where from her bed she looks on his ; no more
Able to rise, poor little soul ! than he.
  Rufus.   Who would disturb them, child or father ? where
Is the churchyard thou speakest of ?
  Tyrrel.   Among   200
Yon nettles : we have level'd all the graves.
  Rufus.   Right : or our horses might have stumbled on
     them.
  Tyrrel.   Your grace oft spares the guilty ; spare the
     innocent !
  Rufus.   Up from the dew ! thy voice is hoarse already.
  Tyrrel.   Yet God hath heard it.   It entreats again,
Once more, once only ; spare this wretched house.
  Rufus.   No, nor thee neither.
  Tyrrel.   Speed me, God ! and judge
O thou ! between the oppressor and opprest !
                    [*He pierces* Rufus *with an arrow.*

THE PARENTS OF LUTHER.

John Luther.   I left thee, Margaretta, fast asleep,
Thou, who wert always earlier than myself,
Yet hast no mine to trudge to, hast no wedge
To sharpen at the forge, no pickaxe loose
In handle.
    Come, blush not again : thy cheeks
May now shake off those blossoms which they bore
So thick this morning that last night's avowal
Nestles among them still.
      So, in few months   10
A noisier bird partakes our whispering bower?
Say it again.
 Margaretta.   And, in my dream, I blush'd !
 John.   Idler ! wert dreaming too ? and after dawn ?
 Marg.   In truth was I.
 John.   Of me ?
 Marg.   No, not of you.
 John.   No matter ; for methinks some Seraph's wing
Fann'd that bright countenance.
 Marg.   Methinks it did. 20
And stir'd my soul within.
     How could you go
And never say good-bye, and give no kiss ?
 John.   It might have waken'd thee.   I can give more
Kisses than sleep : so thinking, I heav'd up
Slowly my elbow from above the pillow,
And, when I saw it woke thee not, went forth.
 Marg.   I would have been awaken'd for a kiss,
And a good-bye, or either, if not both.

John.   Thy dreams were not worth much then.   30
Marg.   Few dreams are ;
But . .
John.   By my troth ! I will intrench upon
The woman's dowry, and will contradict,
Tho' I should never contradict again.
I have got more from dreams a hundred-fold
Than all the solid earth, than field, than town,
Than (the close niggard purse that cramps my fist)
The mine will ever bring me.
Marg.   So have I,   40
And so shall each indeed, if this be true.
John.   What was it then ? for when good dreams befall
The true of heart, 'tis likely they come true.
A vein of gold ? ay ? silver ? copper ? iron ?
Lead ? sulphur ? alum ? alabaster ? coal ?
Shake not those ringlets nor let down those eyes,
Tho' they look prettier for it, but speak out.
True, these are not thy dainties.
Marg.   Guess again.
John.   Crystalline kitchens, amber-basted spits,   50
Whizzing with frothy savory salamanders,
And swans that might (so plump and pleasant-looking)
Swim in the water from the mouths of knights ;
And ostrich-eggs off coral woods (the nests
Outside of cinnamon, inside of saffron,
And mortar'd well, for safety-sake with myrrh),
Serv'd up in fern-leaves green before the Flood ?
Marg.   Stuff ! you will never guess it, I am sure.
John.   No ? and yet these are well worth dreaming of.
Marg.   Try once again.   60
John.   Faith ! it is kind to let me.
Under-ground beer-cascades from Nuremberg ?
Rhine vintage stealing from Electoral cellars,
And, broader than sea-baths for mermaid brides,
With fluits upon the surface strides across,
Pink conchs, to catch it and to light it down ;
And music from basaltic organ-pipes
For dancing ; and five fairies to one man.

Marg.   Oh his wild fancies ! . . Are they innocent ?
John.   I think I must be near it by that shrug.   70
Spicy sack-posset, roaring from hot springs
And running off like mad thro' candied cliffs,
But catching now and then some fruit that drops . .
Shake thy head yet ? why then thou hast the palsy.
Zooks ! I have thought of all things probable
And come to my wits' end.   What canst thou mean ?
Marg.   Nay, I have half a mind now not to tell.
John.   Then it is out . . Thy whole one ill could hold it.
A woman's mind hates pitch upon its seams.
Marg.   Hush ! one word more, and then my lips are
    closed.   [80
John.   Pish ! one more word, and then my lips . .
Marg.   O rare
Impudent man ! . . and such discourse from you !
I dreamt we had a boy . .
John.   A wench, a wench . .
A boy were not like thee.
Marg.   I said a boy.
John.   Well, let us have him, if we miss the girl.
Marg.   My father told me he *must* have a boy,
And call him Martin (his own name) because   90
Saint Martin both was brave and cloth'd the poor.
John.   Hurrah then for Saint Martin ! he shall have
Enough to work on in this house of ours.
Marg.   Now do not laugh, dear husband ! but this dream
Seem'd somewhat more.
John.   So do all dreams, ere past.
Marg.   Well, but it seems so still.
John.   Ay, twist my fingers,
Basketing them to hold it.
Marg.   Never grave !   100
John.   I shall be.
Marg.   That one thought should make you now.
John.   And that one tap upon the cheek to boot.
Marg.   I do believe, if you were call'd to Heaven
You would stay toying here.
John.   I doubt I should.

Methinks I set my back against the gate
Thrown open to me by this rosy hand,
And look both ways, but see more heaven than earth:
Give me thy dream: thou puttest it aside: 110
I must be feasted: fetch it forth at once.
 Marg. Husband! I dreamt the child was in my arms,
And held a sword, which from its little grasp
I could not move, nor you: I dreamt that proud
But tottering shapes in purple filigree
Pull'd at it, and he laught.
 John.   They frighten'd thee?
 Marg. Frighten'd me! no: the infant's strength pre-
  vail'd.
Devils, with angels' faces, throng'd about;
Some offer'd flowers, and some held cups behind,   120
And some held daggers under silken stoles.
 John. These frighten'd thee, however.
 Marg.   He knew all;
I knew he did.
 John.   A dream! a dream indeed!
He knew and laught!
 Marg.   He sought his mother's breast,
And lookt at them no longer.
        All the room
Was fill'd with light and gladness.   130
 John.   He shall be
Richer than we are; he shall mount his horse . .
A feat above his father; and be one
Of the duke's spearmen.
 Marg.   God forbid! they lead
Unrighteous lives, and often fall untimely.
 John. A lion-hearted lad shall Martin be.
 Marg. God willing; if *his* servant; but not else.
I have such hopes, full hopes, hopes overflowing.
 John. A grave grand man, half collar and half cross, 140
With chain enough to hold our mastiff by,
Thou fain wouldst have him. Out of dirt so stiff
Old Satan fashioneth his idol, Pride.
 Marg. If proud and cruel to the weak, and bent

To turn all blessings from their even course
To his own kind and company, may he
Never be great, with collar, cross, and chain ;
No, nor be ever angel, if, O God !
He be a fallen angel at the last.			[*After a pause.*
Uncle, you know, is sacristan ; and uncle			150
Had once an uncle who was parish priest.
 John.	He was the man who sung so merrily
Those verses which few scholars understand,
Yet which they can not hide away, nor drive
The man from memory after forty years.
 Marg. (sings).	“ Our brightest pleasures are reflected
  pleasures.
And they shine sweetest from the cottage-wall.”
 John.	The very same.
 Marg.			*We* understand them, John !
 John.	An inkling.	But your uncle sacristan			160
Hath neither sword nor spur.
 Marg.			It was a sword,
A flaming sword, but innocent, I saw ;
And I have seen in pictures such as that,
And in the hands of angels borne on clouds.
He may defend our faith, drive out the Turk,
And quench the crescent in the Danaw stream.
 John.	Thou, who begannest softly, singest now
Shrill as a throstle.			170
 Marg.			Have we then no cause
To sing as throstles after sign thus strange ?
 John.	Because it was so strange, must we believe
The rather ?
 Marg.	Yes ; no fire was in the house,
No splinter, not a spark.	The Virgin's chin
Shone not with rushlight under it ; 'twas out.
For night was almost over, if not past,
And the Count's chapel has not half that blaze
On the Count's birthday, nor the hall at night.			180
Ah surely, surely fare like ours sends up
No idle fumes ; nor wish nor hope of mine
Fashion'd so bright a substance to a form

So beautiful.   There must be truth in it.
    John.   There shall be then.   Your uncle's sacristy
Shall hold the armour quite invisible,
Until our little Martin some fine day
Bursts the door open, spurr'd, caparison'd,
Dukes lead his bridle, princes tramp behind.
He may be pope . . who knows?   190
    Marg.   Are you in earnest?
But if he should be pope, will he love *us* ?
Or let us (O yes, sure he would!) love *him* ?
Nor slink away, ashamed?   Pope, no; not pope,
But bishop (ay?) he may be?   There are few
Powerfuller folks than uncle Grimmermann.
Promise he scarce would give us, but a wink
Of hope he gave, to make a chorister.
    John.   "If thou wilt find materials," were his words.
    Marg.   I did not mark the words; they were too light: 200
And yet he never breaks his troth.
    John.   Not he:
No, he would rather break his fast ten times.
Do not look seriously . . when church allows,
I mean; no more; six days a week; not seven.
I *have* seen houses where the Friday cheese
Was not (in *my* mind) cut with Thursday knife.
    Marg.   O now for shame! such houses can not stand.
Pr'ythee talk reason.   As the furnace-mouth
Shows only fire, so yours shows laughter only.   210
Choristers have been friars; ours may be;
And then a father abbot.
    John.   At one leap,
As salmon up Schaffhausen.
    Marg.   Just the same . .
Then . .
    John.   Ring the bells! Martin is pope, by Jove!

ANDREA OF HUNGARY, GIOVANNA OF NAPLES, AND FRA RUPERT: A TRILOGY.

————✱————

ANDREA OF HUNGARY.

CHARACTERS.

ANDREA. FRA RUPERT. CARACCIOLI. CARAFFA. BOCCACCIO. MAXIMIN, *a Soldier.* KLAPWRATH, ZINGA, PSEIN, *Hungarian Officers.* PAGE, GARISENDO, *a Peasant.* GIOVANNA, *Queen.* SANCIA, *Queen Dowager.* MARIA, *Sister of Giovanna.* MARIA OF SICILY, *Half-sister.* FLAMMETTA. FILIPPA, *Foster-mother.* PETRONILLA, *a Peasant.*

PROLOGUE.

My verse was for thine eyes alone,
  Alone by them was it repaid;
And still thine ear records the tone
  Of thy grey minstrel, thoughtful maid!

Amid the pomps of regal state,
  Where thou, O Rose! art call'd to move,
Thee only Virtue can elate,
  She only guide thy steps to Love.

Sometimes, when dark is each saloon,
  Dark every lamp that crown'd the Seine,
Memory hangs low Amalfi's moon
  And lights thee o'er Salerno's plain.

And onward, where Giovanna bore
  Keen anguish from envenom'd tongues:
Her fame my pages shall restore,
  Thy pity shall requite her wrongs.

ACT I.   SCENE I.

PALACE AT NAPLES.

ANDREA *and* GIOVANNA.

Andrea.   What say you now, Giovanna! shall we go
And conquer France?   Heigho?   I am sadly idle;
My mighty mind wants full activity.
Giovanna.   Andrea! be contented; stay at home;
Conquer? you've conquer'd me.
Andrea.   Ah rebel queen!
I doubt it: we have had war first, however,
And parleys, and all that.
Giovanna.   You might have more
Before you conquer the strong cities there.   10
Andrea.   England, they tell me, hath as much of France
As France hath.   Some imagine that Provenza
Is half-and-half French land.   How this may be
I can not tell; I am no theologian.
Giovanna . . in your ear . . I have a mind
To ride to Paris, and salute the king,
And pull him by the beard, and make him fight.
Giovanna.   Know that French beards have stiffer hairs
      than German,*
And crackle into flame at the first touch.
Andrea.   'Sblood! like black cats!   But only in the
      dark?   [20
Giovanna.   By night or day, in city or in field.
Andrea.   I never knew it: let the Devil lug them
For me then! they are fitter for his fist.
Sure, of all idle days the marriage-day
Is idlest: even the common people run
About the streets, not knowing what to do,
As if they came from wedding too, poor souls!
This fancy set me upon conquering France.
Giovanna.   And one hour only after we are united?

* Hungary and Germany were hostile.

ACT I.   SCENE II.

Maria enters.

Andrea.   Maria! where are you for?   France or Naples?
She heard, she smiled . . Here's whispering . . This won't
   do . .   [*Going ; but stops, pacified.*
She may have secrets . . they all have . . I'll leave 'em.
  Giovanna.   Unsisterly! unfriendly!   [*Goes.*
  Maria.   Peace! Giovanna!
  Giovanna.   That word has sign'd it.   I have sworn to
   love him.
  Maria.   Ah, what a vow!
  Giovanna.   The harder to perform
The greater were the glory : I will earn it.
  Maria.   How can we love . .   10
  Giovanna (interrupting).   Mainly, by hearing none
Decry the object ; then, by cherishing
The good we see in it, and overlooking
What is less pleasant in the paths of life.
All have some virtue if we leave it them
In peace and quiet ; all may lose some part
By sifting too minutely bad and good.
The tenderer and the timider of creatures
Often desert the brood that has been handled
And turn'd about, or indiscreetly lookt at.   20
The slightest touches, touching constantly,
Irritate and inflame.
  Maria.   Giovanna mine!
These rhetoric-roses are supremely sweet,
But hold! the jar is full.   I promise you
I will not steal up with a mind to snatch,
Or pry too closely where you bid me not . .
But for the nest you talk about . .
  Giovanna.   For shame!
What nest?
  Maria.   That nest your blushes gleam upon.   30
O! I will watch each twig, each feather there,

And, if my turning, tossing, hugging, does it,
Woe to Giovanna's little bird, say I.
   Giovanna.   Seriously, my sweet sister!
   Maria (iuterrupting).   Seriously
Indeed! What briars ere we come to that!
   Giovanna.   I am accustomed to Andrea's ways,
And see much good in him.   40
   Maria.   I see it too.
   Giovanna.   Fix upon that your eyes; they will grow
     brighter,
Maria, for each beauty they discover.

ACT I. SCENE III.

ANOTHER ROOM IN THE PALACE.

ANDREA, FRA RUPERT.

   Andrea.   Well met again, Fra Rupert! Why not, though,
At church with us? By this humility
You lost the prettiest sight that ever was.
   Fra Rupert.   I know what such sights are.
   Andrea.   What?
   Fra Rupert.   Vanity.
   Andrea.   Exact the thing that everybody likes.
   Fra Rupert.   You young and heedless!
   Andrea.   We pass lightly over,
And run on merrily quite to the end;   10
The graver stumble, break their knees, and curse it:
Which are the wiser? Had you seen the church!
The finest lady ever drest for court
A week-day peasant to her! By to-morrow
There's not a leg of all the crowd in Naples
But will stand stiff and ache with this day's tiptoe;
There's not a throat will drop its paste-tape down
Without some soreness from such roaring cheers;
There's not a husband but whose ears will tingle
Under his consort's claw this blessed night   20
For sighing "What an angel is Giovanna!"

Fra Rupert. Go, go!   I can not hear such ribaldry.
Andrea.   Rather should you have heard, as there you might,
Quarrelsome blunder-headed drums, o'erpower'd
By pelting cymbals; then complaining flutes,
And boy-voiced fifes, lively and smart and shrill;
Then timbrels, where tall fingers trip, but trip
In the right place, and run along again;
Then blustering trumpets, wonder-wafting horns,
Evvivas from their folks, *hurrahs* from ours,   30
And songs that pour into both ears long life
And floods of glory and victory for ever.
Fra Rupert.   What signify these fooleries?   In one word,
Andrea, art thou king?
Andrea.   I fancy so.
The people never give such hearty shouts
Saving for kings and blunders.
Fra Rupert.   Son! beware,
Lest while they make the one they make the other.
Andrea.   How must I guard against it?   40
Fra Rupert.   Twelve whole years
Constantly here together, all the time
Since we left Hungary, and not one day
But I have labour'd to instil into thee,
Andrea! how wise kings must feel and act.
Andrea.   But, father, who let *you* into the secret?
Fra Rupert.   I learnt it in the cloister.
Andrea.   Then no doubt
The secret is worth knowing; many are
(Or songs and fables equally are false)   50
Among those whisper'd there.
Fra Rupert.   Methinks, my son,
Such words are lighter than beseems crown'd heads,
As thine should be, and shall be, if thou wilt.
Andrea.   Ay, father, but it is not so as yet;
Else would it jingle to another crown,
With what a face beneath it!   What a girl
Is our Giovanna!
Fra Rupert. . By the saints above!
I thought it was a queen, and not a girl.   60

Andrea.   There is enough in her for both at once.
A queen it shall be then the whole day long.
                         [FRA RUPERT, *impatient.*
Nay, not a word, good Frate! the whole day;
Ave-Maria ends it; does it not?
I am so glad, so gamesome, so light-hearted,
So fond, I (sure!) am long steps off the throne.
    Fra Rupert.   And ever may'st be, if thou art remiss
In claiming it.
    Andrea.   I can get anything
From my Giovanna.   You would hardly guess   70
What she has given me.   Look here!
    Fra Rupert.   A book?
    Andrea.   ' *King Solomon.* '
    Fra Rupert.   His *Song?*   To seculars?
I warrant she would teach it, and thou learn it.
    Andra.   I'll learn it through, I'll learn it every verse.
Where does the *Song* begin?   I see no rhymes.
    Fra Rupert.   ' *The Proverbs !* '   Not so bad!
    Andrea.   Are songs then proverbs?
And what is this hard word?   80
    Fra Rupert.   ' *Ecclesiastes.* '
    Andrea.   But look! you have not seen the best of it.
What pretty pictures! what broad rubies! what
Prodigious pearls! seas seem to roll within,
And azure skies, as ever bent above,
Push their pink clouds, half-shy, to mingle with 'em.
    Fra Rupert.   I am not sure this book would do thee harm,
But better let me first examine it.   [*He takes it.*
    Andrea.   You shall not have it; give it me again.
    Fra Rupert.   Loose it, I say, Andrea!   90
    Andrea.   I say *no !*
    Fra Rupert.   To me?
    Audrea.   Dost think I'd say it to Giovanna?
Beside, she gave it me: she has read in it
With her own eyes, has written Latin in it
With her own fingers, . . for who else could write
Distinctly such small letters? . . You yourself,
Who rarely have occasion for much Latin,

Might swear them to be Latin in ten minutes.
Another thing . . the selfsame perfume clings   100
About those pages as about her bosom.
    Fra Rupert (starts).   Abomination ! Know all that !
    Andrea.   Like matins.
Thence, tho' she turn'd quite round, I saw her take it
To give it me.   Another thing . . the people
Bragg'd of my metal half an hour ago,
And I will show I have it, like the best.
Another thing . . forgettest thou, Fra Rupert,
I am a husband ?
    Fra Rupert.   Seven years old thou wert one.*   110
    Andrea.   Ha, but ! ha, but ! seven years upon seven years
Could not make me the man I am to-day.
    Fra Rupert.   Nor seventy upon seven a tittle wiser.
    Andrea.   Why did not you then make me while you could ?
You taught me nothing, and would let none touch me,
No, not our king himself, the wisest man
In his dominions, nor more wise than willing.
Forsooth ! you made a promise to my father
That nobody should filch my faith and morals,
No taint of learning eat skin-deep into me !   120
And good king Robert said, " If thus my brother
Must have it . . if such promise was exacted . . "
    Fra Rupert.   All have more knowledge than they well
      employ.
Upbraidest thou thy teacher, guardian, father ?
    Andrea.   Fathers may be, alas ! too distant from us,
Guardians may be too close . . but, teacher ? teacher ?
    Fra Rupert.   Silence !
    Andrea (retreating).   He daunts me : yet, some day, *cospetto !*
    Fra Rupert.   What mutterest thou ?
    Andrea (to himself).   I will be brave, please God !   130
    Fra Rupert (suppressing rage).   Obstinate sinners are alone
      unpardon'd :
I may forgive thee after meet repentance,
But must confer with thee another time

* Andrea and Giovanna were contracted when he was seven, she five.

On that refractory untoward spirit.
    Andrea (*to himself*).   He was then in the right (it seems)
       at last.
    Fra Rupert.   I hear some footsteps coming hitherward.

ACT I.   SCENE IV.

Giovanna *and* Filippa.

    Fra Rupert (*turns his back to them*).   O those pestiferous
       women !
    Andrea.   Ay, well spoken.
The most religious of religious men
Lifts up his arms and eyes, my sweet Giovanna,
Before your wond'rous charms.
       [*The* Friar *looks at him with rage and scorn.*
    Giovanna.   Simple Andrea !
Are they more wond'rous than they were before ?
Or are they more apparent now the robes
Are laid aside, and all those gems that made
My hair stand back, chiefly that mischievous   10
Malignant ruby (some fierce dragon's eye
Turn'd into stone) which hurt your finger so
With its vile crooked pin, for touching me,
When you should have but lookt, and not quite that.
    Fra Rupert (*who had listened*).   Come hither ; didst thou
       hear her ?
    Andrea.   Every word ;
And bear no rancour to her, though she scolds.
    Fra Rupert.   She might have waited twenty years beyond
This day, before she thought of matrimony ;
She talks so like a simpleton.   20
    Andrea.   She does
Indeed : yet, father ! it is very true :
The pin did prick me : she is no simpleton
As far as memory goes.
       [*The* Friar *looks up, then walks about impatiently.*
Now, won't you mind me ?

She is but very young, scarce seventeen ;
When she is two years older, just my age,
Then shall you see her ! more like me perhaps.
She might have waited . . . you say well . . . and would
Willingly, I do think ; but I am wiser,   30
And warmer.   Our Hungarian blood (ay, Frate !)
Is not squeez'd out of March anemones.
    Filippa.   Since, friar Rupert ! here are met together
The lofty and the lowly, they and we,
If your austerity of life forbade
To mingle with the world's festivities,
Indulge, I pray you, in that luxury
Which suits all seasons, sets no day apart,
Excludes from its communion none, howe'er
Unworthy, but partakes of God indeed . .   40
Indulge in pardon.
    Fra Rupert.   Does a seneschal's
Wife bend before me ?   Do the proud ones beg ?
    Filippa.   Too proud I may be : even the very humblest
May be too proud.   I am, 'tis true, the widow
Of him you mention.   Do I beg ?   I do.
Our queen commands me to remove ill-will.
    Fra Rupert.   There are commands above the queen's.
    Filippa.   There are,
O holy man ! obey we both at once !   50
    Giovanna (calls ANDREA).   Husband !
    Fra Rupert.   And not our king ? most noble lady !
    Giovanna.   He, or I much mistake him, is my husband.
    Andrea.   Mistake me ! not a whit : I am, I am.
    Giovanna.   If, O my husband ! that dear name has power
On your heart as on mine, now when first spoken,
Let what is love between us shed its sweets
A little wider, tho' a little fainter ;
Let all our friends this day, all yours, all mine,
Be one another's, and not this day only.   60
Persuade them.
    Andrea.   Can I ?
    Giovanna.   You persuaded *me.*
    Andrea.   Ay, but you did not hate me ; and your head

Is neither grey nor tonsured ; these are odds.
I never could imagine well how folks
Who disagree in other things, agree
To make each other angry.   What a game !
To toss back burs until the skin is full
On either side ! Which wins the stake, I wonder ?   70
    Fra Rupert (*bursting away*).   I have no patience.
    Andrea.   I have, now he's gone.
How long were you contriving this grand scheme
To drive away the friar ?   Do you think
                              [*Whispers to* GIOVANNA.
He won't come after supper ?   Does he know
Our chamber ?
    Giovanna.   Hush ! Andrea !
    Andrea.   In good earnest
I fear him, and the fleas about his frock.
Let me go after him : he went in wrath :   80
He may do mischief, if he thinks it right,
As these religious people often do.   [ANDREA *goes.*
    Filippa.   Happy Andrea ! only fleas and friars
Molest him : little he suspects the snares
About his paths ; the bitter jealousies
Of Hungary ; how pertinaciously
Mail'd hands grasp sceptres, how reluctantly
Loose them ; how tempting are our milder clime
And gentler nation ! He deserves our pity.
    Giovanna.   O ! more than pity. If our clime, our nation, 90
Bland, constant, kind, congenial with each other,
Were granted him, how much more was withheld !
Sterile the soil is not, but sadly waste.
What buoyant spirits and what pliant temper !
How patient of reproof ! how he wipes off
All injuries before they harden on him,
And wonders at affronts, and doubts they can be !
Then, his wild quickness ! O the churl that bent it
Into the earth, colourless, shapeless, thriftless,
Fruitless, for ever !   Had he been my brother,   100
I should have wept all my life over him ;
But, being my husband, one hypocrisy

I must put on, one only ever will I.
Others must think, by my observance of him,
I hold him prudent, penetrating, firm,
No less than virtuous : I must place myself
In my own house (now indeed his) below him.
   Filippa.   I almost think you love him.
   Giovanna.   He has few
Even small faults, which small minds spy the soonest ;   110
He has, what those will never see nor heed,
Wit of bright feather, but of broken wing ;
No stain of malice, none of spleen, about it.
For this, and more things nearer . . . for the worst
Of orphancy, the cruellest of frauds,
Stealth of his education while he played
Nor fancied he could want it ; for our ties
Of kindred ; for our childhood spent together ;
For those dear faces that once smiled upon us
At the same hour, in the same balcony ;   120
Even for the plants we rear'd in partnership,
Or spoil'd in quarrel, I do love Andrea.
But, from his counsellors ! . . . .
   Filippa.   We shall elude
Their clumsy wiles perhaps.   The youth, methinks,
Is tractable.
   Giovanna.   May wise men guide him then !
It lies beyond my duty.
   Filippa.   But the wise
Are not the men who guide the tractable.   130
The first bold hand that seizes, holds them fast ;
And the best natures melt into the bad
'Mid dances and carousals.
   Giovanna.   Let Andrea
Be sparing of them !
   Filippa.   Evil there may be
Where evil men preside, but greatly worse
Is proud austerity than princely glee.
   Giovanna.   Heaven guard us !   I have entered on a course
Beleaguered with dense dangers : but that course   140
Was first ordained in earth, and now in heaven.

My father's spirit filled his father's breast,
And peace and union in our family
(They both foresaw) would be secured by ours.
   Filippa.   She who forgets her parent will forego
All later duties : yes, when love has lost
The sound of its spring-head, it grows impure,
Tortuous, and spent at last in barren sand.
I owe these generous kings the bread I broke,
The letters I pickt up : no vile sea-weed   150
Had perisht more neglected, but for them.
They would heap affluence on me ; they did heap it ;
Next, honours : for these only I am ungrateful.
   Giovanna (smiling).   Ungrateful ? thou ? Filippa !
   Filippa.   Most ungrateful.
With humble birth and humbler intellect
The puff-ball might have bounced along the plain
And blinded the beholder with its dust :
But intellect let down on humble birth
Writhes under titles, shrinks from every glance,   160
At every question turns one fibre fresh
For torture, and, unpullied and adrift,
Burns its dull heart away in smouldering scorn.
   Giovanna.   Where no ethereal spirit fills the breast . .
   Filippa. . . Honours are joys great as such breast can hold.
   Giovanna.   The happy then in courts are numberless ;
We hear the contrary.
   Filippa.   Never believe
This, nor another ill report of them.
   Giovanna.   What ?   170
   Filippa.   That the great are not great to their valets ;
'Tis but their valets who can find their greatness.
   Giovanna.   I know that you have enemies.
   Filippa.   Thank God !
I might have else forgotten what I am,
And what he gave me ere he placed me here.
   Giovanna.   I never shall, Filippa !
   Filippa.   Think of those
Who rais'd our souls above us, not of me.
   Giovanna.   Oh ! if my soul hath risen, if the throbs   180

Of gratitude now tell it me, if they
Who rais'd it must be thought of . . to my heart,
Filippa ! for the heart alone can think.
   Filippa.   I first received thee in these arms ; these arms
Shall loose thee last of living things, Giovanna.

ACT II.   SCENE I.

IN THE PALACE.

GIOVANNA, FIAMMETTA, MARIA.

   Maria.   And now, Fiammetta, tell me whence that name
Which tickles thee so.
   Fiammetta.   Tell indeed ! not I.
   Maria (to GIOVANNA).   Sister ! you may command
   Giovanna.   Command a sister ?
Secrets are to be won, but not commanded.
I never heard the name before. . *Fiammetta* . .
Is that it ?
   Maria.   That is it.
   Fiammetta.   For shame, Maria !   10
Never will I entrust you with a secret.
   Maria.   I do believe you like this one too well
Ever to let another mingle with it.
   Fiammetta (to herself).   I do indeed, alas !
   Giovanna. · Some gallant knight
Has carried off her scarf and bared her heart.
But to this change of name I must withhold
Assent, I like *Maria* so much better.
   Fiammetta (points to MARIA).   There is Maria yet.
   Giovanna.   But where twin-roses   20
Have grown so long together, to snap one
Might make the other droop.
   Fiammetta.   Ha ! now, Maria !
Maria ! you are springed, my little quail !
   Giovanna.   Fiammetta ! if our father were here with us,
He would suspect some poet friend of his,
Dealer in flames and darts, their only trade,

Enchanted his Sicilian.
   Maria.   Ho! ho! ho!
Proserpine never blusht such damask blushes   30
When *she* was caught.
   Fiammetta.   I am quite cool.
   Maria.   The clouds
May be quite cool when they are quite as red ;
Girls' faces, I suspect, are somewhat less so.
                               [Fiammetta *runs off.*
   Giovanna.   Maria! dear Maria! She is flown.
Is the poor girl in love then ?
   Maria.   Till this hour
I thought it but a fancy, such as all
We children have : we all choose one ; but, sure,   40
To run out of the room at the mere shadow !
   Giovanna.   What would *you* do ?
   Maria.   Wait till he came himself.
   Giovanna.   And then ?
   Maria.   Think seriously of running off,
Until I were persuaded it was civil.

ACT II.   SCENE II.

   Andrea.   What have ye done to little Sicily ?
She ran so swiftly by me, and pusht back
My hand so smartly when I would have stopt her,
I think you must have vext her plaguily
Among you.
   Maria.   She was vext, but not by us.
   Andrea.   Yes, many girls are vext to-day.   One bride
Sheds fifty thorns from each white rose she wears.
I did not think of that.   (*To* Maria.)   *You* did, no doubt ?
   Maria.   I wear white roses too, as well as she :   10
Our queen's can have no thorns for us.
   Andrea.   Not one ?
   Maria.   No, nor for any in this happy realm.
   Andrea.   Ah now ! this happy realm ! Some people think
That I could make it happier.

Giovanna.　　I rejoice
To hear it.
　　Andrea.　　Are you glad, my little bride?
　　Giovanna.　　Most glad.　O never disappoint their hopes!
The people are so kind! they love us so!　　　　　　20
　　Andrea.　　They are a merry race: ay, very crickets,
Chirruping, leaping.　What they eat, God knows;
Sunshine and cinders, may be: he has sent
Plenty of these, and they are satisfied.
　　Giovanna.　　Should *we* be, if they are?
　　Andrea.　　O then! a boon!
To make them happy all their lives.
　　Giovanna. The boon
To make them happier Heaven alone can grant.
Hearken!　If some oppressions were removed,　　　　30
Beyond my strength to manage, it were done.
　　Andrea.　　Nothing so easy.　Not your strength indeed,
But mine, could push a buffalo away.
I have a little favour to request.
　　Giovanna.　　Speak.
　　Andrea.　　Give me then this kingdom, only this.
I do not covet mountains to the north,
Nor cities over cities farther west,
Casal or Monferrato or Saluzzo,
Asti or Coni, Ceva or Torino,　　　　　　　　　40
Where that great river runs which spouts from heaven,
Nor Aix nor Toulon, nor Marseille nor Nice
Nor Avignon, where our good pope sits percht;
I only want this tidy little kingdom,
To make it happy with this sword upon it.
　　Giovanna.　　The people and their laws alone can give it.
　　Andrea.　　Well, we can make the laws.
　　Giovanna.　　And people too?
　　Andrea.　　Giovanna! I do think that smile could make
A thousand peoples from the dullest clay,　　　　50
And mould them to thy will.
　　Giovanna.　　Pure poetry!
　　Andrea.　　Don't say it! or they knock me on the head!
I ought to be contented: but they would

Insist upon it.   I have askt: here ends
My duty: I don't want it for myself . .
And yet those cities lookt like strings of bird-eggs,
And tempted me above my strength.   I only
Repent of learning all their names for nothing.
Let them hang where they are.   60
   Giovanna.   Well said.
   Andrea.   Who wants 'em?
I like these pictures better.   What a store!
Songs, proverbs, and a word as hard as flint,
Enough for fifty friars to ruminate
Amid their cheese and cobnuts after dinner,
Read it me.
   Giovanna.   Which?   [ANDREA *points.*
   Giovanna.   ' *Ecclesiastes.*'
   Andrea.   Right!   70
As you pronounce it, scarce a word of ours
In Hungary is softer.   What a tongue!
Round, juicy, sweet, and soluble, as cherries.
When Frate Rupert utter'd the same word,
It sounded just as if his beard and breast,
And all which there inhabit, had turn'd round
Into his throat, to rasp and riddle it.
I never shall forget *Ecclesiastes!*
Only two words I know are pleasanter.
   Giovanna.   And which are they?   80
   Andrea (*saluting her*).   *Giovanna* and *Carina.*
   Maria.   Unmanner'd prince!
   Andrea.   Now the white rose sheds thorns.

ACT III.   SCENE III.

SANCIA *and* FILIPPA.

   Sancia (*smiling*).   Step-mothers are not always quite at
    home
With their queen-daughters.
   Giovanna.   Yet queen-mothers are.

Step-mother you have never been to me,
But kindest, fondest, tenderest, truest mother.
   Maria.   Are we not all your children?
   Sancia.   All.   Where then
Is fled our lively Sicily?
   Giovanna.   She is gone
To her own chamber.   10
   Maria.   To read poetry.
   Sancia.   Where poetry is only light or flattering
She might read some things worse, and many better.
I never loved the heroes of Romance,
And hope they glide not in among the leaves.
   Maria.   And love you then their contraries?
   Sancia.   Those better.
What clever speech, Maria, dost thou ponder?
I see we differ.
   Maria.   Rather.   20
   Sancia.   Why so grave?
Surely no spur is tangled in *thy* hem!
   Maria.   No, my regrets were all for you.   What pity
Andrea dropt upon our globe too late;
A puissant antipode to all such heroes!
   Giovanna (smiling).   Intolerable girl! sad jealous creature!
   Sancia.   Where is he? I was seeking him.
   Maria.   There now!
   Sancia.   Or else I should not have return'd so soon
After our parting at the Benediction.   *[Goes.* 30
   Maria.   Sister! I fear my little flippancy
Hurried Queen Sancia: why just now want *sposo?*
   Giovanna.   She did not smile, as you do, when she went.
Fond as she is, her smiles are faint this morning.
A sorrowing thought, pure of all gloom, o'erspread
That saintly face.
   Maria.   It did indeed.
   Giovanna.   She loves
Us all, she loves our people too, most kindly.
   Maria.   Seeing none other than Hungarian troops   40
At church about us, deeply did she sigh
And say "Ah! where are ours?"

  Giovanna. You pain me sadly.
Queens, O Maria! have two hearts for sorrow;
One sinks upon our Naples. Whensoever
I gaze ('tis often) on her bay, so bright
With sun-wove meshes, idle multitudes
Of little plashing waves; when air breathes o'er it
Mellow with sound and fragrance, of such purity
That the blue hills seem coming nearer, nearer,   50
As I look forth at them, and tossing down
Joyance for joyance to the plains below . .
To think what mannerless, unshorn, harsh-tongued
Barbarians from the Danube and the Drave
Infest them, I cast up my eyes to Heaven
Impatiently, despondently, and ask
Are such the guests for such festivities?
But shall they dare enthral my poor Andrea?
Send, send for him: I would not he were harm'd,
Much less degraded. O for ministers   60
To guide my counsels and protect my people!
I would call round me all the good and wise.
  Sancia (returning). Daughter! no palace is too small to
    hold them.
The good love other places, love the fields,
And ripen the pale harvest with their prayers.
Solitude, solitude, so dread a curse
To princes, such a blight to sycophants,
Is *their* own home, their healthy thoughts grow in it.
The wise avoid all our anxieties:
The cunning, with the tickets of the wise,   70
Push for the banquet, seize each vacant chair,
Gorge, pat their spaniel, and fall fast asleep.
  Giovanna. Ah then what vigils are reserved for me!
  Maria. Hark! spears are grounded.
  Giovanna. Officer! who comes?
  Officer. Lady! the friar mounts the stairs; behind him
Those potent lords, Caraffa and Caraccioli.
  Giovanna. Your chair, Queen Sancia, stands unoccupied:
We must be seated to receive the lords.
Is it not so?   80

Sancia. The queen must.
Giovanna. One queen only?
The younger first? we can not thus reverse
The laws of nature for the whims of court.

[SANCIA *is seated.*

There's our kind mother! Just in time! They come.

ACT II.   SCENE IV.

FRA RUPERT, CARAFFA, *and* CARACCIOLI.

Lady! these nobles bring me with them hither,
Fearing they might not win an audience
On what concerns the welfare of the state,
In such an hour of such a day as this.
   Giovanna. Speak, gentlemen! You have much wronged
      yourselves,
And me a little, by such hesitation.
No day, methinks, no hour, is half so proper,
As when the crown is placed upon my brow,
To hear what are its duties.
   Caraffa. Gracious queen !   10
We come to represent . .
   Fra Rupert (behind). Speak out . . wrongs . . rights . .
Religion.
   Caraffa (to him). You distract me.
   Fra Rupert (to CARACCIOLI*).* Speak then thou.
See how attentively, how timidly,
She waits for you, and blushes up your void !
   Caraccioli. 'Tis therefore I want words.
   Fra Rupert. Hear mine then, boys !

[*Walks toward* GIOVANNA.

Imprest with awe before such majesty,   20
The hopes of Naples, whom their fathers deem
On this occasion, this gay hour, from high
Nobility, from splendour of equipments,
Beauty of person, gracefulness of mien,
And whatsoever courts are courtly by,

Most fitted, and most likely to prevail
Against those ancient frauds and artifices
Which certain dark offenders weave about them . .
These unsophisticated youths, foredoom'd
Longest and most impatiently to suffer,   30
Lay humbly at the footstool of your throne
A list of grievances yet unredrest.
    Giovanna.   Give it me, gentlemen, we will peruse it
Together.
    Fra Rupert.   They are more than scribe could pen.
    Giovanna (*to* Fra Rupert).   Are they of native or imported
        growth ?
Your Reverence hath some practice in the sorting.
Permit me to fill up your pause, Fra Rupert !
On this occasion, this gay hour, methinks
To urge impatience and foredoom of suffering   40
Is quite untimely.   High nobility
And splendour of equipment are the last
Of merits in Caraffas and Caracciolis   [*To them.*
The delicacy that deferr'd the tender
Of your important service, I appreciate,
Venturing to augur but a brief delay.
Gentlemen ! if your fathers bade you hither,
I grieve to owe them more than I owe you,
And trust, when next we see you, half the pleasure,
Half, if not all, may be your own free gift.   50
                              [*She rises, they go.*

ACT II.   SCENE V.

PALACE GARDEN.

Fra Rupert, Caraffa, *and* Caraccioli.

Fra Rupert.   The losel !
Caraccioli.   Saints ! what graciousness !
Caraffa.   Was ever
So sweet a girl ?   He is uglier than old Satan,
Andrea . . I abhor him worse than ever . . .

Curse on that Tartar, Turk, Bohemian,
Hungarian !   I could now half-strangle him.
   Fra Rupert.   We are dismist.
   Caraffa.   My speech might have done wonders.
   Fra Rupert.   Now, who (the mischief!) stops a dead
     man's blood ?   [10
Wonders ! ay truly, wonders it had done !
Thou wert agape as money-box for mass,
And wantedst shaking more.   What are our gains ?
   Caraffa.   A vision the strain'd eyes can not inclose,
Or bring again before them from the senses,
Which clasp it, hang upon it, nor will ever
Release it, following thro' eternity.
   Caraccioli.   I can retain her image, hear her words,
Repeat, and tone them on each fibre here,
Distinctly still.   20
   Caraffa.   Then hast thou neither heart
Nor brain, Caraccioli !   No strife so hard
As to catch one slight sound, one faintest trace,
Of the high beauty that rules over us.
Who ever seized the harmony of heaven,
Or saw the confine that is nearest earth ?
   Fra Rupert.   I can bear youthful follies, but must check
The words that run thus wide and point at heaven.
We must warn laymen fairly off that ground.
Are ye both mad ?   30
   Caraffa.   One is ; I swear to one :
I would not be the man that is not so
For empires girt with gold, worlds starr'd with women :
A trance is that man's life, a dream be mine !
Caraccioli's an ice-pit, cover'd o'er
With straw and chaff and double-door'd and thatcht,
And wall'd, the whole dark space, with earthen wall.
Why ! Frate ! all those groans of thine for heaven ?
Art toucht ?
   Fra Rupert.   I have been praying fervently . .   40
Despairingly I fear to say . . 'twere rash,
Ungrateful, and ungodly.
   Caraffa.   He has brought

The whole Maremma on me at one breath.
My cold fit now comes over me.   But, Frate!
If we do feel, may we not say we do?
   Fra Rupert.   To feel is harm; to say it, may be none,
Unless 'tis said with levity like thine.
   Caraffa.   Ah faith! I wish 'twere levity!   The pagan
That heaves up Etna, calls it very differently.   50
I think the dog is better off than I am;
He groans upon the bed where lies his torment;
I very far away from where lies mine.
   Fra Rupert.   Art thou a Christian?
   Caraffa.   Father! don't be serious.
   Fra Rupert.   I must be.
   Caraffa.   Have not I most cause?
   Fra Rupert. Yea truly.
   Caraffa.   I am not over-given to complain,
But nettles will sting all . .   60
   Fra Rupert . . who put their hands in.
Caraccioli! be warn'd by this our friend
What sufferings may arise from lawless love.
Thine passeth its due bounds; it doth, Caraccioli!
But thou canst conquer every wild desire;
A high emprize! what high emprize but suits
A true Caraccioli!   We meet again . .
I have some warnings, some reproofs, for him.
                    [Caraccioli *goes.*

ACT II.   SCENE VI.

Fra Rupert, Caraffa.

   Fra Rupert.   Where walls are living things, have ears,
     eyes, mouths,
Deemest thou, son Francesco! I alone
Heard those most violent words about Andrea?
   Caraffa.   What words?   I never thought about the man;
About his wife some little; true enough.
Some little? criminal it were to say it:

He who thinks little of such . . such perfection,
Has left his thoughts among the worms that creep
In charnel-houses, among brainless skulls,
Dry bones, without a speck of blood, a thread   10
Of fibre, ribs that never cased a heart.
The volumes of the doctors of the church
Could not contain a tithe of it: their clasps,
Strong enough to make chains for Saracens,
Their timbers to build argosies, would warp
And split, if my soul's fire were pent within.
    Fra Rupert.   Remember, son Francesco! prince Andrea,
King rather (such the husband of a queen
Is virtually, and should be) king Andrea
Lives under my protection.   20
    Carraffa.   Well, what then?
    Fra Rupert.   What?   Into mine own ear didst thou not
        breathe
Traitorous threats?
    Caraffa.   I?   Threats?   About his queen?
    Fra Rupert.   Filthy! most filthy!
    Caraffa.   No, no: wandering thoughts
Fluttered in that direction; one thought, rather.
Doves have hot livers.
    Fra Rupert.   Be adultery
Bad as it will, yet treason, son Francesco!   30
Treason is far more difficult to deal with.
    Caraffa.   I do suspect it may be.
    Fra Rupert.   Saidst thou not
Thou couldst half-strangle that Hungarian?
    Caraffa.   Spake I so rashly?
    Fra Rupert.   I am a Hungarian.
    Caraffa.   Evident: but that noble mien would daunt
Moor, Usbeck, Abyssinian: and that strength!
A Switzer bear could not half-strangle it.
    Fra Rupert.   'Twere martyrdom, 'twere martyrdom.
        The life   40
Of kings hath swords and scaffolds round about it;
A word might fling thee on them.

Caraffa.   Such a word
Must fall from holy lips, thenceforth unholy.
  Fra Rupert.   Guided by me and courage, thou art safe.

ACT III. SCENE I.

IN THE PALACE.

ANDREA *and* FILIPPA.

Andrea.   Many the stories you've repeated to me,
Lady Filippa ! I have clean forgotten 'em ;
But all the bloody giants every girl
Before our bed-time threw into my night-cap,
Lie safe and sound there still.
  Filippa.   I quite believe
You've not the heart to drive them out, my prince.
  Andrea.   Not I indeed.   And then your sage advice !
  Filippa.   Is all that too forgotten ?
  Andrea.   No, not all ;   10
But, dear Filippa, now that I am married,
And sovran (one may say) or next door to it,
You must not give me any more advice . .
Not that I mind it ; but to save appearances.
                    [*She bends : he goes, but returns suddenly.*
Lady Filippa ! lady seneschal !
  Filippa.   My prince ! command me.
  Andrea.   Solve me one more question.
How happens it (while old men are so wise)
That any foolish thing, advice or story,
We call it an old woman's ?   20
  Filippa.   Prince Andrea !
I know not as for stories and advice ;
I only know, when *we* are disappointed
In any thing, or teazed with it, we scoff
And call it an old man's.
  Andrea.   Ah spiteful sex !
  Filippa.   Here comes Maria : ask her no such questions.

Andrea.   I wish Fra Rupert heard your words.
Filippa.   To prove them?
Maria.   Give him a nosegay at the door.   30
Andrea.   He spurns
Such luxury.
  Maria.   Since his arrival here,
Perfumes, they tell me, are more general
And tenfold dearer: everybody wears them
In self-defence: men take them with their daggers;
Laundresses sprinkle them on vilest linen,
Lest they be called uncleanly; round the churches
What once were clouds of incense, now are canopies
Of the same benzoin; kites could not fly thro';   40
The fainting penitents are prone to catch
At the priest's surplice as he passes by,
And cry, above their prayers to heaven for mercy,
Stop! stop! turn back! waft me a little yet.
  Andrea.   The father is indeed more fox than civet,
And stinks out sins like sulphur and stale eggs.
(*To* Maria.)   You will not run away with him?
  Maria.   Tarantola!
Worse than most venomous tarantola,
He bites, and will not let us dance for it.   50

ACT. III.   SCENE II.

IN THE GARDENS OF CAPO DI MONTE.

Boccaccio *and* Fiammetta.

Fiammetta.   I do not know whether it be quite right
To listen, as I have, morn after morn
And evening after evening.
  Boccaccio.   Are my sighs
Less welcome in the garden and the bower,
Than where loud organ bellow'd them away,
And chorister and waxlight ran between?
  Fiammetta.   You sadly interrupted me at vespers:

Never do that again, sir!   When I pray,
I like to pray with all my heart.   Bold man!   10
Do you dare smile at me?
    Boccaccio.   The bold man first
Was smiled at; was he not?
    Fiammetta.   No, no such thing:
But if he was, it was because he sigh'd
At the hot weather he had brought with him.
    Boccaccio.   At the cold weather he fear'd coming on
He sighed.
    Fiammetta.   And did it come?
    Boccaccio.   Too gracious lady!   20
    Fiammetta.   Keep *gracious lady* for dull drawing-rooms;
Fiammetta is my name; I would know yours.
    Boccaccio.   Giovanna.
    Fiammetta.   That I know (*aside*).   I ought, alas!
Often with Acciaioli and Petrarca
I've seen you walking, but have never dared
To ask your name from them; your house's name
I mean of course; our own names stand for nothing.
You must be somebody of high estate.
    Boccaccio.   I am not noble.   30
    Fiammetta (shrinking back).   Oh! . . then! . .
    Boccaccio.   I must go!
That is the sentence, is it not?
    Fiammetta (runs and takes his hand).   Don't tell me
Thou art not noble: say thou art most noble:
Norman . . half-Norman . . quarter-Norman . . say it.
    Boccaccio.   Say an untruth?
    Fiammetta.   Only this one; my heart
Will faint without it.   I will swear to think it
A truth, wilt thou but say it.   'Tis a truth: 40
Thy only falsehood thou hast told already,
Merely to try me.   If thou art not noble . .
Noble thou art, and shalt be!
        [*She sobs and pauses: he presses her hand to his bosom.*
Who gainsays it?
    Boccaccio.   A merchant's son, no better, is thy slave,
Fiammetta!

Fiammetta (smiling).   Now art thou disguised indeed.
Come, show me specimens of turquises,
Amethysts, emeralds, diamonds . . out with them.
   Boccaccio.   A merchant's, and poor merchant's son am I ;
Gems I have none to offer, but pure love   [50
Proof to the touchstone, to the crucible.
   Fiammetta.   What then or who is noble, and thou not ?
I have heard whispers that myself am not so
Who am king Robert's daughter.   We may laugh
At those who are, if thou and I are none.
Thou art my knight, Giovanni !   There now ; take
                              [*Giving him her scarf.*
Thy patent of nobility, and wear it.
   Boccaccio (kisses it).   What other but were cobweb after
      this ?
   Fiammetta.   Ha ! kiss it ! but take care you don't kiss
   me.   [60
                              [*Runs away.*

ACT III.   SCENE III.

IN THE PALACE.

SANCIA *and* FILIPPA.

Sancia.   Even you, my dear Filippa, are alert
As any of the girls, and giddy too :
You have dropt something now you can not find.
   Filippa.   I have been busy, looking here and there
To find Andrea.
   Sancia.   Leave him with his bride,
Until they tire of saying tender things.
   Filippa.   Untender things, I fear, are going on.
He has been truant to the friar Rupert
Of late, who threatens him with penances   10
For leaving some injunction unperform'd.
And more perhaps than penances are near :
For sundry captains, sundry nobles, meet
At friar Anselm's cell ; thither had sped

Fra Rupert.   In the garden of Saint Clara
Voices were heard, and threats; then whispers ran
Along the walls.   They walkt out, one by one,
Soldiers with shuffling pace unsoldierly,
Friars with folded hands, invoking heaven,
And hotly calm as night ere burst Vesuvius.   20
   Sancia.   Beyond the slight affronts all princes bear
From those who miss what others have obtain'd,
Andrea shall fear nothing: Heaven protects him.
   Filippa.   Heaven, in its equal dispensation, gives
The pious palms, the prudent length of days.
We seek him not then with the same intent
Of warning?
   Sancia.   With the same of warning; you,
Where the good angels guard; I, where the bad
Seduce him.   Having reign'd, and having heard   30
That thither tend his wishes . .
   Filippa.   Momentary.
   Sancia.   But lawless wishes have returning wings
Of speed more than angelic.   I would win
His private ear, lest courtiers take possession;
I would persuade him, with his lovely bride
To share all other troubles than the crown's.

ACT III. SCENE IV.

IN THE PALACE.

ANDREA *and* MARIA.

   Andrea.   Are we then going up to Capo-Monte?
How long shall we remain there? all the night?
   Maria.   Until the evening.
   Andrea.   And where then?
   Maria.   Aversa.
   Andrea.   Ay, because there I askt her if she loved me:
Beside . . the strangest thing on earth . . young brides
Fly from the altar and roost anywhere
Rather than near it.   What should frighten them?

But, if we go, why not set off directly?　　　10
　　Maria.　We stay because the people round the gates,
Who left too late their farms and villages
To see our queen and you, expect at noon
To follow the procession.
　　Andrea.　What procession?
Is there another marriage?　O rare sport!
　　Maria (continuing).　From Castel-Nuovo far as Capo-
　　　Monte.
　　Andrea.　O glorious!　But we really shall be let
Into the gardens and the groves?
　　Maria.　Why not?　　　20
Who should prevent us?
　　Andrea.　Into all?　Among
The marble men and women who stand there,
And only stir by moonlight?　I don't think
They stir at all : I am half-sure they don't.
　　Maria.　I have been always of the same opinion.
　　Andrea (shakes his head).　Although he said it who says
　　　mass, I doubt it.
　　Maria.　Ah! but to doubt is not to be half-sure :
The worse end may stick fast, like broken tooth.
　　Andrea.　Now if you laugh, you make an unbeliever.　30
You girls are . .
　　Maria.　Pray what are we?
　　Andrea.　Cunninger.
Fra Rupert told me he would break their bones.
　　Maria.　Did he?
　　Andrea.　As bad.　He'd tumble them down headlong,
If ever he once caught me looking up
Again at those who stood alert for swimming.
　　Maria.　When?
　　Andrea.　Four years back.　To me they seem'd pure
　　　marble,
　　　　　　[40
But Frate Rupert never could have spited
Mere marble so, although they lookt like women.
I scarcely would believe him when he said
They once were devils, but could do no harm
Now the salt water had been sprinkled on 'em,

Unless we look at them as worshippers.
    Maria.   I am sure you did not.
    Andrea.   No ; upon my faith !
    Maria.   We never stand about them ; we walk on.
    Andrea (in a low voice).   What ! when you are but one or
      two together ?   [50
I like their looks : the women are quite lovely,
And the men too (for devils) not amiss.
I wonder where they laid their plaguy scourges ;
They must have had them, or were never worshipt.
    Maria.   Did not the Frate tell you ?
    Andrea.   Ask the Frate !
He would have found them in a trice, and held
The scourges good enough, though not the devils.
    Maria.   I think you mind him less than formerly.
    Andrea.   I am a married man.   60
    Maria.   But married men
Fear priests and friars more than single ones.
    Andrea.   He is the holiest monk upon God's earth,
And hates you women most.
    Maria.   Then the least holy.
    Andrea.   Dost think it ?   If I thought him so, I'd fear
The beast no longer, broad as are his shoulders,
His breath . . pho ! . . like a water-snake's, his fist
Heavy as those big books in chapter-houses,
And hairy as the comet ; for they say   70
'Twas hairy ; though I saw no hairs upon it.
    Maria.   Whenever love comes upon *thee*, Andrea,
Art thou not kinder ?
    Andrea.   Kinder, but not holier.
    Maria.   Is not thy heart more grateful ?
    Andrea.   As may happen ;
A little thing would make it so.
    Maria.   And, tell me,
Art thou not readier to give alms ?
    Andrea.   Tell *me*   80
How long, Maria, those bright eyes have seen
Into my thoughts ? Fra Rupert knows not half one
Unless he question for an hour or better

And stamp and threaten, nor then more than half one.
I'll never fear him now : I'll tell him so.
   Maria.   Be not too hasty: tell him no such thing.
But fear him not : fear rather those about him.
                       [FRA RUPERT *is prying.*

   Andrea.   Whom ?
   Maria.   His Hungarians.
   Andrea.   They're my countrymen.   90
   Maria.   Should they make all us dread them ?
   Andrea.   Me ?
   Maria.   Even you,
Under Fra Rupert, like the best, or worst.
Should they possess our kingdom ?
   Andrea.   My wife's kingdom ?
No, by the Saints ! they shall not touch her kingdom.
   Fra Rupert (crossing the farther part of the stage).   They
     shall not touch her kingdom . . and shalt thou ?
   Andrea.   I heard a voice.
   Maria (laughing).   No doubt, no doubt, the Frate's. 100
   Andrea.   I hear and feel him farther off than thou dost.
   Maria.   Andrea ! were thy ears as quick to hear
Thy friends as enemies.
   Andrea.   Still would that eye
Glare over me, like the great open one
Above the throne at church, of gold and azure,
With neither brows nor lashes, but black clouds
Round it, and nought beside.
   Maria.   The three eyes match,
May-be ; but is there anything in church   110
So like his voice ?
   Andrea.   The organ bellows are,
Without the keys.   That was not much unlike it . .
A little softer . . and not too soft, neither.
   Maria.   I heard no voice whatever, not a sound.
Are you still half afraid ?
   Andrea.   No, if thou are not.
   Maria.   Are you convinced ?
   Andrea.   I was not very soon.
Men weigh things longer than you women do.   120
Maria ! take my word, I am quite sated

Of fearing, tho' (thank God!) the worst is past.
 Maria. I praise this manliness, this resolution.
 Andrea. Dost thou? Already am I grown more manly,
More resolute. O! had your praise come earlier,
And heartily as now, another man
In thought and action might have been Andrea!
But will you tell Giovanna what you think?
 Maria. I will indeed, and joyfully.
 Andrea. Her praise   130
Is better still: yours screws the spur on heel,
Hers scarfs the neck and lifts the lance to hand.
What's all this tinkling?
    [*Guitars in the next chamber; the door opens.*
 Maria (smiling). O! again Fra Rupert!
One of these voices surely must be his!
Which of them? can not you distinguish it?
 Andrea (calls out). Who sings there?
 Maria. Do not stop them: let us hear.

Petronilla.
Ah! do not go! ah do not go
 Among the silly and the idle!
A lover surely should not so
 From her who loves him slip and sidle.

Garisendo.
The *saltarella** waits for me,
 And I must go and I must play . .
Come! do not dance, but hear and see,
 To-morrow we will love all day.

 Andrea. Now she is reasonable, he might spare her ·
A handful of his ribbons, or that net   140
Silver and blue there dangling down his nape.
Who is he? I don't know him.
 Maria. Garisendo.
 Andrea. And t'other?
 Maria. Petronilla.
 Andrea. Nor her neither.
 Maria. I and Giovanna know here every face.
 Andrea. And every name?
 Maria. Every one.

* The favourite Neapolitan dance.

Andrea.   Clever creatures!   150
Maria.   By all those twitchings at the two guitars,
And tappings of fore-finger on the wrist,
They seem to be at fault.
Andrea.   No harm, no matter,
Zooks! they are up again; he first . . that's odd.
Maria.   Nay, but he only tells her what to sing.

Petronilla.
There is a lad upon the sea,
　There is, O Mary! such a lad!
And all he thinks of, it is me.

Garisendo.
Why then, my jewel! he is mad.

Petronilla.
Mad! he is no more mad than you.

Garisendo.
Unless he stamps, and stares, and cries,
As certain pretty creatures do,
　And stain their cheeks and spoil their eyes.

Petronilla.
I love, I love him with my whole . .   [*Sobbing.*

Garisendo.
Go on, go on : you mean to say
(I'd lay a wager) heart and soul,
　And very well, no doubt, you may.

Petronilla.
No, I may not, you cruel man!
　He never did what you have done,
Yet, say and do the worst you can,
　I love, I love, but you alone.

Maria.   He has not much offended.
Andrea.   Who can tell?
I am quite sorry they have fallen out.
What almanack can calculate fine weather   160
In those strange fickle regions where God plants
A man and woman, and sticks love between!
Maria.   All the man's fault.
Andrea.   All hers : she went and teased him :
With my own eyes I saw it; so might you.

Maria. You do not always look so melancholy
At music ; yet what music can be gayer
Than this is ?
 Andrea. Gayer, say you ? Ay, the music.
But if folks quarrel so in joke, what will they   170
In earnest ? If, before they're man and wife . .
Ah ! Heaven be praised ! there's time to break it off.
Look, look at them !
 Maria. She seems more reconciled.
 Andrea. Reconciled ! I should say . .
 Maria. Pray, don't say anything.
 Andrea. Ready for . . By my troth ! 'twas a salute.
 Maria. Now what things run into your head, Andrea !
 Andrea. It was as like as pea to pea, if not . .
However, let them know, another time   180
They must not sing about the house in that way.
 Maria. Why not ?
 Andrea. Giovanna might not like it now.
 Maria. So ! you would do then all she likes ?
 Andrea. I would :
But if she ever hears that wicked song,
She might not do all *I* like. Sweet Maria !
Persuade them, when you see them, to forget it ;
And, when you go to bed, turn on your pillow,
First drop it from one ear, then from the other,   190
And never pick it up again, God love you !
 Maria. I'll run to them directly with your wishes.
 Andrea. Stay : the last verse is clever : pick out that.
 Maria. And nothing more ?
 Andrea (anxiously). Don't overload your memory.

ACT III. SCENE V.

FRA RUPERT'S CELL.

ANDREA *and* FRA RUPERT.

Fra Rupert. What ! am I never to be left alone,
Andrea ? Let me have my pleasures too,
Such as they are.

Andrea. They're very much like mine.
Have we not prayed and scourged and wept together?
  Fra Rupert. Ah! were that now the case!
  Andrea. Well, father, well!
I would not stand between you and your duty:
But I thought, being prince . .
  Fra Rupert (sneering). Thou, being prince,   10
Thoughtest! Thou verily not only toppest
Thyself, but most among thy fellows, lad!
And so, Andrea! being prince, thou thoughtest?
  Andrea. Good-bye, thou art as brave and blithe as ever.
                                              [*Goes, but turns back.*
I had one little thing upon my conscience.
  Fra Rupert. I am quite ready: let me know the whole:
Since yesterday? Nod? wink? to me?
  Andrea (to himself). He chafes me.
  Fra Rupert. And throw thy head back thus?
  Andrea. My head's my own.   20
  Fra Rupert. Wonderful! be not over-sure of that.
                                              [*Aside.*
If thou art contrite, go!
  Andrea. I will not go;
I am not contrite.
  Fra Rupert. I am in a maze!
  Andrea. A scrape thou'rt in.
  Fra Rupert. A scrape! Who could betray me?
                                              [*To himself.*
  Andrea. Thou'st lost thy lamb, old shepherd! no great
    pet.
  Fra Rupert. No, nor great loss: when lambs, tho', lose
    their shepherd
They find the shambles nearer than the fold.   30
  Andrea. Father! you said you must confer with me
Another time?
  Fra Rupert. I did so.
  Andrea. Why not now?
  Fra Rupert. I see not why: but soon Caraccioli,
And first Caraffa, must unbosom here.
Thou hast much power, Andrea! thou canst do

Anything now to glorify thy country.
   Andrea.   Suppose I wish to swim to Ischia; could I?
   Fra Rupert.   My boy! thou hast not wind enough for
     that.   40
Am I to be evaded, taunted, posed?
Or thinkest thou, Andrea, that because
A silly girl espouses thee . .
   Andrea.   By Peter!
She who espouses me shall ne'er be call'd
A silly girl.   I am a husband, Frate!
I am a boy no longer: I can cope
With women: and shall men then, even tho' friars,
Pretend to more?   I will go back and call
The maidens: they shall pelt you from the palace   50
If ever you set foot within its walls.
   Fra Rupert.   Should every stone from maiden hit my
     nose,
A grain of dust would hurt it tenfold more.
   Andrea.   Know, they have tongues that yours could never
     meet.
   Fra Rupert.   Andrea! wouldst thou kill me with un-
     kindness?
   Andrea.   Gad! he sheds tears! . . Now at him!
. . Yes, I would.
   Fra Rupert.   And bring down these grey hairs . .
   Andrea.   Which hairs are they?
The skull's are shaven, and the beard's are dirty;   60
They may be grey though.
   Fra Rupert.   Shame upon thy mirth!
I am a poor old man.
   Andrea.   'Tis your vocation.
Beside, I have heard say that poverty
Is the best bargain for the best place yonder
In Paradise.   All prick their feet before
They clamber upward into that inclosure:
'Tis well worth while.
   Fra Rupert.   Age too (alas how heavy!)   70
To serve my loving ward, my prince's son,
I would support still longer, willingly.

Andrea.   Frate ! 'tis more than I can say for it.
                    [RUPERT *creeps supplicatingly toward him.*
Out of my sight ! crawl back again . . I loathe thee.

ACT III.   SCENE VI.

Fra Rupert (alone).   I have no malice in me : if I know
My secret heart, no heart so pure of malice :
But all my cares and vigils, hopes and dreams,
Blown by a boy, spurn'd by a brute, away !
So ends it ?   Blessed Stephen ! not so ends it.
It ends with him, and with him only : me
No sword can touch.   Why are not come those fools ?
I thought the other would have kept them off.
I will have power without him, and not thro' him.
They must have clean forgotten.   'Tis the hour . .   10
'Tis past it . . no, not past it . . just the hour ;
The bell now strikes for noon.   [*A knocking.*
One comes at last.   [*Opens the door :* CARAFFA *enters.*
    Fra Rupert.   Exactly to the moment.
    Caraffa.   I was walking
About the cloister till I heard the bell,
For Father Rupert's hours are golden ones.
    Fra Rupert.   May my friends spend them profitably for
        me !
Caraffa ! thine are number'd.
    Caraffa.   All men's are.   20
    Fra Rupert.   But some are not notcht off like schoolboy's
        days
Anxious to see his parent.   Thou may'st see
Thy parent too.
    Caraffa.   I left him but just now.
    Fra Rupert.   We all have one, one whom we all have left
Too often.   Hast thou not some sins for me ?
    Caraffa.   As many as a man could wish to have.
    .*Fra Rupert.*   Are there none dangerous ? none involving
        life ?

Hast thou forgotten our last conference?
   Caraffa.   No, nor shall ever.   But what danger there? 30
   Fra Rupert.   Need I to say, Francesco, that no breath
Transpired from me?   We both were overheard.
   Caraffa.   I think you hinted it.
   Fra Rupert.   I fear'd it only.
Thou knowest my fond love . . I will not say
For thee . . thou art but second in my breast . .
Poor, poor Andrea!
   Caraffa.   Never fear about him.
Giovanna, even tho' she did not love,
(O that she did not!) yet would never wrong him.   40
   Fra Rupert.   Nay, God forbid she should!   'Twas not
      for me
To mark her looks, her blushes, gestures . . how
Faltered the word "Caraffa" as she spoke it.
Thy father then said nothing?
   Caraffa.   Not a word;
What should he?
   Fra Rupert.   Not a word.   Old men are close:
And yet I doubted . . I am apt to doubt . .
Whether he might not . . for ambition stirs
Most fathers . . just let slip . . Why didst thou falter? 50
For never faltered child as thou didst falter.
Thou knowest then her mind better than we?
   Caraffa.   I know it?   I divine it?   Would I did!
   Fra Rupert.   Nay, rather let the bubble float along
Than break it: the rich colours are outside.
Everything in this world is but a bubble,
The world itself one mighty bubble, we
Mortals, small bubbles round it!
   Caraffa.   Frate! Frate!
Thou art a soapy one!   No catching thee!   [*Aside.* 60
[*Aloud.*] What hopes thou showest me!   If these were solid
As thou, most glorious bubble who reflect'st them,
Then, then indeed, to me from this time forth
The world, and all within the world, were bubbles.
   Fra Rupert.   A knight art thou, Caraffa! and no title
(Secular title, mind! secular title)
Save only royalty, surpasses knighthood.

There is no condescension in a queen
Placing her foot within the palm of knight,
And springing from it on her jewel'd saddle :   70
No condescension is there if she lend
To theirs the sceptre who lent hers the sword.
Knights there have been, and are, where kings are not,
Kings without knights what are they ?
   Caraffa.   Norman blood
Runs in my veins as in her own : no king
(Savage or tame) shall stand above those knights
Who raised his better to the throne he won :
Of such am I.   But what am I before
Giovanna ! to adore, to worship her,   80
Is glory far above the chiselling
Of uncouth kings, or dashing them to earth :
O be it mine !
   Fra Rupert.   Perhaps some other Norman
May bear less tamely the new yoke ; perhaps
A Filangieri may, this very night . .
   Caraffa.   No Filangieri ever stoopt to treachery.
No sword of Norman ever struck by night.
Credulous monk ! to me name Filangieri !
Quellers of France and England as we are,   90
And jealous of precedency, no name
(Offence to none) is higher than Filangieri.
   Fra Rupert.   Boaster !
   Caraffa.   I boast of others ; few do that
Who merit such a title.
   Fra Rupert.   Lower thy crest ;
Pause ! thou art in my hands.
   Caraffa.   I am in God's.
   Fra Rupert (mildly, after hesitation).   Who knows but
     God hath chosen thee, amid
His ministers of wrath, to save thy country   100
And push oppression from her !   Dreams and signs
Miraculous have haunted me.
   Caraffa.   Thee, Frate !
   Fra Rupert.   Me, even me.   My ministry is over :
Marriage ends pupilage, and royalty

Ends friendship.   Little is it short of treason
To say that kings have friends.
    Caraffa.   How short of treason
I know not, but I know how wide of truth.
    Fra Rupert.   Listen !   There are designs against the life
Of young Andrea.   [110
    Caraffa.   By the saints above !
I hope there are not.
    Fra Rupert.   If thy name be found
Among conspirators (and those are call'd
Conspirators who vindicate their country)
Where thy sword is, there must thy safety be.
The night for vengeance is the marriage-night.
    Caraffa.   *I* draw the sword without defiance first ?
I draw the sword uninjured ? Whom against ?   120
Against a life so young ! so innocent
Of any guile ! a bridegroom ! in his bed !
O ! is this horror only at the crime ?
Or is it . . No, by heaven ! 'tis heaven's own horror
At such unmanly deed.   *I*, Frate ! *I*,
Caraffa, stain with tears Giovanna's cheek !
I sprinkle poison on the flowers she smells !
    Fra Rupert (resolutely).   Hark ye, Caraffa !   If the public
      good . .
    Caraffa.   Away with public good !   Was never book
Put in my hand ? was never story told me ?   130
Show me one villain vile beyond the rest,
Did not that villain talk of public good ?
    Fra Rupert.   Only at friars are Caraffa's stabs.
Valiant and proud and wealthy as thou art,
Thou may'st have nothing left on earth to-morrow.
    Caraffa.   I shall have more to-morrow than to-day.
My honour may shoot up all in one night,
As did some tree we read of.
    Fra Rupert.   Thou art rash.
    Caraffa.   Rashness may mellow into courage ; time   140
Is left me.
    Fra Rupert.   For thy prayers.
    Caraffa.   My prayer then is,

Peace, safety, glory, joy, to our Giovanna!
  Fra Rupert. Thou may'st depart.
  Caraffa (indignantly). For ever.   [*Goes.*
  Fra Rupert. He says well.

CARACCIOLI *enters.*

  Fra Rupert (smiling and embracing him). Caraccioli! with-
    out our friend Caraffa!
  Caraccioli. He should have been here first.
  Fra Rupert (aside). Perfectly safe!   150
I did not follow him into the cloister.
  Caraccioli. Father! you seem as pondering to yourself
How that wild fellow kept his word so ill;
Caraffa-like!
  Fra Rupert. I keep mine well with him.
  Caraccioli. He should have thought of that.
  Fra Rupert. He had no time.
  Caraccioli. Always so kind! so ready with your plea
For little imperfections! Our Francesco,
Somewhat hot-headed, is warm-hearted too.   160
  Fra Rupert. His petty jealousy about the queen
(Were there no sin behind it) we might smile at.
Caraffa stands not with Caraccioli.
  Caraccioli. On the same level . . there particularly.
  Fra Rupert. Ho! ho! you laugh and jeer about each
    other?
  Caraccioli. We might. How she would laugh at two such
    ninnies!
  Fra Rupert. At one, most certainly. But laughing girls
Often like grave men best. There's something grand
As well as grave even in the sound " Caraccioli."
  Caraccioli. I have no hopes.   170
  Fra Rupert. How I rejoice to hear it!
Hopes are but wishes, wishes are but sin,
And, fed with ranker exhalations, poison.
  Caraccioli. The subtilest consumes me.
  Fra Rupert. What?
  Caraccioli. Despair.
  Fra Rupert. Violets and primroses lie under thorns

Often as asps and adders; and we find
The unexpected often as the expected,
The pleasant as the hideous.   180
    Caraccioli.   That may be,
But what avails your lesson? whither tends it?
    Fra Rupert.   My son! I hear from those who know the
        world
And sweep its noisome litter to my cell,
There are mild days when love calls love abroad
As birds call birds, and even leaves call leaves:
Moments there are, my poor Caraccioli!
Moments in which the labyrinth of the ear
At every turn of its proclivity
Grows warmer, and holds out the clue, itself: 190
Severity should not beget despair.
I would not much encourage thee, nor yet
Dash all thy hopes, however inconsiderate,
For hopes there may be, though there should not be,
Flickering even upon despondency.
There may be sounds in certain names to smite
The stagnant heart, and swell its billows high
Over wide spaces, over distant years . .
There may; but who would utter them and know it?
Delicate is the female sense, yet strong   200
In cherishing and resenting; very prompt
At hiding both, and hating the discoverer.
Never, my Paolo! look too deeply in,
Or thou may'st find what thou art looking for.
Not that she ever said one word against thee;
She even lower'd her voice in naming thee,
Seeing her sister and the rest sit giggling,
"Anything else! anything else!" said she,
And snapt the thread she workt with, out of spite.
A friend, who hopes the best, may tell the worst.   210
Patience will weary; even Giovanna's patience.
I could go farther, and relate . . but why
Why ('tis too light to touch upon) relate
The little hurt she gave Filippa's ancle
With that lark heel of hers, by twitching it

Uneasily?   O the impatient sex !
She did shed . . tears I will not say . . a tear . .
Shed it ! no, I am wrong : it came, it stayed,
As hangs one star, the first and only one,
Twinkling, upon some vernal evening.   220
    Caraccioli.   I am but clay beneath her feet.   Alas !
Clay there would quicken into primal man,
Glorified and immortal once again.
    Fra Rupert.   Thou art too hot, my Paolo !   One pulse less
In the half-hour might have been rather better.
Lovest thou our Francesco ?
    Caraccioli.   Like a brother.
    Fra Rupert.   He should not then have brought thy life in
        peril.
Andrea is quite furious : all at court
Are sworn upon thy ruin.   230
    Caraccioli.   Upon mine ?
I will then calmly tell them they are wrong.
    Fra Rupert.   Will they as calmly hear ?   Francesco said,
Imprudent youth ! you boasted of remembering
Every the lightest mole about Giovanna.
    Caraccioli.   *I* say it ?
    Fra Rupert.   Those were not your words ?
    Caraccioli.   My words !
    Fra Rupert.   Certainly not . . precisely.
    Caraccioli.   Holy Mary !   240
Is there in Naples, Hungary, or Hell,
The monster who dares utter them ?
    Fra Rupert.   ’Tis hard
Our friend should be the very man.
    Caraccioli.   ’Tis false,
Frate ! ’tis false : my friend is not the man.   [*Bursts away.*
    Fra Rupert (*sneering*).   I will not follow *him* into the
        cloister.

ACT IV.   SCENE I.

IN THE GARDEN OF CAPO DI MONTE.

BOCCACCIO *and* FIAMMETTA.

Boccaccio (sings).

If there be love on earth, 'tis here,
  O maid of royal line!
Should they who spring from heroes, fear?
  Be scornful the divine?

Shine not the stars upon the sea.
  Upon the fountain too?
O! let your eyes then light on me,
  And O! let mine see you.

      [FIAMMETTA *comes forward.*

How kind to come!
 Fiammetta. To come into the air?
I like it. They are all at their *merenda.**
The smell of melon overpowers me quite;
I could not bear it; therefore I just come
Into the air to be revived a little.
And you too here? Sly as the satyr-head [*Affecting surprise.*
Under yon seat!
 Boccaccio. Did you not tell me?
 Fiammetta. I?   10
You dreamt it.
 Boccaccio. Let me dream then on? Without
Such dreams, Fiammetta, dull would be the sleep
Call'd life.
 Fiammetta (looking round timidly). *I* must be broad awake.
 Boccaccio. You must.
 Fiammetta (nodding). And you. All are indulgent to me;
  most
Of all queen Sancia and Giovanna.
 Boccacio. One
A saint, the other better.   20
 Fiammetta. Then the grave.

  * *Merenda* (meridiana) the mid-day repast.

Filippa . .
   Boccaccio.   Grave and watchful.
   Fiammetta.   Not a word
Against her!   I do hold her in my heart,
Although she gives me good advice sometimes.
   Boccaccio.   I'm glad to hear it; for the very worthy
Are very rarely general favourites.
   Fiammetta.   Some love our friend most cordially; those
     know her:
Others there are who hate her; those would know her   30
And can not: for she stands aloof and thanks them:
Remoter, idler, neither love nor hate,
Nor care about her; and the worst and truest
They say of her, is, that her speech is dark.
   Boccaccio.   Doubtless, the vulgar eye will take offence
If cedar chambers are unwasht with lime.
   Fiammetta.   But why are you come here?
   Boccaccio.   To gaze, to sigh,
And, O Fiammetta! tell me if . . to live.
   Fiammetta (laughing).   I never saw more signs of life in
     any.   40
   Boccaccio.   Cruel!
   Fiammetta.   To find the signs of life in you?
   Boccaccio.   To scoff them out.
   Fiammetta.   I am incapable.
        [Boccaccio *rises, and steps back, gazing fondly.*
O now, Giovanni! I am terrified!
Why! you sprang up . . as if you sprang to kiss me!
Did ever creature think of such a thing?
   Boccaccio.   The drooping blades of grass beneath your feet
Think of it; the cold runlet thinks of it;
The pure sky (how it smiles upon us!) thinks of it . .   50
I will no more then think of it.   [*Kisses her.*
   Fiammetta.   Giovanni!
Ah! I shall call you (wretch!) to task for this.
   Boccaccio.   Call; and, by heaven! I'll come, tho' from
     the grave.
   Fiammetta.   Any one now would say you thought me
     handsome.

Boccaccio.   Earth has two beauties ; her Bellagio
And Anacapri ; earth's inhabitants
Have only one among them.
   Fiammetta.   Whom ?
   Boccaccio.   Fiammetta.   [*Going.*   60
   Fiammetta.   Where are you running now ?   Stay ! tho'
    quite angry,
I am not yet so angry as I should be :
But, if you ever take such liberties
Again !
   Boccaccio.   O never ! . . till we reach Aversa.
   Fiammetta.   And will you there ? and tell me to my face ?
                              [*Is departing.*
Wait, wait for pardon.   Must we part ? so soon ?
So long a time ?
   Boccaccio.   Till star-light.
   Fiammetta.   Stay a moment.   70
   Boccaccio.   Gladly a life : but my old mule loves
    walking
And meditation.   Now the mask and dress,
And boy to carry them, must all be found.
   Fiammetta.   Boy, mask, dress, mule ! speed, gallop, to
    Aversa !
   Boccaccio.   So many kisses lie upon this hand,
Mine hardly reach it.
   Fiammetta.   Lips there may have been ;
Had there been kisses, I must sure have felt them,
As I did yours . . at least I thought I did . .
But go, for I am half afraid of you . .   80
That is, of your arriving yonder late.
Go, else the crowd may stop you ; and perhaps
I might delay you for some sudden fancy,
Or . . go your ways . . not let you go at all.

ACT IV.   SCENE II.

FRA RUPERT'S CELL.

FRA RUPERT, *alone.*

I wisht him power ; for what was his was mine ;
I wisht him jealousy, distrust, aversion

For his pert bride, that she might have no share.
I never fail'd before this wretched day.
Fail'd! I have not: I will possess my rights,
Spring over him, and never more be spurn'd.
They who had rais'd his seat shall stablish mine,
Without those two vain boys: O! had they done it!
And not been where they are! The fault was theirs.

MAXIMIN enters.

Fra Rupert.   Maximin! since thy services may soon   10
Be call'd for, satchel on thee my experience,
Then set about thy work.   My Maximin!
Mind how thou liest!   Know, if lie thou must,
Lies, while they sap their way and hold their tongues,
Are safe enough: when breath gets into them,
They, and the work about them, may explode.
Maximin! there are more lies done than said.
Son! when we hesitate about the right,
We're sure to do the wrong.
  Maximin.   I don't much hesitate.   20
  Fra Rupert.   To chain a dog and to unchain a dog
Is hazardous alike, while the deaf beast
Stands barking: he must sleep; then for the cord.
  Maximin.   What! are my services in some farm-yard?
I am a soldier.
  Fra Rupert.   All great statesmen have been.
How large a portion of the world is each
In his own eyes.
  Maximin.   Am I so proud in saying
I am a soldier?   30
  Fra Rupert.   *I* am proud of thee:
Be that sufficient.   Give thou every man
What he requires of thee.
  Maximin.   A world to each?
  Fra Rupert.   Not so: yet hold not up to him a glass
That shows him less, or but some digits greater.
  Maximin.   Honestly now, Fra Rupert, by my cross!
No gull art thou.   I knew that trick myself,
And (short the digits) told it word for word.

Fra Rupert.   I will be sworn for thee.   Being minister.   40
(Not that I think it certain just at present,
For when the sage and honest are most wanted,
That is the chink of time they all drop through)
But when thou art so, mind this precept.   One
Not wise enough to keep the wiser off
Should never be a minister of state.
   Maximin.   Fra Rupert! presto! make me one to-day.
Give fifty precepts, there they go [*Blowing*] but this,
I 'll kiss the cross and the queen's hand, and keep.
   Fra Rupert.   *I* make thee minister!   50
   Maximin.   You can make kings.
   Fra Rupert.   Not even those! I might have made Andrea
What thou and every true Hungarian
Wisht him to be, ere he show'd hoof for claw,
And thought to trample down his countrymen.
   Maximin.   Andrea bloody-minded! turtle-doves
Are bloody-minded then, and leave their elm,
The first day's mating, for the scent of gore.
   Fra Rupert.   Maximin! here is no guitar for thee,
Else mightest thou sip that pure poetry   60
Preciously warm and frothy from the udder.
   Maximin.   Father! if any in our troop call'd me
A poet, he should sing for it.
   Fra Rupert.   Thou 'rt brave,
Maximin! and Andrea is not bloody.
But there are princes, or have been within
Our memory, who, when blood gusht forth like water
From their own people, stood upon some bridge
Or island, waving their plumed caps, and drank
The cries of dying men with drunken ears.   70
   Maximin.   Curses, eternal curses, man's and God's,
Upon such heathens!
   Fra Rupert.   Nay, they were not heathens;
Happily they were christians, Maximin!
Andrea, though myself instructed him,
Is treacherous. Better were this pasty people
Dissolved, washt down, than brave Hungarians perish.
   Maximin.   No truer word prophet or saint e'er spoke.

Fra Rupert (*sighing*).   Saint hath not spoken it: O may
  not prophet!
Maximin.   I, being neither, can not understand you.   80
Fra Rupert.   The innocent, the helpless, are surrounded.
Maximin.   Andrea?
Fra Rupert.   My Andrea would betray us.
Maximin.   To whom?   Are we the helpless? we the
  innocent?
Fra Rupert.   While he is yonder at Aversa, we
Are yelling thro' these very streets for mercy.
Maximin.   I cry *you* mercy, father!   When I yell,
I 'll borrow whistles from some thirty good
Neapolitans, who 'll never want them more.
Fra Rupert.   Be ready then! be ready for Aversa!   90
Glory stands there before thee; seize the traitor,
Win wealth, win jewels, win . . What have not palaces
For brave young men upon such nights as these?
Maximin.   Would'st bid me stick Andrea?
Fra Rupert.   Hungary,
Not I; our country, not revenge.
Maximin.   Bids murder?
I will proclaim thy treason thro' the camp.
Fra Rupert.   Unhappy son, forbear!   By thy sweet
  mother!
Upon my knees!   Upon my knees before   100
A mortal man!   Yea, Rupert! bend thy head;
Thy own son's hand should, and shall, spill thy blood.
          [MAXIMIN *starts, then hesitates, then rushes at him.*
Maximin.   Impudent hound!   I 'll have thy throat for that.
Fra Rupert (*guards his throat*).   Parricide! make me not
  cry murder . . love
Forbids it . . rather die!   My son! my son!
Hide but thy mother's shame; my shame, not hers.
                    [MAXIMIN *relaxes his grasp.*
Maximin! stand between the world and it?
Oh! what avails it! sinner as I am!
Other worlds witness it.   [MAXIMIN *looses hold.*
My Maximin?   [RUPERT *embraces him.*   110
  Maximin.   Why, how now, Frate! hath some wine-vault
  burst

And fuddled thee ? we know thou never drinkest.
   Fra Rupert.   That lighter sin won't save me.
   Maximin.   If light sins
Could save us, I have many a bushelful,
And little need your sentry-boxes yonder.
   Fra Rupert (*very mildly*).   I must reprove (my own dear
     child !)   (*Passionately*) . . I must
Reprove, however gently, such irreverence.
Confessionals *are* sentry-boxes ! true !
And woe betide the sentry that naps there !   120
Woe, if he spare his voice, his prayer, his curse !
   Maximin.   Curses we get dog-cheap ; the others, reason-
     able.
   Fra Rupert.   Sweet Maximin ! whatever my delight
In gazing on those features (for sharp shame,
When love blows over it from lands afar,
Tingles with somewhat too, too like delight !)
We must now part.   Thy fortune lies within
My hands.   To-night, if thy own officers
Command thee to perform a painful office . .
   Maximin.   Good father ! what know we of offices ?   130
Let them command a duty, and 'tis done.
   Fra Rupert.   Discreet tho' ! Maximin ! discreet ! my
     marrow !
Let not a word escape thee, not a breath.
Blessings, my tender kid !   We must walk on
(I love thee so !) together thro' the cloister.
   Maximin.   No, father ! no ; too much !
   Fra Rupert.   Too much for thee !
     [Rupert *precedes, speaks to three men, who bow and*
       retire ; he disappears.
   Maximin (*loitering in the cloister*).   Incredible ! yet friars
     and cockroaches
Creep thro' all rooms, and like the closet best.
Let me consider ! can it be ? how can it ?   140
He is bare fifty ; I am forty-one.

ACT IV.   SCENE III.

THE GARDEN OF FRIAR ANSELM'S CONVENT.

FRA RUPERT, KLAPWRATH, ZINGA, *and* PSEIN.

Fra Rupert.   Ye brave supporters of Hungarian power
And dignity! O Zinga! Klapwrath! Psein!
Becomes it me to praise (we may admire
Those whom to praise were a temerity)
Such men as you.
   Psein.   Us? we are only captains.
   Zinga.   After hard service we are nothing more.
   Klapwrath.   Twenty-three years hath Klapwrath rid and
     thirsted.
   Fra Rupert.   Ingratitude! the worst of human crimes,
Hardly we dare to say; so flat and stale,   10
So heavy with sick sobs from mouth to mouth,
The ejaculation.   To my mind scarce witchery
Comes up to it.
   Psein.   Hold! father!   For that sin
Either we deal with devils or old women.
   Fra Rupert.   Man was created of the dust; to make
The fragile mass cohesive, were employed
The bitter waters of ingratitude.   *[Affects to weep.*
   Klapwrath.   Weeping will never rinse that beaker, Frate!
   Fra Rupert.   It is not for myself.   20
   Zinga.   We see it is not.
   Fra Rupert.   Ye can not see deep into me.
   Psein.   Few can.
   Fra Rupert.   Ye can not see the havoc made within
By ever-dear Andrea.
   Zinga.   Havoc?
   Fra Rupert.   Havoc!
   Klapwrath.   I like the word: purses and rings hang
     round it,
Necklaces, brooches, and indented armlets.
   Psein.   But, ere we reach 'em, ugly things enough,   30

Beside the broken swords that lie below
And brave men brandisht in the morning light.
   Klapwrath.   Brave men then should not cross us; wise
  men don't.
   Fra Rupert.   Your spirit all attest; but those the least
Whose safety hangs upon your saddle-skirts.
Men are not valued for their worth in Italy:
Of the same price the apple and the peach,
The service and the fig.
   Zinga.   Well, there they beat us.
   Psein.   Whatever they may be, we can not help it.   40
   Fra Rupert.   Help it, I say, ye can; and ye shall help it,
Altho' I perish for ye.
   Klapwrath.   Then indeed,
Frate! some good might come of it; but wilt thou?
   Fra Rupert.   Abandon to his fate my poor Andrea!
Has he not slept upon this bosom?
   Klapwrath.   Has he?
He must have had some scratches on his face.
   Fra Rupert.   Has he not eaten from this hand?
   Klapwrath.   Why then,   50
He'll never die for want of appetite.
   Fra Rupert.   Have we not drunk our water from one bowl?
   Klapwrath.   Father! you were not very liberal;
He might have drunk the whole of mine, and welcome.
   Fra Rupert.   How light ye make of life!
   Zinga.   Faith! not so light;
I think it worth a tug, for my part of it;
Nor would I leave our quarters willingly.
   Psein.   O the delight of floating in a bath,
One hand athwart an orange-bough, the other   60
Flat on the marble pavement, and our eyes
Wandering among those figures round the arch
That scatter flowers, and laugh at us, and vie
With one another which shall tempt us most!
Nor is it undelightful, in my mind,
To let the curly wave of the warm sea
Climb over me, and languishingly chide
My stopping it, and push me gently away.

Klapwrath.   Water, cold, tepid, hot, is one to me.
The only enemy to honest wine   70
Is water ; plague upon it !
    Zinga.   So say I.
    Fra Rupert.   Three braver friends ne'er met.   Hei ! hei !
        hei ! hei !
The very name of friend !   You can not know
What love I bear Andrea !
    Psein.   All the world
Knows it.
    Frate.   The mischief he designs, who guesses ?
    Psein.   All boys are mischievous.
    Fra Rupert.   Alas ! but mischief   80
There might be without treachery.
    Psein.   Poor Andrea !
So little fit for it !
    Fra Rupert.   Frank generous souls
Always are first to suffer from it, last
To know it when they meet it.
    Klapwrath.   Who shall harm
Our own king's colt ? Who moves, speaks, looks, against him,
Why ! that man's shroud is woven, and spread out.
    Fra Rupert.   Let mine then be ! would it had been so
        ere   90
I saw this day !
    Psein.   What has he done ?
    Fra Rupert.   To me
All kindness ever.   Why such mad resolves
Against the lives of his most sure defenders ?
Against his countrymen, his guards, his father's
Most chosen friends ?
    Zinga.   Against your life ?
    Fra Rupert.   No ! no !
Heaven protects *me ;* he sees it ; nor indeed   100
(To do him justice) has he such a heart.
But why ask *me* to aid him ? Why ask *me*
Whether he was as strong at heart as Zinga,
Dexterous at sword as Klapwrath, such a fool . .
Pardon ! your pardon, gentlemen !   [*Looking at* Psein.

Psein.   As Psein.
Fra Rupert.   The very word!   Who else dared utter it?
I give him up!   I almost give him up!
   Klapwrath.   He shall not rule us.   The best blood of
      Hungary
Shall not be pour'd this night upon the wine.   110
   Fra Rupert.   If you must leave the country . . and
      perhaps
No worse may reach the greater part of you . .
   Psein.   I have no mind to leave it.
   Zinga.   None shall drive us.
   Klapwrath.   The wines of Hungary strive hard with these,
Yet Klapwrath is contented; he hates change.
   Zinga.   Let us drink these out first, and then try those.
   Fra Rupert.   Never will come the day when pine-root fire
And heavy cones puff fragrance round the room,
And two bluff healthy children drag along   120
(One by the ear, the other by the scut)
A bulging hare for supper; where each greyhound
Knows his own master, leaps up, hangs a foot
Inward, and whimpers piteously to see
Flagons go round, then off for bread and lard.
Those were your happy times; unless when foray
Stirr'd ye to wrath, and beeves and swine and trulls
(Tempting ye from propriety) heapt up
A mount of sins to strive against; abduction
Of linen-chests, and those who wove the linen;   130
And shocking oaths obscene, and well-nigh acts;
Fracture of cellar-doors, and spinning-wheels;
And (who can answer for you) worse, worse, worse!
   Klapwrath.   'Sblood!   Frate!   runs no vine-juice in our
      arteries?
Psein's forehead starts wry veins upon each side;
His nostrils blow so hot they'll crack my boots.
   Zinga.   Must we move hence?
   Fra Rupert.   To die like sheep? like conies?
Ye shall not die alone; I will die with you.
There have been kings who sacrificed their sons.   140
Abraham would have done it; Pagans have;

But guardians such as I am! . .
   Klapwrath.   Frate! Frate!
Don't tear those tindery rags, or they will quit thee
With only horse-hair under, and some stiffer.
   Fra Rupert.   You conquer me, you conquer me, I yield.
He was not bloody.   Could it end with one!
And we knew which . . or two, or three.
   Zinga.   But us?
   Fra Rupert.   "If once the captains of the companies," 150
Said he . . and then, I own, he said no more:
He saw me shudder, and he sped away.
   Klapwrath.   Are we to hold our throats out to the knife?
   Fra Rupert.   Patience! dear doubtful Klapwrath! mere
     suspicion!
He did not say the knife, or sword, or halter,
He might have meant the scaffold; nothing worse;
Deprive you he might not of all distinction,
Nay, might spare one or other of you yet:
Why then prevent what may need no prevention?
Slyer are few; many more sanguinary: 160
Must we (don't say it) give him up?   I hope
He's mischievous through weakness, not malignity.
   Zinga.   What matters that?   A feather-bed may stifle us
(If we will let it) with a babe to press it.
Is there no other prince in Hungary
Fit to maintain us here?
   Fra Rupert.   The very thought
That came into my head!
   Psein.   But when ours fall,
What matters it who leaps upon his horse   170
To overlook our maintenance?   A fool
I may be; can his wisdom answer that?
   Zinga.   He doubts my courage, bringing thus his own
Against it.   He's a boy: were he a man,
No injury, no insult, no affront . .
Every man is as brave as I . . Stop there!
By all my saints! (*He shows several about him*) by all my
     services!
This hilt shall smash his teeth who dares say, "*braver.*"

Klapwrath.   What I am you know best, at battling it ;
Nothing is easier : but I've swum two nights   180
And days together upon Baian wine,
And so have ye : 'twould swamp that leaky nump-skull.
Behead us ; good ! but underrate us ; never !
  Fra Rupert.   Having thus clear'd our consciences, and
    shown
Our purity in face of day, we swear . .   [*Hesitates.*
  Zinga.   Frate, if *you* don't grudge an oath or two . .
  Fra Rupert.   Death to Andrea ! loyalty to Lewis !
  All.   Hurrah !
  Fra Rupert.   Sweet friends ! profane not thus the cloister !
Leave me to weep for him ! the cruel boy !   190

ACT IV.   SCENE IV.

PALACE OF AVERSA ; SALOON OVERLOOKING THE GARDEN.

SANCIA, FILIPPA, MARIA, FIAMMETTA.

Maria.   Ha ! here they come again.   See ! lady Sancia
Leaning upon Filippa.   They are grown
Wiser, and will not barter songs for griefs.

Boccaccio sings.

A mellow light on Latmos fell :
It came not from the lowly cell,
   It glided from the skies ;
It lighted upon one who slept,
Some voice then askt him why he wept,
   Some soft thing prest his eyes.

Another might have wondered much,
Or peer'd, or started at the touch,
   But he was far too wise ;
He knew the light was from above,
He play'd the shifting game of love,
   And lost at last three sighs.

Fiammetta (*to* FILIPPA).   I wish he would come nearer,
    just to see
How my hair shines, powder'd with dust of gold :

I think he then would call me . .
  Maria.   What?
  Fiammetta.   Fiammetta.
  Filippa.   He hardly . . poet as he seems to be . .
Such as he is . . could feign a better name.   10
He does not seem to be cut out for singing.
  Fiammetta.   I would not have his voice one tittle altered.
The poetry is pretty . . She says nothing.
The poetry is charming . . Now she hears me.
The most delightful poetry! . . O lady
Filippa! not one praise for it! not one!
I never dreamt you were yourself a poet.
  Filippa. These summer apples may be palatable,
But will not last for winter; the austere
And wrinkle-rinded have a better chance.   20
Throw a whole honeycomb into a haystalk,
It may draw flies, but never will feed horses.
From these same cogs (eternally one tune)
The mill has floured us with such dust all over
As we must shake off, or die apoplectic.
Your gentle silken-vested swains may wish
All poetry one sheepfold.
  Maria.   Sheep are well,
Like men and most things, in their proper places,
But when some prancing knight would entertain us,   30
Some gallant, brightening every gem about him,
I would not have upon the palace-steps
A hind cry out, "Make way there for my sheep."
They say (not speaking of this woolsy race)
They say that poets make us live for ever.
  Filippa.   Sometimes the life they lend is worse than none,
Shorn of its glory, shrivel'd up for want
Of the fresh air of virtue.
  Fiammetta.   Yet, to live!
O! and to live by those we love so well!   40
  Filippa.   If such irregularities continue
After to-night, when freedoms are allowed,
We must lock up the gardens, rigorously
Forbidding all the inmates of the palace

To use the keys they have.
   Fiammetta.   The good king Robert
Sooner had driven out the nightingales
Than the poor timid poets.
   Filippa.   Timid poets!
What breed are they of?   50
   Fiammetta.   Such as sing of love.
   Filippa.   The very worst of all; the boldest men!
   Maria.   Nay; not the boldest; very quarrelsome,
Tragic and comic, hot and cold, are so;
And so are nightingales; the gardener
Has told me; and the poets do no worse
Than they do.   Here and there they pluck a feather
From one another, here and there a crumb;
But, for hard fighting, fair straightforward fighting,
With this one nosegay I could beat them all.   60
In good king Robert's day were lute and lyre;
Nor hardly dare we hang them on the nail,
But run away and throw them down before
The boisterous drum and trumpet hoarse with rage.
Let poetry and music, dear Filippa,
Gush forth unfrozen and uncheckt!
   Filippa.   Ah child!
Thy fancy to some poet hath inflamed:
Believe me they are dangerous men.
   Maria.   No men   70
Are dangerous.
   Filippa.   O my child!
   Maria.   The very creatures
Whom God has given us for our protection.
   Filippa.   But against whom?
   Maria.   I never thought of that.
   Fiammetta.   Somebody told me once that good king Robert
Gave keys to three or four, who neither were
Nor would be constant inmates of the court.
   Maria.   Who might and would not!   This is an
      enigma.   80
They must have felt then very low indeed.
Among our glass-house jewels newly set,

I have seen vile ones, and have laught to think
How nicely would my slipper pat their faces ;
They never felt thus low.
   Sancia.   We feel it for them.
Prescriptively, we leave to our assayers
To stamp the currency of gold and brass.
   Fiammetta (to Filippa).   Have you not prais'd the king
     your very self
For saying to Petrarca, as he did,   90
" Letters are dearer to me than my crown,
And, were I forced to throw up one or other,
Away should go the diadem, by Jove ! "
   Sancia.   Thou art thy very father.   Kiss me, child !
His father said it, and thy father would.
When shall such kings adorn the throne again !
   Fiammetta.   When the same love of what Heaven made
     most lovely
Enters their hearts ; when genius shines above them,
And not beneath their feet.   [*Goes up to* Giovanni.
   Sancia (to Filippa).   Rapturous girl !   100
Warmth ripens years and wisdom.   She discourses
Idly as other girls on other things.
   Filippa.   That ripening warmth fear I.
   Sancia.   Portending what ?
   Filippa.   Ah, gracious lady ! sweetest fruits fall soonest . .
   Sancia.   (Who sweeter ?)
   Filippa.   And are bruised the most by falling.
   Maria (joining them).   Sicily and myself are disagreed.
Surely the man who sang must have thick fingers.
He play'd so badly : but his voice is sweet,   110
For all its trembling.
   Fiammetta.   Now I think the trembling
Makes it no worse.   I wish he would go on.
   Maria.   Evidently the song should finish there.
   Fiammetta.   Evidently it should go on . . (*aside*) for
     ever.
   Maria.   Ho ! ho ! you are not cruel to the knight ?
   Fiammetta.   It is no knight at all.
   Sancia.   How know you that ?

Maria.   You would be frightened . .
Fiammetta.   He could never frighten.   120
Maria.   If tilting. .
Fiammetta.   Nobody would hurt Giovanni.

ACT IV.   SCENE V.

ANDREA, MARIA, *and* FIAMMETTA.

Andrea.   So ! you too have been listening, every soul,
I warrant ye.
   Maria.   And have you too, Andrea ?
   Andrea.   From that snug little watch-tower : 'twas too
      high ;
I only lookt upon the tops of trees.
See ! him there ! maskt ! under the mulberry !
   Fiammetta.   I do not see him . . Look for him elsewhere :
That is a shadow.
   Andrea.   Think you so ?   It may be.
And the guitar ?   10 ·
   Fiammetta.   What ! that great yellow toad-stool ?
   Andrea.   How like is everything we see by starlight !
   Fiammetta (aside).   If there were not a star in all the sky,
Every one upon earth would know Giovanni !
   Andrea.   I wish the mulberries were not past, that dozens
Might drop upon him, and might speckle over
His doublet : we should see it like a trout
To-morrow, white and crimson, and discover
The singer of this nonsense about light.
   Fiammetta.   If you don't like it, pray don't listen to it.   20
   Maria (maliciously).   Then let us come away.
   Fiammetta. Pray do.
   Maria (taking her arm).   Come.
   Fiammetta (peevishly).   No.
   Maria.   Listen ! another song !
   Fiammetta.   Hush ! for Heaven's sake !
O ! will you never listen ?   All this noise !
   Maria.   Laughter might make some ; smiles are much too
      silent.

Fiammetta.   Well; you have stopt him; are you now
    content?
Maria.   Quite, quite; if you are.   30
    Fiammetta.   He begins again!
Hush! for the hope of Paradise!   O hush!

Boccaccio sings.
List! list ye to another tale!

Fiammetta.
No; he who dares tell one
To other ears than one's shall fail.

Boccaccio.
I sing for her alone.

Andrea.   I have a mind to be . .
Maria.   What? prince!
Andrea.   What? angry.
Maria.   Not you.
Andrea.   Not I?   Why, who should hinder me?
Maria (coaxing).   No, no; you won't be angry, prince!
Andrea.   I said
Half-angry, and resolve to keep my word.   40
    Maria.   Anger is better, as pomegranates are,
Split into halves, and losing no small part.
    Andrea.   I never heard such truth about pomegranates!
What was the other thing we reason'd on?
Ho! now I recollect, as you shall see.

[Goes : all follow.

ACT IV.   SCENE VI.

GARDEN.

Andrea, Maria, Fiammetta, *and* Boccaccio.

Andrea.   Keep back: where thieves may be, leave men
    alone.
Now for drawn swords!   Where are they; slipt behind
The mulberry: wisely schemed! 'twon't do! come forth!

Yield ! tremble like a poplar-leaf !   Who art thou ?
                                   [*Seizing* Boccaccio.

   Boccaccio.   King Robert, sir, respected me.
   Andrea.   Did *he ?*
Did *he ?*   Then far more highly should Andrea.
Sicily ! treat him kindly.   We may all,
Even you and I, commit an indiscretion.
How the stars twinkle ! how the light leaves titter !   10
And there are secret quiverings in the herbs,
As if they all knew something of the matter,
And wisht it undisturb'd.   To-night no harm
Shall happen to the worst man in Aversa.

ACT V.   SCENE I.

PALACE OF AVERSA.

ANDREA *and* GIOVANNA.

   Giovanna.   How gracefully thou sattest on thy horse,
Andrea !
   Andrea.   Did I ?
   Giovanna.   He curveted so,
Sidled and pranced and croucht and plunged again,
I almost was afraid, but dared not say it.
   Andrea.   Castagno is a sad curvetting rogue.
   Giovanna.   'Twas not Castagno ; 'twas Polluce.
   Andrea.   Was it ?
How canst thou tell, Giovanna ?   10
   Giovanna.   I can tell.
   Andrea.   All at hap-hazard : I am very sure
'Twas not the horse you lookt at ; nor did I
Think about riding, or about the palfrey,
Crimson and gold, half palfrey and half ostrich.
But thou too ridest like a queen, my dove !
     Giovanna.   So very like one ? Would you make me
     proud ?
   Andrea.   God forbid that !   I love thee more for beauty.

Ne'er put on pride, my heart! thou dost not want it;
Many there are who do; cast it to them   20
Who can not do without it, empty souls!
Ha! how you look! is it surprise or pleasure?
  Giovanna.   Pleasure, my love! I will obey with pleasure
This your first order. But indeed, my husband,
You must not look so fondly when the masks come,
For you and I, you know, shall not be masked.
  Andrea.   A pretty reason for not looking fond!
Must people then wear masks for that?
  Giovanna.   Most do.
I never saw such fondness as some masks   30
Presented.
  Andrea.   Thou hast never seen half mine;
Thou shalt; and then shalt thou sit judge between us.
We have not spoken more to-day, my chuck,
Than many other days, yet thou appearest
Wiser than ever. I have gain'd from thee
More than I gave.
  Giovanna.   And, without flattery,
I am more pleas'd with your discourse than ever.
  Andrea (*fondly*). No, not than ever. In this very room 40
Didst thou not give to me this very hand
Because I talked so well?
  Giovanna.   We foolish girls
Are always caught so.
  Andrea.   Always kept so, too?
Well, we must see about it then, in earnest.
  Giovanna.   Andrea! one thing see to: pray inquire
If, in the crowd that rushed so thro' the gates,
No accident has happen'd. Some cried out,
Some quarrell'd; many horses started off,   50
And bore amid them.
  Andrea.   Never fear.
  Giovanna.   But ask.   [*He goes.*

ACT V.   SCENE II.

Fiammetta, Maria, Filippa, *and* Sancia, *enter.*

Maria.   The bridegroom is among the other grooms,
Asking odd questions: what man's horse broke loose,
Who was knockt down, what fruit-stall overturn'd,
Who quarrell'd, who cried out, struck, ran away.
   Giovanna.   Maria! this is pleasantry.
   Andrea (returning hastily).   They say,
Caraffa and Caraccioli are dead.
   Giovanna.   It can not be: they were both well this
     morning.
   Filippa.   The west-wind blew this morning . . no air now.
   Giovanna.   O but, Filippa! they both came together.   10
Did not queen Sancia tell you?
   Filippa.   I have seen
Two barks together enter the port yonder,
And part together.
   Giovanna.   But to die at once!
   Filippa.   Happy the friends whom that one fate befalls!
   Giovanna.   So soon!
   Filippa.   Perhaps so soon.
   Giovanna.   It may be happy.
It must be strange; awfully strange indeed!   20
                     [Fiammetta *goes out.*
   Andrea.   My darling! how you pity those two youths!
I like you for it.
   Giovanna.   Both have fathers living:
What must they suffer! Each . . I never heard,
But may well fancy . . loved some girl who loves him.
I could shed tears for her.
   Maria.   My dear Giovanna!
Do queens shed tears? and on the wedding-day?
   Sancia.   I see no reason why they should not.
   Filippa (aside).   I,   30
Alas! see far too many why they should.
   Andrea.   What did Filippa say? that brides should cry?

Filippa (*to* GIOVANNA *and* MARIA).   Not idly has the genial
     breath of song
Turn'd into pearls the tears that women shed ;
They are what they are call'd : some may be brighter
Among your gems, none purer, none become
The youthful and the beautiful so well.
     Andrea (*as* FIAMMETTA *enters*).   Here enters one you never
          will teach that,
She is too light for grief, too gay for love,
And neither salt nor mistleto can catch her,   40
Nor springe nor net : she laughs at all of them
Like any woodpecker, and wings away.
I know you women ; I'm a married man :
     Fiammetta.   They will not give the story up : they draw
All different ways, but death they all will have.
     Andrea.   Ay, and one only will not satisfy them.
               [*An Officer enters, and confers apart with him.*
Certain ?
     Giovanna. Some other accident less heavy,
Heaven ! let us hope !
     Andrea.   Strangled ! O what a death !   50
One of them . . one (no matter now which of them)
Disliked me, shunn'd me ; if we met, lookt at me
Straighter and taller and athwart the shoulder,
And dug his knuckles deep into his thigh.
I gave him no offence . . yet, he is gone . .
Without a word of hearing, he is gone !
To think of this ! to think how he has fallen
Amid his pranks and joyances, amid
His wild heath myrtle-blossoms, one might say,
It quite unmans me.   60
     Sancia.   Speak not so, my son !
Let others, when their nature has been changed
To such unwonted state, when they are call'd
To do what angels do and brutes do not,
Sob at their shame, and say they are unmann'd :
Unmann'd they can not be ; they are not men.
At glorious deeds, at sufferings well endured,
Yea, at life's thread snapt with its gloss upon it,
Be it man's pride and privilege to weep.

ACT V.   SCENE III.

GRAND SALOON.

Masks passing.

ANDREA, GIOVANNA, MARIA, FIAMMETTA, FILIPPA.

Filippa.   It may be right, my lady, that you know
What masks are here.
  Giovanna.   I have found out already
A few of them.   Several waived ceremony
(Desirably at masks) and past unnoticed. .
The room fills rapidly.
  Filippa.   Not to detain
My queen (for hundreds anxiously approach),
Pardon! I recognised the Prince Luigi.
  Giovanna.   Taranto?   Tell our cousin to keep on   10
His mask all evening.   Hither! uninvited!
  Maria (out of breath).   Think you the dais will keep the
    masks from hearing?
  Giovanna.   Why should it?
  Maria.   Oh! why should it?   He is here.
Even Filippa could distinguish him.
Every one upon earth must know Taranto.
  Giovanna.   Descend we then : beside the statue there
We may converse some moments privately.
  Maria.   Radiant I saw him as the sun . . a name
We always gave him . . rapid as his beams.   20
I should have known him by his neck alone
Among ten thousand.   While I gazed upon it,
He gazed at three mysterious masks : then rose
That graceful column, ampler, and more wreathed
With its marmoreal thews and dimmer veins.
The three masks hurried thro' the hall ; Taranto
After them (fierce disdain upon his brow)
Darted as Mercury at Jove's command.
No doubt, three traitors who dared never face him
In his own country, are courageous here.   30

Giovanna.   Taranto then, Taranto was unmaskt
Against my orders!
Maria.   Rather say, *before.*
Luigi never disobeyed Giovanna.
Giovanna.   Filippa carried them.
Maria.   I know his answer.
Giovanna.   Repeat it then, for she may not to-night.
Maria.   " Tell her I come the cousin, not the prince,
Nor with pretension, nor design, nor hope ;
I come the loyal, not the fond, Taranto."   40
Why look you round ?
Giovanna.   The voice is surely his.
Maria.   The thoughts are . .
Giovanna (*pressing her hand*).   May, O Heaven! the
      speaker be !   [*Both walk away.*
Fra Rupert (*masked and disguised, to one next*).   I heard
      our gracious queen, espoused to-day,
Give orders that Taranto keep well maskt.
Next Mask (*to another*).   Ho then ! Taranto here !
Second Mask.   What treachery !
Fra Rupert (*masked*).   He could not keep away.   Tem-
      pestuous love
Has tost him hither.   Let him but abstain   50
From violence, nor play the jealous husband,
As some men do when husbands cross their road.
Second Mask.   Taranto is a swordsman to the proof.
First Mask.   Where is he ?
Fra Rupert.   He stood yonder, in sky-blue,
With pearls about the sleeves.
Second Mask.   Well call him Phœbus !
I would give something for a glimpse at what
That mask conceals.
Fra Rupert.   Oh ! could we catch a glimpse   60
Of what all masks conceal, 'twould break our hearts.
Far better hidden from us !   Woman ! woman !   [*Goes off.*
First Mask (*to second*).   A friar Rupert ! only that his
      voice
Breathes flute-like whisperings, rather than reproofs.
Second Mask.   Beside, he stands three inches higher ; his
      girth

Slenderer by much.
    First Mask.   Who thought 'twas really he?
I only meant he talkt as morally.
    Third Mask (coming up to Fourth).   I am quite certain
      there is Frate Rupert.
    Fourth Mask.   Where is he not?   The Devil's ubiquity!
But, like the Devil, not well known when met.   [70
How found you him so readily?   What mark?
    Third Mask.   Stout is he, nor ill-built, tho' the left
      shoulder
Is half a finger's breadth above the right.
    Fourth Mask.   But that man's . . let me look . . That
      man's right shoulder
Stands two good inches highest.
    Third Mask.   Doubt is past . .
We catch him! over-sedulous disguise!

ACT V.   SCENE IV.

    Andrea.   We have a cousin in the house, my queen!
What dost thou blush at? why art troubled? sure
We are quite grand enough for him : our supper
(I trust) will answer all his expectations.
    Maria.   So you have lookt then at the supper-table?
    Andrea.   'Twould mortify me if Giovanna's guests
Were disappointed.
    Giovanna.   Mine! and not yours too?
    Andrea.   Ah sly one! you have sent then for Taranto
And would not tell me!   Cousin to us both,   10
To both he should be welcome as to one.
Another little blush!   Why, thou art mine,
And never shalt, if love's worth love, repent it.
    Giovanna.   Never, my own Andrea! for such trust
Is far more precious than the wealthiest realms,
Or all that ever did adorn or win them.
    Andrea.   I must not wait to hear its value told,
We shall have time to count it out together.
I now must go to greet our cousin yonder,

He waits me in the balcony ; the guards   20
Have sent away the loiterers that stood round,
And only two or three of his own friends
Remain with him.   To tarry were uncourteous.
    Maria (earnestly).   I do believe Luigi is below.
    Andrea.   Do not detain me : we have never met
Since your proud sister spoke unkindly to him,
And, vaulting on his horse, he hurried home.   [*Goes.*
    Maria.   The soldiers there do well to guard the balcony,
And close the folding-doors against intrusion.   [*Cry is heard.*
    Fiammetta.   Ha! some inquisitive young chamber-lady, 30
Who watcht Luigi enter, pays for it.
Those frolicsome young princes are demanding
A fine for trespass.
    Giovanna.   Nay, they are too rude,
Permitting any rudeness.   Struggles ! sobs !
Andrea never caused them.
    Maria.   Shame, Taranto !
    Giovanna.   Stifling of screams !   Those nearer are alarmed ;
Those farther off are running for the staircase ;
And many come this way !   What can they mean ?   40
See, they look angry as they run, and dash
Their hands against their foreheads !   [*Very alarmed.*
Where's a page ?
                [*A page stands masked in the doorway ; crowds
                        of unmasked behind him.*
    Maria.   A page ! a page !
    Page (to himself).   I am one ; and discovered !   [*Advances.*
    Giovanna.   Run ; see what those young courtiers round
        the princes
Are doing in the balcony.   Below ;
Not there.
    Page.   I might mistake the Prince Andrea,
Not having ever seen him.   50
    Maria.   Who then are you ?
    Page.   The Prince Luigi's page, whom I awaited,
To say his groom and horse are near at hand.
    Maria.   He goes then ?
    Page.   Ere it dawn.

Giovanna.   O ! hasten ! hasten
Below, and instantly run back again,
Reporting me what you can discover there.
　Page (*returns*).   Lady ! the lamps about the balcony
Are all extinguisht.   60
　Giovanna.   Is the wind so high ?
What didst thou hear, what didst thou note, beside ?
　Page (*hesitating*).   Against the gentlest, the most virtuous
　　queen,
Opprobrious speech, threats, imprecations . .
　Giovanna.   Pass it.
　Page.   Upon the stairs; none from the gardens.
　Giovanna.   There
What sawest thou ?
　Page.   Over the balcony
Downward some burden swang.   70
　Giovanna.   Some festive wreath
Perhaps.
　Page.   Too heavy ; almost motionless.
　Maria.   Several damask draperies thrown across.
　Page.   May-be. The wind just stirr'd the bottom of them :
I had no time to look : I saw my prince
Fighting.
　Maria.   O heaven ! was ever night like this . .
　Page.   For gallant sword ! it left two proofs behind :
The third man, seeing me (poor help for arm   80
So valiant !) fled.
　Maria.   O ! we are safe then, all.   [*Very joyous.*
　Page.   No cap lost they, nor did the one who fled :
Whose in the world of Naples, can be this ?

> [*He takes from under his richly embroidered
> cloak the cap of* Andrea. Giovanna
> clasps it to her face, and falls with a
> stifled scream.*
> [*Another Page brings in* Andrea's *ermine
> cloak.*

This cloak fell near me from the balusters.
　Maria.   His own ! Ha ! this dark speck is not the ermine's.
　Filippa.   See ! she revives ! Hide it away !   O guests
Of our unhappy festival, retire.

GIOVANNA OF NAPLES.

CHARACTERS.

Lewis, *King of Hungary.* Luigi, *Prince of Taranto.* Acciajoli, *Seneschal of Naples.* Ugo del Balzo. Spinello, *General of Naples.* Rienzi, *Tribune of Rome.* Fra Rupert. Boccaccio. Petrarca. Psein, *a Hungarian Captain.* Pope's Nuncio. Prior of the Celestines. Wife of Rienzi. Filippa of Catania. Sancia, *her Granddaughter.* Princess Maria. Fiammetta.

ACT I.   SCENE I.

GARDEN OF CAPO-DI-MONTE.

Boccaccio *and* Fiammetta.

Boccaccio.   Adieu the starlit gardens of Aversa,
The groves of Capo-Monte!
　Fiammetta.   Why adieu?
　Boccaccio.   One night will throw its gloom upon them
　　long.
　Fiammetta.   It will indeed, but love can dwell in gloom,
And not repine in it.
　Boccaccio.   The generous man,
Who might have much impeded ours, gave way
To bitter impulses.   My face is flusht
To think of his hard doom, and find myself   10
Happy where he was happy, and so lately!
　Fiammetta.   I too have sighs, nor for thee only, now.
Giovanna, had an angel told it me
The other day, I should have disbelieved.
We all are now alike.   Even queen Sancia,[1]

[1 L. reads
　　　　　　　Even Queen Sancia
　　Sancia so calm in sorrow, said, "Death comes
　　To some with flames across his angry brow,
　　To others holds green palm and aureole crown," &c.]

Whose sadness is scarce sadness, so resign'd
Is she to Heaven, at this balustrade
Lean'd and lookt over, hearing some one sing.
" Impatient is the singer there," said she,
" To run thro' his delight, to fill the conch　　　20
Of song up to the brim, and wise were he
Thought he not, O my child, as think he might,
How every gust of music, every air,
Breathing its freshness over youthful breasts,
Is a faint prelude to the choirs above,
And how Death stands in the dark space between,
To some with invitations free and meek,
To some with flames athwart an angry brow ;
To others holds green palm and aureole crown,
Dreadless as is the shadow of a leaf . ."　　　30
But, while she said it, prest my hand and wept,
Then prayed of Heaven its peace for poor Andrea.
　　Boccaccio.　We may think too as wisely as the queen
When we attain her age ; of other flames
And other palms and other crowns just now.
Like every growth, thoughts also have their seasons ;
We will not pluck unripe ones ; they might hurt us.
That lady then was with you ?
　　Fiammetta.　She herself
Led me up hither by the sleeve.　Giovanna　　　40
Is there below, secure, in Castel-Nuovo.
Look you ! what crowds are gathering round about it.
　　Boccaccio.　I see them, and implore you, my Fiammetta,
To tarry here, protected by queen Sancia.
　　Fiammetta.　And will you tarry near me ?
　　Boccaccio.　While the queen
Your sister is quite safe.
　　Fiammetta.　What ! thinkest thou
She ever can be otherwise than safe ?
I will run down to her.　　　50
　　Boccaccio.　There is no danger
At present ; if there should be, my weak aid
Shall not be wanting.　He whom she laments
I too lament : this bond unites me with her ;

And I will keep her in my sight, and follow
(As lighter birds follow the powerfuller)
Where'er the tempest drives her . . not to save,
But break the fall, or warn her from below.
   Fiammetta.   Generously spoken, my own sweet Giovanni!
Do so, and I can spare you ; but remember   60
Others may want a warning too, may want
Some one to break a fall, some one to save . . .
Giovanni! O Giovanni! to save what?
For what is left but love? . . save that, Giovanni!
   Boccaccio.   Were any infelicity near you,
Crowns and their realms might perish : but your sister
Is part of you : had she but lookt into
Your cradle, and no more ; had one kind word,
And only one, fallen from her upon you ;
My life should be the price for it.   70
   Fiammetta.   Your life!
We have but one, we two.   But until she
Is safe again, and happier, you shall keep it.
Go, go then ; follow her ; but soon return.
While you are absent from me, shapeless fears
Must throng upon and keep awake my sorrow.
   Boccaccio.   To grieve for what is past, is idle grief,
Idler to grieve for what may never be.
Courage ! when both most wish it, we shall meet.

ACT I.   SCENE II.

CASTEL-NUOVO.

Giovanna *and* Del Balzo.

   Giovanna.   Ugo del Balzo ! thou art just and firm.
Seek we the murderers out, and bring them forth
Before their God and fellow-men, if God
Or fellow-men have they.   Spare none who did
This cruel deed.   The partner of my throne,
Companion of my days . . until that day . .
Avenge !   In striking low the guilty head

Show mercy to my people.   Take from me
And execute with promptness this commission.
O what a chasm in life hath one day made,   10
Thus giving way with such astounding crash
Under my feet, when all seem'd equable,
All hopeful, not a form of fear in sight.
    Del Balzo.   Lady ! if all could see the pangs within
Which rend your bosom, every voice would pause
From railing and reproach.
    Giovanna.   Reproach who will,
Rail who delight in railing.   Could my arm
Protect the innocent ?
    Del Balzo.   But strange reports   20
(With this commission in my hand I speak it)
Murmur throughout the city.   Kindred, ay,
Close kindred are accused.
    Giovanna.   Such accusations
Have burst upon my ear : they wrong my cousin.
A man more loyal than the brave Taranto
Nor court nor field e'er saw : but even he
Shall not escape if treachery be found
Within the shadow of that lofty mien.
    Del Balzo.   No, by the sword of the archangel ! no .. 30
Altho' his sister smiles this hour upon
Her first-born of my dear and only brother
The Duke of Andria.   Thou must weep, Francesco !
And she and I ; for such dishonour taints
The whole house through, obscuring past and future.
Was he not in Aversa ?
    Giovanna.   He was there.
    Del Balzo.   And were no orders given that he keep on
His mask all evening ?
    Giovanna.   Yes, I gave those orders.   40
    Del Balzo.   The Queen's commission reaches not the
        Queen.
    Giovanna.   Imperfect then is that commission, Ugo !
    Del Balzo.   Freedom of speech is limited.
    Giovanna.   By what ?
    Del Balzo.   The throne.

Giovanna.   For once then push the throne more back,
And let thy words and actions have their scope.
    Del Balzo.   Why was Aversa chosen for the revels?
                    [*The* QUEEN *hesitates and sighs deeply.*
One answer comes from all.   Because the town
Is Norman, the inhabitants are Norman,   50
Sworn enemies to an Hungarian prince;
The very name sounds hostilely; the walls
Built in aversion to the pride of Capua.
    Giovanna.   I could give other answer, which such hearts
Would little understand.   My happiest days
Were spent there . . O that there my last had closed!
Was it not in Aversa we first met?
There my Andrea, while our friends stood round
At our betrothment, fain would show me first
A horse they led for him from Hungary.   60
The hands we join'd were little hands indeed!
And the two rings we interchanged would ill
Let pass the bossy chain of his light hair
Entwisted with my darker, nor without
His teeth were then drawn through it.   Those were days
When none saw quarrels on his side or mine,
Yet were there worse than there were latterly,
Or than since childhood ever.   We have lived
From those days forth without distrust and strife.
All might have seen but now will not know that.   70
    Del Balzo.   Lady! the court and people do remember
That none more courteous, none more beautiful,
Lives than the Prince Luigi . . they acknowledge
That Prince Andrea's qualities fell short . .
    Giovanna.   Del Balzo! cease! he was your prince but
        now . .
His virtues were domestic . . few saw those.
    Del Balzo.   Few, I confess it; not so few the other's.
His assiduities, his love.
    Giovanna.   Do these
Remember too, whate'er advantages   80
The Prince Luigi of Taranto had,
I gave my hand where they who rear'd me will'd,
    VOL. I.   M

That no contention in our family
Might reach my people ? Ugo ! tell me now
To whom show'd I my love ? To them or him ?
   Del Balzo. Lady ! 'twas nobly done. Yet he was seen
To walk among the maskers on that night,
Was ordered to keep on his mask, was known
To watch Andrea in the balcony,
To rush away, to fight below the place   90
Where the inhuman deed was perpetrated,
And then to fly.
   Giovanna. Oh ! if Taranto could
Be guilty ! . . but impossible ! My sister
Saw him pursue three masks : and his own page
Found him in fight with one, where two were slain.
   Del Balzo. Would any court receive such testimony ?
   Giovanna. Examine then more closely. I am lost,
Not in conjectures, for my mind flies off
From all conjecture, but in vague, in wild   100
Tumultuous thoughts, all broken, crost, and crazed.
Go, lose no moment. There are other things
                                [DEL BALZO *goes.*
I could have said . . what were they ? . . there are things . .
Maria . . why not here ! . . She knows there are . .
O ! were the guilty so perplext as I am,
No guilt were undiscover'd in the world !

ACT I.   SCENE III.

FILIPPA, SANCIA TERLIZZI, DEL BALZO.

   Sancia Terlizzi. Gentle and gracious and compassionate,
Companion and not queen to those about her,
Giovanna delegates her fullest powers
To stern Del Balzo ; and already force
Enters the palace gates.
   Filippa. Let them be closed
Against all force. Send for the seneschal.

Sancio Terlizzi. Acciajoli has departed for Aversa,
There to make inquest.

   Filippa. Who dares strike the door?   10

   Del Balzo (entering). The laws.

   Filippa. Count Ugo! is the queen extinct?

   Del Balzo. The prince is. Therefore lead with due
   respect
These ladies, and the rest, away.   *[To an Officer.*

   Filippa. What means
This violence?

   Del Balzo (to the Officer). Let none, I pray, be used.
                      [To Filippa.
Behold the queen's commission! In that chamber
Where close examinations must ensue,
In clear untroubled order let your words   20
Leave us no future violence to be fear'd.

   Filippa (returning the paper). The queen hath acted as she
   always acts,
Discreetly; bravely; it becomes her race
And station: what becomes a faithful subject
Let us do now.   *[The* Queen *enters.*

   Sancia Terlizzi. Turn: lo, the queen herself!

   Del Balzo. Lady! there is one chamber in the realm,
And only one, and that but for one day,
You may not enter.

   Giovanna. Which is that, Del Balzo?   30

   Del Balzo. Where the judge sits against the criminal.

   Giovanna. Criminal! none are here.

   Del Balzo. If all my wishes
Avail'd me, there were none.

   Giovanna. Sure, sure, the palace
Is sacred.

   Del Balzo. Sacred deeds make every place
Sacred, unholy ones make all unholy.

   Giovanna. But these are our best friends.

   Filippa. My royal mistress!   40
The name of friendship and the name of justice
Should stand apart. Permit me to retire.. *[To* Del Balzo.
Whither, sir, you must dictate.

Del Balzo.   Lead them on.

       [*The* QUEEN *throws her arms round* FILIPPA *who*
         gently removes them and goes.

Lady! would you protect the culpable?

   Giovanna.   Ugo del Balzo! would you wrong the queen?

   Del Balzo.   I recognise the lofty race of Robert,

And my arm strengthens and my heart dilates.

   Giovanna.   Perform your duty, sir, and all your duty;

Win praise, win glory . . mine can be but tears.   50

                                 [*Goes.*

ACT I.   SCENE IV.

FRA RUPERT, DEL BALZO.

Fra Rupert.   Confessionals are close; and closer still

The heart that holds one treasure.

   Del Balzo.   Father Rupert!

What brought thee hither at this busy hour?

   Fra Rupert.   My duty: I must not delay my duty.

   Del Balzo.   What is it?

   Fra Rupert.   I would fain absolve from sin

(Far as the Church allows) the worst of sinners.

   Del Balzo.   In few plain words, who sent for thee?

   Fra Rupert.   In fewer,   10

I scorn thy question.

   Del Balzo.   Father! thou must wait.

The prince's death involves some powerful ones,

Whose guilt or innocence shall presently

Be ascertained.

   Fra Rupert.   What! and shall man hear first

The guilty soul confess its secret sin?

Shall not the angels carry up the tale

Before the people catch it?

   Del Balzo.   They, no doubt,   20

Already have done this.

   Fra Rupert.   Not half, not half.

   Del Balzo.   Father! it seems thou knowest more about it

Than I or any else.   Why reddenest thou?

Fra Rupert.   Dost think, Del Balzo, any word escapes
The sanctuary of consciences ? the throne
Of grace and mercy on our earth below ?
The purifier, the confessional ?
So then ! some powerful ones are apprehended
For what they did ! O merciful Del Balzo !   30
Be sparing of a woman's blood, Del Balzo !
And age hath claims upon our pity too ;
And so hath youth, alas ! and early ties
Suddenly broken shock far round about.
Beside ; who knows . . thou canst not certainly . .
If any can . . they may be innocent,
Each of the three, one more, one less, perhaps :
Innocent should be all whose guilt lacks proof.
O my poor child Andrea, pardon me !
Thou wouldst not have sought blood for blood, Andrea !   40
Thou didst love all these women ! most of all
Her . . but there's justice, even on earth, Andrea !   [*Goes.*
   Del Balzo.   'Tis so ! that stern proud bosom bursts with
      grief.

ACT I.   SCENE V.

Maria.   Ah, why, Del Balzo, have you let come in
The filthy monk, Fra Rupert ?   He has frightened
Sancia Terlizzi almost into fainting.
And tell me by what right hath he or any
Ordered her up into her room, and taken
Her mother down below, into those chambers
Which we have always been forbid to enter !
   Del Balzo.   Perhaps to ask some questions ; for the queen
Ought to be satisfied.
   Maria.   Then let me go   10
And ask her : she would tell me in a moment
What they will never get from her.
   Del Balzo.   Perhaps,
O princess ! you may have mistaken.
   Maria.   No :

I never was mistaken in Filippa.
Rudeness can neither move nor discompose her:
A word, a look, of kindness, instantly
Opens her heart and brings her cheek upon you.
   Del Balzo.   The countess has more glorious qualities   20
Than noble birth has given any else.
Whether her heart has all that tenderness . .
   Maria.   Is my heart tender.
   Del Balzo.   Be it not too tender,
Or it may suffer much, and speedily,
And undeservedly.   The queen your sister,
Gentle as you, hath fortitude.
   Maria.   Giovanna
Is tenderer than I am ; she sheds tears
Oftener than I do, though she hides them better.   30
   Del Balzo.   I saw their traces : but more royally
Never shone courage upon grief opprest.
   Maria.   The lovely platane in the garden-walk
Catches the sun upon her buds half-open,
And looks the brightest where unbarkt and unscathed.
O find them out who have afflicted her
With that most cruel blow.
   Del Balzo.   'Tis what she bade me,
And what I now am hastening to perform.   [*Goes.*

GIOVANNA enters.

   Maria.   Courage, Giovanna ! courage, my sweet sister ! 40
Del Balzo will find out those wicked men.
O ! I forgot to tell him what assistance
Fra Rupert might afford him.   Every crime
Is known to him.   But certainly Fra Rupert,
Who loved Andrea so, will never cease
Until he find the slayer of his friend.
Ah my poor sister ! if you had but heard
The praises of Del Balzo, you would soon
Resume your courage and subdue your tears.
   Giovanna.   Before Del Balzo, sister, I disdain   50
To show them or to speak of them.   Be mine
Hid from all eyes !   God only knows their source,

Their truth or falsehood.   In the light of day
Some lose their bitterness, run smoothly on,
And catch compassion, leisurely, serenely:
Never will mine run thus: my sorrows lie
In my own breast; my fame rests upon others,
Who throw it from them now the blast has nipt it.
'Tis ever so.   Applauses win applauses,
Crowds gather about crowds, the solitary   60
Are shunned as lepers, and in haste past by.
  Maria.   But we will not be solitary; we
Are not so easy to pass by in haste;
We are not very leper-looking.
  Giovanna.   Cease,
Maria! nothing on this earth so wounds
The stricken bosom as such sportiveness,
Or weighs worn spirits down like levity.
Give me your hand . . Reproof is not reproach.
I might have done the same . . how recently!   70
  Maria.   Hark! what is all that outcry?
  Giovanna.   'Tis for him
Whom we have lost.
  Maria.   But angry voices mixt
With sorrowful?
  Giovanna.   To him both due alike.

Spinello *enters.*

  Spinello.   Hungarian troops throng every street and lane,
Driving before them the infirm, the aged,
The children, of both sexes.
  Giovanna.   Shelter them.   80
  Spinello.   Such is the hope of those base enemies,
That, unprovided for defence, the castle
May fall into their hands: and very quickly
(Unless we drive them back) our scanty stores
Leave us exhausted.
  Giovanna.   Dost thou fear, Spinello?
  Spinello.   I do: but if my sovran bids me bare
This breast of armour and assail her foes,
Soon shall she see what fears there lie within.

Giovanna.   Let me too have my fears, nor worse than thine,
Loyal and brave Spinello!   Dare I ask   [90
Of God my daily bread nor give it those
Whose daily prayers have earned it for us all ?
I dare not.   Throw wide open every gate
And stand between the last of my poor people
And those who drive them in.
    Spinello.   We then are lost.
    Giovanna.   Not from God's sight, nor theirs who look to
        God.
    Maria.   O sister ! may that smile of yours be parent
Of many.   It sinks back, and dies upon   100
The lovely couch it rose from.   [DEL BALZO *enters.*]   I
        will go ;
Del Balzo looks, I think, more stern than ever.
    Giovanna.   Del Balzo, I perceive thou knowest all,
And pitiest my condition.   [DEL BALZO *amazed.*
    Spinello.   Standest thou,
Lookest thou, thus, before thy sovran, sir ?
    Giovanna.   Be friends, be friends, and spare me one
        affront.
Wiser it were, and worthier, to devise
How tumults may be quell'd than how increast.
On your discretion lies your country's weal.   [*Goes.*   110
    Spinello.   Ugo del Balzo ! thou art strong in war,
Strong in alliances, in virtue strong,
But darest thou, before the queen, before
The lowest of the loyal, thus impute
With brow of scorn and figure fixt aslant,
Atrocious crimes to purity angelic ?
    Del Balzo.   Heard'st thou her words and askest thou this
        question ?
Spinello ! nor in virtue nor in courage
(Our best alliances) have I pretence
To stand before thee.   Chancellor thou art,   120
And, by the nature of thy office, shouldst
Have undertaken my most awful duty :
Why didst thou not?
    Spinello.   Because the queen herself

Will'd otherwise ; because her chancellor,
She thought, might vindicate some near unduly.
   Del Balzo.   She thought so ? what ! of thee ?
   Spinello.   Thus it appears.
But on this subject never word escaped
Her lips to me : her own pure spirit frankly   130
Suggested it : her delicacy shunn'd
All explanation, lacking no excuse.
Thou askest if I heard her at thy entrance :
I heard her, like thyself.   The words before
Thou didst not hear ; I did.   Her last appeal
Was for the wretched driven within the castle,
And doom'd to pine or force us to surrender.
For them she call'd upon thee, never else,
To pity her condition.
   Del Balzo.   Pardon me !   140
I have much wrong'd her.   Yet, among the questioned
Were strange confessions.   One alone spake scornfully
Amid her tortures.
   Spinello.   Is the torture, then,
The tongue of Truth ?
   Del Balzo.   For once, I fear, 'tis not.
   Spinello.   It was Giovanna's resolute design
To issue her first edict through the land
Abolishing this horrid artifice,
Whereby the harden'd only can escape.   150
" The cruel best bear cruelty," said she,
" And those who often have committed it
May once go through it."
   Del Balzo.   And would'st thou, Spinello !
Thus lay aside the just restraints of law,
Abolishing what wise and holy men
Raised for the safeguard of society ?
   Spinello.   The holy and the wise have done such things
As the unwise and the unholy shrink at.   [160
   Del Balzo.   It might be thought a hardship in a country
Where laws want ingenuity ; where scales,
Bandage, and sword, alone betoken Justice.
Ill-furbisht ineffective armoury,

With nothing but cross-shooting shafts of words!
   Spinello.   Since every deed like torture must afflict
A youthful breast, so mild, so sensitive,
Trust it to me, and we will then devise
How the event may best be laid before her.
   Del Balzo.   A clue was given by unwilling hands,
Wherewith we entered the dark narrow chambers   170
Of this strange mystery.   Filippa first,
Interrogated if she knew the murderer,
Denied it : then, if she suspected any ;
" I do," was her reply.   Whom ?   She was silent.
Where should suspicion now (tell me, Spinello !)
Wander or fix ?   I askt her if the Queen
Was privy to the deed.   Then swell'd her scorn.
Again I askt her, and show'd the rack.
" Throw me upon it ; I will answer thence,"
Said with calm voice Filippa.   She was rackt.   180
Screams from all round fill'd the whole vault.   " See,
     children !
How those who fear their God and love their Prince
Can bear this childish cruelty," said she.
Although no other voice escaped, the men
Trembled, the women wail'd aloud.   " To-morrow,"
Said I, " Filippa ! thou must answer Justice.
Release her."   Still the smile was on her face :
She was releast : Death had come down and saved her.
   Spinello.   Faithfullest friend of the unhappy ! plead
For us whose duty was to plead for thee !   190
Thou art among the Blessed ! On, Del Balzo !
   Del Balzo.   Sancia, her daughter's child . .
   Spinello.   The playful Sancia ?
Whose fifteenth birthday we both kept together . .
Was it the sixth or seventh of last March ? . .
Terlizzi's bride two months ago ?
   Del Balzo.   The same.
   Spinello.   And the same fate ?
   Del Balzo.   She never had seen Death :
She thought her cries could drive him off again,   200
Thought her soft lips might have relaxt the rigid,

And her warm tears . .
   Spinello.   Del Balzo ! wert thou there ?
Or tearest thou such dreamery from some book,
If any book contain such ?
   Del Balzo.   I was there ;
And what I saw I ordered to be done.
Justice would have it ; Justice smote my heart,
Justice sustained it too.
   Spinello.   Her husband would   210
Rather have died than hear one shriek from Sancia.
   Del Balzo.   So all men would : for never form so lovely
Lighted the air around it.
   Spinello.   Let us go
And bear her home.
   Del Balzo.   To me the way lies open ;
But much I fear, Spinello, the Hungarians
Possess all avenue to thy escape.
   Spinello.   Escape is not the word for me, my friend.
I had forgotten the Hungarians   220
(It seems) the Queen, myself, captivity . .
I may not hence : relate then if more horrors
Succeeded.
   Del Balzo.   When Terlizzi saw Filippa
Lie stiff before him, and that gentle bride
Chafing her limbs, and shrinking with loud yells
Whenever her soft hand felt some swol'n sinew,
In hopes to finish here and save all else,
He cried aloud, " Filippa was the murderess."
At this she darted at him such a glance   230
As the mad only dart, and fell down dead.
" 'Tis false ! 'tis false ! " cried he.   " Speak, Sancia, speak !
Or hear me say 'tis false."   They dragg'd away
The wavering youth, and fixt him.   There he lies,
With what result of such inconstancy
I know not, but am going to inquire . .
If we detect the murderers, all these pains
Are well inflicted.
   Spinello.   But if not ?
   Del Balzo.   The Laws   240

Have done their duty and struck fear through all.
   Spinello.   Alas! that duty seems their only one.
   Del Balzo.   Among the first 'tis surely.   I must go
And gather up fresh evidence.   Farewell,
Spinello.
   Spinello.   May good angels guide your steps!
Farewell!   That Heaven should give the merciless
So much of power, the merciful so little!

ACT II.   SCENE I.

CASTEL-NUOVO.

GIOVANNA *and* MARIA.

   Maria.   I do not like these windows.   Who can see
What passes under?   Never were contrived
Cleverer ones for looking at the sky,
Or hearing our Hungarians to advantage.
I can not think their songs are pastorals;
They may be; if they are, they are ill-set.
Will nothing do, Giovanna?   Raise your eyes;
Embrace your sister.
   Giovanna.   So, you too, Maria!
Have turgid eyes, and feign the face of joy.   10
Never will joy be more with us . . with you
It may be . . O God grant it! but me! me,
Whom good men doubt, what pleasure can approach?
   Maria.   If good men all were young men, we might
      shudder
At silly doubts, like other silly things
Not quite so cold to shudder at.
   Giovanna.   Again,
Maria! I am now quite changed; I am
Your sister as I was, but O remember
I am (how lately!) my Andrea's widow.   20
   Maria.   I wish our little Sancia would come hither
With her Terlizzi . . those inseparables!
We scarcely could get twenty words from them

All the day long; we caught them after dinner,
And lost them suddenly as evening closed.
   Giovanna.   Send for her.   But   perhaps   she   is   with
     Filippa. . .
   Maria.   Learning sedateness in the matron life.
   Giovanna.   Or may-be with the queen whose name she bears,
And who divides her love, not equally
With us, but almost equally.   30
   Maria.   If so,
No need to seek her; for the queen went forth
To San Lorenzo at the dawn of day,
And there upon the pavement she implores
Peace for the dead, protection for the living.
   Giovanna.   O may her prayers be heard!
   Maria.   If piety
Avails the living or the dead, they will.
   Giovanna.   How, how much calmer than thy sweetest smile
Has that thought made me!   Evermore speak so,   40
And life will almost be as welcome to me
As death itself.
   Maria.   When sunshine glistens round,
And friends, as young as we are, sit beside us,
We smile at Death . . one rather grim indeed
And whimsical, but not disposed to hurt us . .
And give and take fresh courage.   But, sweet sister!
The days are many when he is unwelcome,
And you will think so too another time.
'Tis chiefly in cold places, with old folks,   50
His features seem prodigiously amiss.
But Life looks always pleasant, sometimes more
And sometimes less so, but looks always pleasant,
And, when we cherish him, repays us well.
Sicily says it is the worst of sin
To cast aside what God hath given us,
And snatch at what he may hereafter give
In its due season . . scourges, and such comfits,
Cupboarded for Old-age.   Youth has her games;
We are invited, and should ill refuse.   60
On all these subjects our sweet Sicily

Discourses with the wisdom of a man.
You are not listening: what avails our wisdom?
    Giovanna.   To keep afloat that buoyant little bark
Which swells endanger.   O may never storm
O'ertake it! never worm unseen eat thro'!
    Maria.   I wish we were away from these thick walls,
And these high windows, and these church-like ceilings,
Without a cherub to look down on us,
Or play a prank up there, with psalter-book,   70
Or bishop's head, or fiddle, or festoon.
    Giovanna.   Be satisfied awhile: the nobler rooms
Are less secure against the violence
Of those Hungarians.
    Maria.   I saw one who bowed
Graceful as an Italian.   "Send away
The men below," said I, "then bow again,
And we will try which bows most gracefully."
    Giovanna.   My giddy, giddy sister!
    Maria.   May my head   80
Be ever so, if crowns must steady it!
    Giovanna.   He might have thought . .
    Maria.   Not he; he never thinks.
He bowed and shook his head.   His name is Psein.
Often hath he been here on guard before:
You must remember him.
    Giovanna.   No, not by name.
    Maria.   Effeminate and vain we fancied him,
Because he always had a flower in hand,
Or with his fingers combed his forehead hair.   90
    Giovanna.   No little merit in that sullen race.
    Maria.   If he has merit I will bring it out.
    Giovanna.   Resign that idle notion.   Power is lost
By showing it too freely.   When I want
His services, I order them.   We part.
Too large a portion of the hour already
Has been among the living.   Now I go
To other duties for the residue
Of this sad day.
    Maria.   Unwelcome is Maria   100

Where sorrow is ?
  Giovanna.   Her sorrow is unwelcome ;
Let me subdue my own ; then come and join me.
Thou knowest where the desolate find one
Who never leaves them desolate.   [*Goes.*
  Maria. 'Tis hard
To linger here alone.
  Officer. The Seneschal
Of Naples. Acciajoli.

ACT II.   SCENE II.

ACCIAJOLI *and* MARIA.

  Acciajoli.   By command
Of our most gracious queen, O royal lady !
I come for yours.
  Maria.   That is, to bear me company.
  Acciajoli.   Such only as the humblest bear the highest.
  Maria.   Seneschal ! you excell the best in phrases.
You might let others be before you there,
Content to shine in policy and war.
  Acciajoli.   I have been placed where others would have
    shone.
  Maria.   Come, do not beat me now in modesty.   10
Had I done anything, I might not boast,
Nor should I think I was improving it
By telling an untruth and looking down.
I do not like our lodgment, nor much wish
To see an arrow quivering in that wainscot :
The floors are well enough ; I would not see them
Paved with smooth pebbles from Hungarian slings.
Can not you send those soldiers to their quarters ?
  Acciajoli.   In vain have I attempted it.
  Maria.   Send Pscin   20
To me.
  Acciajoli.   He, like the rest, is an insurgent.
Civilest of barbarians, yet may Pscin
(With horror I must utter it) refuse.

Maria.   Fear of refusal has lost many a prize.

                      [ACCIAJOLI *goes.*

I hope the Seneschal will go himself,
Not send another.   How I wisht to ask it!
But, at my years, to hint an act of delicacy
Is too indelicate.   He has seen courts,
Turn'd over their loose leaves (each more than half   30
Illumination, dulness the remainder),
And knows them from the cover to the core.

ACT II.   SCENE III.

PSEIN *conducted by* ACCIAJOLI, *who retires.*

The queen commands my presence here.
   Maria.   The queen
Desires your presence; I alone command it.
Eyes have seen *you*, commander Psein!
   Psein.   Impossible!
   Maria.   Yes, eyes have seen you, general Psein! they have,
And seen that they can trust you.
   Psein.   By my troth
To all that's lovely!
   Maria.   Ah, sad man! swear not . .   10
Unless you swear my words.
   Psein.   To hear and swear
And treasure them within this breast, is one.
   Maria (PSEIN *repeating*).   "I swear to love and honour
     and obey" . .
Ha! not the hand . . it comes not quite so soon . .
   Psein.   I have but little practice in the form;
Pardon me, gracious lady!
   Maria.   Earn your pardon
By your obedience.   Now repeat again.
" Whatever perils may obstruct her path,   20
I give safe-conduct to my royal mistress,
Giovanna, queen of Naples."   (*He starts.*)   Have you taken
Me for my sister all this while?   I told you
It was not she commanded you, 'twas I.

Psein.   Oaths are sad things!   I trot to church so seldom
They would not let me out of mine for little
(Not they!) like any good old customer.
    Maria.   And so! you would deceive me, general?
    Psein (aside).   I am appointed! that sounds well: but
        general!
She said the same before: it must be true.   30
    Maria.   Tell me at once, nor hesitate.   Another
May reap the harvest while you whet the sickle.
    Psein.   But I have sworn to let none pass, before
The will of my superiors be announced.
    Maria.   Behold them here! their shadow fills this palace,
And in my voice, sir, is their will announced.
    Psein.   I swore.
    Maria.   I heard you.
    Psein.   But before.
    Maria.   Before   40
Disloyalty, now loyalty.   Are brave
And gallant men to ponder in the choice?
    Psein.   Devoted as I am to you, O lady!
It can not be.
    Maria.   Is that the phrase of Psein?
We love the marvellous; we love the man
Who shows how things which can not be can be.
Give me this glove again upon the water,
And queen Giovanna shall reward you for it.
    Psein.   Upon the water or upon the fire,   50
The whirlpool or volcano . . By bad luck
(What fools men are! they always make their own!)
The troops are in revolt.   Pride brightens zeal
But not invention.   How shall we contrive
To manage them at present?
    Maria.   Tell the troops
We will have no revolts.   Sure, with your powers
Of person and persuasion, not a man
Would hesitate to execute his duty.
    Psein.   We are but three . .   60
    Maria.   We are but two: yet, Psein!
When two are resolute they are enough.

Now I am resolute, and so are you,
And if those soldiers dare to disobey
It is rank mutiny and halbert-matter.
Await the Seneschal: he now returns.   [*Goes.*
  Psein.   She knows the laws of war as well as I,
And looks a young Minerva, tho' of Naples.

ACT II.   SCENE IV.

Acciajoli *and* Psein.

  Acciajoli.   Sorrow and consternation are around.
  Psein.   Men could not have cried louder had they lost
Policinello, who begets them fun,
While princes but beget them blows and taxes.
When will they see things straightly, and give these
Their proper station?
  Acciajoli.   Have you not *your* king?
  Psein.   O! quite another matter!   We have ours,
True; but his taxes are for us; and then
The blows . . we give and take them, as may happen.   10
  Acciajoli.   We too may do the same, another day.
                    [*Psein expresses contempt.*
So! you imagine that your arms suffice
To keep this kingdom down!   War is a game
Not of skill only, not of hazard only,
No, nor of both united.
  Psein.   What the ball
Is stuft with, I know not, nor ever lookt;
I only know it is the very game
I like to play at.
  Acciajoli.   Many are the chances.   20
  Psein.   Without the chances I would throw it up.
Play me at Naples only five to one,
I take the odds.
  Acciajoli.   All are not Neapolitans.
  Psein.   Then strike off three.
  Acciajoli.   Some Normans.

Psein.   Then my sword
Must be well whetted and my horse well fed,
And my poor memory well poked for prayers.
And, hark ye! I should like one combatant   30
As well as twenty, of that ugly breed.
Lord Seneschal, be ready at your post.
  Acciajoli.   I trust I shall be.
  Psein.   At what hour?
  Acciajoli.   Not yet.
  Psein.   Ay, but the queen must fix it.
  Acciajoli.   She inclines
To peace.
  Psein.   I know it; but for flight ere peace.
  Acciajoli.   Flight is not in the movements of our queen.   40
  Psein.   Departure then.
  Acciajoli.   Sir! should she will departure,
Breasts are not wanting to repell the charge
Of traitor or intruder.
  Psein.   Here is one,
Lord Seneschal! as ready to defend her
As any mail'd with iron or claspt with gold.
Doubtest thou? Doubt no longer.   [*Shows the glove.*
  Acciajoli.   Whose is that?
  Psein.   The names we venerate we rarely speak;   50
And love beats veneration out and out.
I will restore it at the vessel's side,
And ask it back again when she is safe
And the less happy lady whom you serve.
It then behoves me to retrace my steps
And rally my few countrymen for safety.

ACT II.   SCENE V.

A HERALD *enters.*   PSEIN *goes.*

  Acciajoli.   Whence come you, sir?
  Herald.   From Gaeta.
  Acciajoli.   What duty?
  Herald.   To see the queen.

Acciajoli.   The queen you can not see:
Her consort died too lately.
    Herald.   Therefore I
Must see the queen.
    Acciajoli.   If you bring aught that throws
Light upon that dark treason, speak at once.   10
    Herald. The light must fall from Rome.   Cola Rienzi,
Tribune of Rome, and arbiter of justice
To Europe, tarrying on the extremest verge
Of our dominions, to inspect the castles,
Heard the report, brought with velocity
Incredible, which man gave man along
The land, and ship gave ship along the coast.
    Acciajoli. Then 'twas prepared: and those who spread the news
Perpetrated the deed.
    Herald. Such promptitude.   20
Could not escape the Tribune.   He demands
The presence of Giovanna queen of Naples,
To plead her cause before him.
    Acciajoli.   Is Rienzi
A king? above a king?
    Herald.   Knowest thou not
Rienzi is the tribune of the people?
    Acciajoli.   Sir! we have yet to learn by what authority
He regulates the destiny of princes.
    Herald.   The wisest men have greatly more to learn   30
Than ever they have learnt: there will be children
Who in their childhood shall know more than we do.
Lord Seneschal! I am but citizen
In my own city, nor among the first,
But I am herald here, and, being herald,
Let no man dare to question me.   The king
Of Hungary is cited to appear,
Since in his name are accusations made
By some at Naples, which your queen must answer.
    Acciajoli.   Her dignity and wisdom will decide,   40
I am well pleas'd that those around the castle
Threw no obstruction in your way.
    Herald.   The soldiers

Resisted my approach ; but instantly
Two holy friars spread out their arms in front,
And they disparted like the Red-sea waves,
And grounded arms before me.
    Acciajoli.   Then no hindrance
To our most gracious queen, should she comply ?
    Herald.   None ; for Rienzi's name is spell against it.   50
    Giovanna (enters).   O ! is there one to hear me patiently ?
Let me fly to him !
    Acciajoli. .Hath our sovran heard
The order of Rienzi ?
    Giovanna.   Call it not
An order, lest my people be incenst.
    Herald.   Lady ! if plainly hath been understood
The subject of my mission, the few words
Containing it may be unread by me.
Therefore I place them duly in the hands   60
Of the Lord Seneschal.   With brief delay
Your presence were desirable.
    Giovanna.   What time
Return you, sir ?
    Herald.   This evening.
    Giovanna.   And by sea ?
    Herald.   In the same bark which brought me.
    Giovanna.   If some ship
More spacious be now lying at the mole,
I will embark in that ; if not, in yours,   70
And we will sail together.   You have power
Which I have not in Naples ; and the troops,
And those who seem to guide them, hear your words.
    Herald.   Lady ! not mine ; but there are some they hear.
    Giovanna.   Entreat them to let pass the wretched ones
Who fancied I could succour them within,
Whom famine must soon seize.   Until they pass
I can not.   Dear is fame to me ; but far
Be Fame that stalks to us o'er hurried graves.
Lord Seneschal ! see Rome's ambassador   80
Be duly honoured : then, whatever else
Is needful for departure, be prepared.

ACT III.   SCENE I.

ROME. CAPITOL.

Rienzi *and the* Pope's Nuncio.

Nuncio.   With infinite affliction, potent Tribune !
The Holiness of our Lord the Sovran Pontiff
Learns that Andrea, prince of Hungary,
Hath, in the palace of Aversa, been
Traitorously slain.   Moreover, potent Tribune !
The Holiness of our Lord the Sovran Pontiff,
Hears sundry accusations : and, until
The guilt or innocence of those accused
Be manifested, in such wise as He,
The Holiness of our Lord, the Sovran Pontiff   10
Shall deem sufficient, he requires that troops
March from his faithful city, and possess
Otranto and Taranto, Brindisi
And Benevento, Capua and Bari,
Most loving cities and most orthodox.
And some few towns and villages beside,
Yearning for peace in his paternal breast,
He would especially protect from tumult.
Laying his blessing on your head thro' me
The humblest of his servitors, thus speaks   20
The Holiness of our Lord the Sovran Pontiff.
    Rienzi (seated). Lord Cardinal ! no truer stay than me
Hath, on Italian or Provenzal ground,
The Holiness of our Lord the Sovran Pontiff.
The cares that I have taken off his hands
The wisdom of his Holiness alone
Can measure and appreciate.   As for troops,
That wisdom, seeing them so far remote,
Perhaps may judge somewhat less accurately.
The service of his Holiness requires   30
All these against his barons.   Now, until
I hear the pleas of Hungary and Naples,

My balance is suspended.   Those few cities,
Those towns and villages, awhile must yearn
For foreign troops among them ; but meantime
Having the blessing of his Holiness,
May wait contentedly for any greater
His Holiness shall opportunely grant.
Kissing the foot of his Beatitude,
Such, my lord Cardinal, is the reply   40
From his most faithful Cola di Rienzi,
Unworthy tribune of his loyal city.
    Nuncio.   We may discuss anew this weighty question
On which his Holiness's heart is moved.
    Rienzi.   If allocution be permitted me
To his most worthy Nuncio, let me say
The generous bosom would enfold about it
The friend, the neighbour, the whole human race,
And scarcely then rest satisfied.   With all
These precious coverings round it, poisonous tongues   50
Can penetrate.   We lowly men alone
Are safe, and hardly we.   Who would believe it ?
People have heretofore been mad enough
To feign ambition (of all deadly sins
Surely the deadliest) in our lord the pope's
Protecting predecessors !   Their paternal
Solicitude these factions thus denounced.
Ineffable the pleasure I foretaste
In swearing to his Holiness what calm
Reluctance you exhibited ; the same   60
His Holiness himself might have exprest,
In bending to the wishes of those cities
So orthodox and loving ; and how fully
You manifested, by your faint appeal,
You sigh as deeply to decline, as they
Sigh in their fears and fondness to attain.
                    [Nuncio *going.*
Help my lord Cardinal.   This weather brings
Stiffness of joints, rheums, shooting pains.   Way there !

ACT III.   SCENE II.

CAPITOL.

Rienzi, Acciajoli, Petrarca, *and* Boccaccio.

Boccaccio.   If there was ever upon throne one mind
More pure than other, one more merciful,
One better stored with wisdom, of its own
And carried from without, 'tis hers, the queen's.
Exert, my dear Francesco, all that eloquence
Which kings and senates often have obeyed
And nations have applauded.
Petrarca.   My Boccaccio!
Thou knowest Rome, thou knowest Avignon:
Altho' so brief a time the slave of power,   10
Rienzi is no longer what he was,
Popes are what they have ever been.   They all
Have families for dukedoms to obey.
Boccaccio.   O! had each holy father twenty wives
And each wife twenty children! then 'twere hard
To cut out dukedoms for so many mouths,
And the well-furred tiara could not hatch
So many golden goose-eggs under it.
Petrarca.   We must unite our efforts.
Boccaccio.   Mine could add   20
Little to yours; I am not eloquent.
Petrarca.   Thou never hast received from any court
Favour or place; I, presents and preferments.
Boccaccio.   I am but little known : for dear to me
As fame is, odious is celebrity.
Petrarca.   I see not why it should be.
Boccaccio.   If no eyes
In the same head are quite alike, ours may
Match pretty well, yet somewhat differ too.
Petrarca.   Should days like yours waste far from men and
    friends?
                                                                    [30
Boccaccio.   Leave me one flame ; then may my breast dilate

To hold, at last, two (or almost two) friends:
One would content me: but we must, forsooth,
Speculate on more riches than we want.
Moreover, O Francesco! I should shrink
From scurril advocate, cross-questioning
Whom knew I in the palace? whence my knowledge?
How long? where first? whence introduced? for what?
Since in all law-courts I have ever entered,
The least effrontery, the least dishonesty,　　40
Has lain among the prosecuted thieves.
　　Petrarca.　We can not now much longer hesitate;
He hath his eye upon us.
　　Boccaccio.　Not on me;
He knows me not.
　　Petrarca.　On me it may be then,
Altho' some years, no few have intervened
Since we last met.
　　Boccaccio.　But frequent correspondence
Retains the features, nay, brings back the voice;　　50
The very shoe creaks when the letter opens.
　　Petrarca.　Rienzi was among those friends who sooner
Forget than are forgotten.
　　Boccaccio.　They who rise
Lose sight of things below, while they who fall
Grasp at and call for anything to help.
　　Petrarca.　I own I cease to place reliance on him.
Virtue and Power take the same road at first,
But they soon separate, and they meet no more.
　　Usher.　The Tribune, ser Francesco! claims your presence.
　　Rienzi.　Petrarca! pride of Italy! most welcome!　　[60
　　Petrarca.　Tribune of Rome! I bend before the fasces.
　　Rienzi.　No graver business in this capitol,
Or in the forum underneath its walls,
Or in the temples that once rose between,
Engaged the thoughts of Rome. No captive queen
Comes hither, none comes tributary, none
Courting dominion or contesting crown.
Thou knowest who submits her cause before
The majesty that reigns within this court.　　70

Petrarca.   Her, and her father, and his father knew I,
Nor three more worthy of my love and honour
(Tho' born to royalty) adorn our earth.
Del Balzo hath supplied the facts : all doubts
On every side of them hath Acciajoli
Clear'd up.
Rienzi.   But some will spring where others fall,
When intellect is strongly exercised.
Petrarca.   The sources of our intellect lie deep
Within the heart ; what rises to the brain   80
Is spray and efflorescence ; they dry up.
Rienzi.   However, we must ponder.   So then truly,
Petrarca ! thou dost think her innocent ?
Petrarca.   Thou knowest she is innocent, Rienzi !
Write then thy knowledge higher than my belief :
The proofs lie there before thee.
Rienzi.   But these papers
Are ranged against them.
Petrarca.   Weigh the characters
Of those who sign them.   90
Rienzi.   Here the names are wanting.
Petrarca.   Remove the balance then, for none is needed.
Against Del Balzo, upright, stern, severe,
What evidence can struggle ?
Rienzi.   From Del Balzo
The Queen herself demands investigation
Into the crime, and bids him spare not one
Partaker.
Petrarca.   Worthy of her race !   Now ask
If I believe her guiltless.   100
Rienzi.   May we prove it !
Acciajoli.   She shall herself, if needful.   Should more
        answers
Be wanted from me, I am here before
That high tribunal where the greatest power
And wisdom are united ; where the judge
Gives judgment in the presence of such men
As Rome hath rarely seen in ancient days,
Never in later.   What they hear, the world

Will hear thro' future ages, and rejoice
That he was born in this to raise an arm   110
Protecting such courageous innocence.
    Rienzi.   Lord Seneschal of Naples, Acciajoli!
We have examined, as thou knowest, all
The documents before us, and regret
That death withholds from like examination
(Whether as witnesses or criminals)
Some inmates of your court, the most familiar
With queen Giovanna.
    Acciajoli.   Did she then desire
Their death? as hidden enemies accuse her   120
Of one more awful.   I presume the names
Of the young Sancia, count Terlizzi's bride,
And hers who educated that pure mind
By pointing out Giovanna, two years older,
Filippa of Catana.
    Rienzi.   They are gone
Beyond our reach.
    Acciajoli.   Sent off, no doubt, by one
Who loved them most, who most loved her! sent off
After their tortures, whether into Scotland   130
Or Norway or Laponia, the same hand
Who wrote those unsign'd papers may set forth.
    Rienzi.   I cannot know their characters.
    Acciajoli.   I know them
Loyal and wise and virtuous.
    Rienzi.   But Filippa
Guided, 'tis said, the counsels of king Robert.
    Acciajoli.   And were those counsels evil? If they were,
How happens it that both in life and death
The good king Robert was his appellation?   140
    Rienzi.   How many kings are thrust among the stars
Who had become the whipping-post much better?
    Acciajoli.   Was Robert one?
    Rienzi.   We must confess that Robert
Struck down men's envy under admiration.
    Acciajoli.   If then Filippa guided him, what harm?
    Rienzi.   She might have fear'd that youth would less obey

Her prudent counsels than experience did.
    Acciajoli.   Well might she : hence for many a year her cares
Have been devoted to our queen's instruction,   150
Together with queen Sancia, not without :
And neither of these ladies (I now speak
As president) have meddled with our councils.
    Rienzi.   When women of low origin are guides
To potentates of either sex, 'tis ill.
    Acciajoli.   I might have thought so ; but Filippa showed
That female wisdom much resembles male ;
Gentler, not weaker ; leading, not controlling.
Again ! O tribune ! touching low estate.
More vigorously than off the downier cradle   160
From humble crib springs up the lofty mind.
    Rienzi.   Strong arguments, and cogent facts, are these !
                                   [*To an Usher.*

Conduct the queen of Naples into court.
    Acciajoli.   That, by your leave, must be my office, sir !

ACT IV.   SCENE III.

Rienzi, Acciajoli, Giovanna, *and* Prior *of the* Celestines.

    Rienzi.   Giovanna, queen of Naples ! we have left you
A pause and space for sorrow to subside ;
Since, innocent or guilty, them who lose
So suddenly the partner of their hours,
Grief seizes on, in that dark interval.
Pause too and space were needful, to explore
On every side such proofs as may acquit
Of all connivance at the dreadful crime
A queen so wise, and held so virtuous,
So just, so merciful. It can not be   10
(We hope) that she who would have swept away
Playthings of royal courts and monkish cells,
The instruments of torture, that a queen
Who in her childhood visited the sick,
Nor made a luxury or pomp of doing it,

Who placed her little hand, as we have heard,
In that where fever burnt, nor feared contagion,
Should slay her husband.
   Acciajoli.   Faintness overpowers her,
Not guilt.   The racks you spoke of, O Rienzi!   20
You have applied, and worse than those you spoke of.
   Rienzi.   Gladly I see true friends about her.
   Acciajoli.   Say
About her not; say in her breast she finds
The only friend she wants . . her innocence.
   Rienzi.   People of Rome! your silence, your attention,
Become you.   With like gravity our fathers
Beheld the mighty and adjudged their due.
Sovran of Naples, Piedmont, and Provence,
Among known Potentates what other holds   30
Such wide dominions as this lady here,
Excepting that strong islander whose sword
Has cut France thro', and lies o'er Normandy,
Anjou, Maine, Poictou, Brittany, Touraine,
And farthest Gascony; whose hilt keeps down
The Grampians, and whose point the Pyrenees?
Listen! she throws aside her veil, that all
May hear her voice, and mark her fearless mien.
   Giovanna.   I say not, O Rienzi! I was born
A queen; nor say I none but God alone   40
Hath right to judge me.   Every man whom God
Endows with judgment arbitrates my cause.
For of that crime am I accused which none
Shall hide from God or man.   All are involved
In guilt who aid, or screen, or spare, the guilty.
Speak, voice of Rome! absolve me or condemn,
As proof, or, proof being absent, probability,
Points on the scroll of this dark tragedy.
Speak, and spare not: fear nought but mighty minds,
Nor those, unless where lies God's shadow, truth.   50
   Rienzi.   Well hast thou done, O queen, and wisely chosen
Judge and defenders.   Thro' these states shall none
Invade thy realm.   I find no crime in thee.
Hasten to Naples! for against its throne

Ring powerful arms and menace thy return.
           [*Acciajoli leads the Queen out.*
    Prior of the Celestines.   Thou findest in that wily queen no
      crime.
So be it ! and 'tis well.   But tribune, know,
Ill chosen are the praises thou bestowest
On her immunity from harm, in touching
The fever'd and infected.   She was led   60
Into such places by unholy hands.
I come not an accuser : I would say
Merely, that Queen Giovanna was anointed
By the most potent sorceress, Filippa
The Catanese.
    Rienzi.   Anointed Queen ?
    Prior.   Her palms
Anointed, so that evil could not touch them.
Filippa, with some blacker spirits, helpt
To cure the sick, or comfort them unduly.   70
    Rienzi.   Among the multitude of sorceresses
I find but very few such sorceries,
And, if the Church permitted, would forgive them.
    Prior.   In mercy we, in mercy, should demur.
    Rienzi.   How weak is human wisdom ! what a stay
Is such stout wicker-work about the fold !
    Prior.   Whether in realms of ignorance, in realms
By our pure light and our sure faith unblest,
Or where the full effulgence bursts from Rome,
No soul, not one upon this varied earth,   80
Is unbeliever in the power of sorcery :
How certain then its truth, the universal
Tongue of mankind, from east to west, proclaims.
    Rienzi.   With reverential and submissive awe,
People of Rome ! leave we to holy Church
What comes not now before us, nor shall come,
While matters which our judgments can decide
Are question'd, while crown'd heads are bowed before us.

ACT IV. SCENE I.

RIENZI'S OWN APARTMENT IN THE CAPITOL.

RIENZI, FRIAR ANSELMO, *and poor* NEAPOLITANS.

Rienzi.   Who creeps there yonder with his fingers folded?
Hither; what wantest thou? who art thou, man?
  Anselmo.   The humblest of the humble, your Anselmo.
  Rienzi.   Mine?
  Anselmo.   In all duty.
  Rienzi.   Whence art thou?
  Anselmo.   From Naples.
  Rienzi.   What askest thou?
  Anselmo.   In the most holy names
Of Saint Euphemia and Saint Cunigund!   10
And in behalf of these poor creatures ask I
Justice and mercy.
  Rienzi.   On what count?
  Anselmo.   On life.
  Rienzi.   Who threatens it in Rome?
  Anselmo.   In Rome none dare
Under the guardianship of your tribunal.
But Naples is abandoned to her fate
By those who ruled her.   Those, alas! who ruled her
Heaven has abandoned.   Crimes, outrageous crimes,   20
Have swept them from their people.   We alone
In poverty are left for the protection
Of the more starving populace.   O hear,
Merciful Tribune! hear their cries for bread!   [*All cry out.*
  Anselmo (to them).   Ye should not have cried now, ye
    fools! and choak ye!
  Rienzi.   That worthy yonder looks well satisfied:
All of him, but his shoulder, seems at ease.
  Anselmo.   Tommaso! art thou satisfied?
  Tommaso.   Not I.
A fish upon my bread, at least on Friday,   30
Had done my body and my soul some good,

And quicken'd one and t'other at thanksgiving.
Anchovies are rare cooks for garlic, master!   [*To* RIENZI.
   Anselmo.   I sigh for such delusion.
   Rienzi.   So do I.
How came they hither?
   Anselmo.   By a miracle.
   Rienzi.   My honest friends! what can we do for you
At Rome?
   Anselmo.   Speak.   Does the Devil gripe your tongues?   40
   Mob.   We crave our daily bread from holy hands,
And from none other.
   Rienzi.   Then your daily bread
Ye will eat hot, and delicately small.
Frate Anselmo, what means this?
   Anselmo.   It means,
O tribune, that the lady, late our queen,
Hath set aside broad lands and blooming gardens
For hospitals; which, with unrighteous zeal,
She builds with every church.   There *Saint Antonio*   50
Beyond the gate of Capua! there *Saint Martin*
On *Mount Saint-Eremo!* there *Saint Maria*
Incoronata!   All their hospitals!
No one hath monastery! no one nuns!
   Rienzi.   Hard, hard upon you!   But what means were
     yours
To bring so many supplicants so long
A journey with you?
   Anselmo.   'Twas a miracle.
   Rienzi.   Miracles never are of great duration.
Hurry them back!   Hurry ye while it lasts!   60
I would not spoil it with occult supplies,
I reverence holy men too much for that,
And leave them to the only power above them.
Possibly quails and manna may not cross you
If you procrastinate.   But, setting out
To-morrow, by whichever gate seems luckiest,
And questioning your honest mules discreetly,
I boldly answer for it, ye shall find
By their mild winking (should they hold their tongues)

The coin of our lord Clement on the back					70
Of one or other, in some well-thonged scrip.
	Anselmo (aside). Atheist!
	Tommaso. Ah no, father! Atheists
Never lift up their eyes as you and he do.

							[*Going together.*

I know one in a twinkling.   For example,
Cosimo Cappa was one.   He denied
A miracle his mother might have seen
Not twelve miles from his very door, when she
Was heavy with him; and the saint who workt it,
To make him one, cost thirteen thousand ducats.					80
There was an atheist for you! that same Cappa . .
I saw him burnt . . a fine fresh lusty man.
I warrant I remember it: I won
A heap of chestnuts on that day at morra.
A sad poor place this Rome! look where you will,
No drying paste here dangles from the windows
Across the sunny street, to make it cheerful;
And much I doubt if, after all its fame,
The nasty yellow river breeds anchovies.

ACT IV.   SCENE II.

RIENZI'S OWN APARTMENT IN THE CAPITOL.

RIENZI *and his* WIFE.

	Rienzi. I have been sore perplext, and still am so.
	Wife. Yet falsehood drops from truth, as quicksilver
From gold, and ministers to purify it.
	Rienzi. The favour of the people is uncertain.
	Wife. Gravely thou givest this intelligence.
Thus there are people in a northern isle
Who tell each other that the weather changes,
And, when the sun shines, say the day looks bright,
And, when it shines not, there are clouds above.
	Rienzi. Some little fief, some dukedom, we'll suppose,	10

Might shelter us against a sudden storm.
   Wife.   Not so: we should be crusht between two rocks,
The people and the barons.   Both would hate thee,
Both call thee traitor, and both call thee truly.
   Rienzi.   When we stand high, the shaft comes slowly up;
We see the feather, not the point; and that
Loses what venom it might have below.
   Wife.   I thought the queen of Naples occupied
Thy mind entirely.
   Rienzi.   From the queen of Naples   20
My hopes originate.   The pope is willing
To grant me an investiture when I
Have given up to him, by my decree,
Some of her cities.
   Wife.   Then it is untrue
Thou hast acquitted her of crime.
   Rienzi.   I did;
But may condemn her yet: the king of Hungary
Is yet unheard: there are strong doubts: who knows
But stronger may arise!   My mind misgives.   30
Tell me thou thinkest her in fault.   One word
Would satisfy me.
   Wife.   *Not* in fault, thou meanest.
   Rienzi.   In fault, in fault, I say.
   Wife.   No, not in fault,
Much less so foully criminal.
   Rienzi.   O! could I
Absolve her!
   Wife.   If her guilt be manifest,
Absolve her not; deliver her to death.   40
   Rienzi.   From what the pope and king of Hungary
Adduce . . at present not quite openly . .
I must condemn her.
   Wife.   Dost thou deem her guilty?
   Rienzi.   O God! I wish she were! I must condemn her.
   Wife.   Husband! art thou gone mad?
   Rienzi.   None are much else
Who mount so high, none can stand firm, none look
Without a fear of falling: and, to fall! . .

No, no, 'tis not, 'tis not the worst disgrace.　　50
　　Wife.　What hast thou done?　Have thine eyes seen
　　　corruption?
　　Rienzi.　Thinkest thou gold could move Rienzi? gold
(Working incessantly demoniac miracles)
Could chain down Justice, or turn blood to water?
　　Wife.　Who scorns the ingot may not scorn the mine.
Gold may not move thee, yet what brings gold may.
Ambition is but avarice in mail,
Blinder, and often weaker.　Is there strength,
Cola! or speed, in the oblique and wry?
Of blood turn'd into water talkest thou?　　60
Take heed thou turn not water into blood
And show the pure impure.　If thou do this,
Eternal is the stain upon thy hand;
Freedom thro' thee will be the proud man's scoff,
The wise man's problem; even the slave himself
Will rather bear the scourge than trust the snare.
Thou hast brought large materials, large and solid,
To build thy glory on: if equity
Be not the base, lay not one stone above.
Thou hast won the influence over potent minds,　　70
Relax it not.　Truth is a tower of strength,
No Babel one: it may be rais'd to heaven
And will not anger God.
　　Rienzi.　Who doubts my justice?
　　Wife.　Thyself.　Who prosecutes the criminal?
Thyself?　Who racks the criminal?　Thyself.
Unhappy man! how maim'd art thou! what limb
Proportionate! what feature undisfigured!
Go, bathe in porphyry . . thy leprosy
Will never quit thee: thou hast eaten fruit　　80
That brings all sins, and leaves but death behind.
　　Rienzi.　But hear me.
　　Wife.　I have heard thee, and such words
As one who loves thee never should have heard.
　　Rienzi.　I must provide against baronial power
By every aid, external and internal,
For, since my elevation, many friends

Have fallen from me.
   Wife.   Throw not off the rest.
What! is it then enough to stand before   90
The little crags and sweep the lizards down
From their warm basking-place with idle wand,
While under them the drowsy panther lies
Twitching his paw in his dark lair, and waits
Secure of springing when thy back is turned?
Popular power can stand but with the people:
Let them trust none a palm above themselves,
For sympathy in high degrees is frozen.
   Rienzi.   Such are my sentiments.
   Wife.   Thy sentiments!   100
They were thy passion.   Are they sentiments?
Go! there's the distaff in the other room.
   Rienzi.   Thou blamed'st not what seemed ambition in me.
   Wife.   Because it gave thee power to bless thy **country.**
Stood tribunitial ever without right?
Sat ever papal without perfidy?
O tribune! tribune! whom weak woman teaches!
If thou deceivest men, go, next enslave them;
Else is no safety.   Would'st thou that?
   Rienzi.   To make   110
Any new road, some plants there must be crusht,
And not the higher only, here and there.
Whoever purposes great good, must do
Some partial evil.
   Wife.   Thou hast done great good
Without that evil yet.   Power in its prime
Is beautiful, but sickened by excess
Collapses into loathsomeness; and scorn
Shrivels to dust its fierce decrepitude.
   Rienzi.   Am I deficient then in manly deeds,   120
Or in persuasion?
   Wife.   Of all manly deeds
Oftentimes the most honest are the bravest,
And no persuasion so persuades as truth.
   Rienzi.   Peace! peace! confound me not.
   Wife.   The brave, the wise,

The just are never, even by foes, confounded.
Promise me but one thing.   If in thy soul
Thou thinkest this young woman free from blame,
Thou wilt absolve her, openly, with honour,   130
Whatever Hungary, whatever Avignon,
May whisper or may threaten.
  Rienzi.   If my power
Will bear it ; if the sentence will not shake
This scarlet off my shoulder.
  Wife.   Cola ! Cola !

ACT IV.   SCENE III.

TRIBUNAL IN THE CAPITOL.

RIENZI, CITIZENS, &c.

  Citizen.   There is a banner at the gates.
  Rienzi.   A banner !
Who dares hoist banner at the gates of Rome ?
  Citizen.   A royal crown surmounts it.
  Rienzi.   Down with it !
  Citizen.   A king, 'tis said, bears it himself in hand.
  Rienzi.   Trample it in the dust, and drag him hither.
What are those shouts ?   Look forth.
  Usher (having looked out).   The people cry
Around four knights who bear a sable flag :   10
One's helm is fashion'd like a kingly crown.
  Rienzi.   Strike off his head who let the accursed symbol
Of royalty come within Roman gate :
See this be done : then bind the bold offenders.
                    [LEWIS *of* HUNGARY *enters.*
Who art thou ?
  Lewis.   King of Hungary.
  Rienzi.   What brings thee ?
  Lewis.   Tribune ! thou knowest well what brings me hither.
Fraternal love, insulted honour, bring me.
Thinkest thou I complain of empty forms   20
Violated to chafe me ? thinkest thou

'Tis that I waited in the port of Trieste
For invitation to my brother's wedding,
Nor invitation came, nor embassy?
Now creaks the motive.   Silly masquerade
Usurpt the place of tilt and tournament;
No knight attended from without, save one,
Our cousin of Taranto: why he came,
Before all earth the dire event discloses.
　　Rienzi.　Lewis of Hungary! it suits not us　　　　30
To regulate the laws of chivalry
Or forms of embassies.   We know there may be
Less folly in the lightest festival
Than in the sternest and severest war.
Patiently have we heard; as patiently
Hear thou, in turn, the accused as the accuser;
Else neither aid nor counsel hope from me.
　　Lewis.　I ask no aid of thee, I want no counsel,
I claim but justice; justice I will have,
I will have vengeance for my brother's death.　　　　40
　　Rienzi.　My brother too was murdered.   Was my grief
Less deep than thine?   If greater my endurance,
See what my patience brought me! all these friends
Around, and thee, a prince, a king, before me.
Hear reason, as becomes a Christian knight.
　　Lewis.　Ye always say to those who suffer wrong,
Hear reason!   Is not that another wrong?
He who throws fuel on a fiery furnace
Cries, *Wait my signal for it! blaze not yet!*
Issue one edict more: proclaim, O tribune,　　　　50
Heat never shall be fire, nor fire be flame.
　　Rienzi.　King Lewis! I do issue such an edict
(Absurd as thou mayest deem it) in this place.
Hell hath its thunders, loud and fierce as Heaven's,
Heaven is more great and glorious in its calm:
In this clear region is the abode of Justice.
　　Lewis.　Was it well, tribune, to have heard the cause,
Nay and to have decided it, before
Both sides were here?   The murderess hath departed,
And may have won her city from the grasp　　　　60

Of my brave people, who avenge their prince,
The mild Andrea.   Justice I will have,
I will have vengeance.
    Rienzi.   Every man may ask
If what I do is well : and angry tones,
Tho' unbecoming, are not unforgiven
Where virtuous grief bursts forth.   But, king of Hungary,
We now will change awhile interrogations.
I ask thee was it well to bring with thee
Into our states a banner that blows up   70
The people into fury ? and a people
Not subject to thy sceptre or thy will ?
We knew not of thy coming.   When thy friends
In Naples urged us to decide the cause,
'Twas in thy name, as guardian to thy brother,
Bringing against the queen such accusations,
And so supported, that we ordered her
To come before us and defend herself.
She did it, nor delayed.   The cardinal
Bishop of Orvieto and the Cardinal   80
Del Sangro on their part, on hers Del Balzo
And Acciajoli, have examined all
The papers, heard the witnesses, and signed
Their sentence under each.   These we suggest
To the approval of thy chancery.
    Lewis.   Chanceries were not made for murderesses.
    Rienzi.   I am not learned like the race of kings,
Yet doth my memory hold the scanty lore
It caught betimes, and there I find it written,
Not in Hungarian nor in Roman speech,   90
Vengeance is mine.   We execute the laws
Against the disobedient, not against
Those who submit to our award.   The queen
Of Naples hath submitted.   She is free,
Unless new proof and stronger be adduced
To warrant her recall into my presence.
    Lewis.   Recall'd she shall be then, and proof adduced.
    Rienzi.   We have detected falsehood in its stead.
    Lewis.   I will have justice, come it whence it may.

Rienzi.   Cecco Mancino! read the law against   100
Those who accuse maliciously or lightly.
  Mancino. (reads).   "Who shall accuse another, nor make
      good
His accusation, shall incur such fine,
Or such infliction of the scourge, as that
False accusation righteously deserves."
  Rienzi.   Fine cannot satisfy the wrongs that royalty
Receives from royalty.
  Lewis.   Wouldst thou inflict
The scourge on kings?
  Rienzi.   The lictor would, not I.   110
  Lewis.   What insult may we not expect ere long!
And yet we fare not worst from demagogues.
Those who have risen from the people's fist
Perch first upon their shoulders, then upon
Their heads, and then devour their addled brain.
  Rienzi.   We have seen such of old.
  Lewis.   Hast thou seen one
True to his feeder where power whistled shriller,
Shaking the tassels and the fur before him?
  Rienzi.   History now grows rather dim with me,   120
And memory less vivacious than it was:
No time for hawks, no tendency to hounds!
  Lewis.   Cold sneers are your calm judgments! Here at
      Rome
To raise false hopes under false promises
Is wisdom! and on such do we rely!
  Rienzi.   Wisdom with us is not hereditary,
Nor brought us from the woods in ermine-skins,
Nor pinned upon our tuckers ere we chew,
Nor offered with the whistle on bent knee,
But, King of Hungary! we can and do   130
In some reward it and in all revere;
We have no right to scoff at it, thou hast.
Cecco Mancino!
  Mancino.   Tribune most august!
  *Rienzi (turning his back, and pointing to the eagles over his
      tribunal).*   Furl me that flag.   Now place it underneath

The eagles there.   When the king goes, restore it.
                              [*Walks down from the tribunal.*

ACT V.   SCENE I.

PALACE ON THE SHORE NEAR NAPLES.

GIOVANNA, ACCIAJOLI, DEL BALZO, LUIGI OF TARANTO,
            KNIGHTS.

Acciajoli.   My queen! behold us in your native land
And lawful realm again!
   Giovanna.   But other sounds
Than greeted me in earlier days I hear,
And other sights I see; no friends among them
Who guided me in childhood, warn'd in youth,
And were scathed off me when that thunderbolt
Fell down between us.   Are they lost so soon!
So suddenly!   Why could they not have come?
                              [*To* DEL BALZO.
Where is Filippa? where Terlizzi? where   10
Maternal Sancia?
   Del Balzo.   Such her piety,
Nor stranger nor insurgent hath presumed
To throw impediment before her steps.
For friends alike and enemies her prayers
Are daily heard among the helpless crowd,
But loudest for Giovanna; at which name,
Alone she bends upon the marble floor
That saintly brow, and stirs the dust with sighs.
   Giovanna (*to Acciajoli*).   Arms only keep her from me.
      Whose are yonder?   20
   Acciajoli.   I recognise Calabrian; Tarantine.
   Giovanna.   Ah me! suspicion then must never cease!
Never, without Luigi, Tarantine
Arms glitter in the field.   Even without him
(Which can not be) his troops in my defence
Would move again those odious thoughts, among
My easy people, guileless and misled.

Del Balzo.   His duty and his fealty enforce
What loyalty and honour would persuade.
Taranto is a fief: Taranto's prince   30
Must lead his army where his suzerain
Commands, or where, without commanding, needs.
   Acciajoli.   He can not see your city in your absence
A prey to lawless fury, worse than war.
   Del Balzo.   Ay, and war too: for those who came as
      pilgrims
And penitents, to kiss the holy frock
Of father Rupert, spring up into soldiers;
And thus are hundreds added to the guards
Which that most powerful friar placed around
Him whom we mourn for.   Three strong companies   40
(Once only eight score each) are form'd within
The conquered city.   Canopies of state
Covered with sable cloth parade the streets,
And crucifixes shed abundant blood
Daily from freshened wounds; and virgins' eyes
Pour torrents over faces drawn with grief.
What saint stands unforgotten ? what uncall'd ?
Unincenst !   Many have come forth and walkt
Among the friars, many shouted loud
For vengeance.   Even Luigi's camp stood wavering.   50
Only when first appeared your ship afar,
And over the white sail the sable flag,
Flapping the arms of Anjou, Naples, Hungary,
'Twas only then the rising mutiny
Paus'd, and subsided ; only then Luigi,
Pointing at that trine pennant, turn'd their rage
Into its course.
   Acciajoli.   Perhaps the boat I see
Crossing the harbour, may bring some intelligence ;
Perhaps he may, himself . .   60
   Giovanna.   No ! not before . .
No ! not at present . . Must I be ungrateful ?
Never ! . . ah, must I seem so ?

ACT V.   SCENE II.

An Old Knight.   From the prince
Commanding us, O lady! I am here
To lay his homage at his liege's feet.
He bids me say, how, at the first approach
Of that auspicious vessel, which brought hither
Before her city's port its lawful queen,
His troops demanded battle.   In one hour
He places in your royal hands the keys
Of your own capital, or falls before it.
   Giovanna.   God grant he fall not!   O return! return!
Tell him there are enow . . without, within . .   [10
And were there not enow . . persuade, implore . .
Show how Taranto wants him; his own country,
His happy people . . they must pine without him!
O miserable me!   O most ungrateful!
Tell him I can not see him . . I am ill . .
The sea disturbs me . . my head turns, aches, splits . .
I can not see him . . say it, sir! repeat it.
   Knight.   May-be, to-morrow . .
   Giovanna.   Worse, to-morrow! worse!   20
Sail back again . . say everything . . thanks, blessings.
   Knight.   Too late!   Those thundering shouts are our
      assault . .
It was unfair without me; it was hard . .
Those are less loud.
   Giovanna.   Luigi is repulst!
Perhaps is slain! slain if repulst . . he said it.
Yes; those faint shouts . .
   Knight.   Lady, they are less loud
Because the walls are between him and us.
   Giovanna (falls on her knees).   O! every saint in heaven
      be glorified!   [30
Which, which hath saved him? [*Rises.*] Yet, O sir! if
      walls
Are between him and us, then he is where

His foes are !   That is not what you intend ?
What is it ?   Cries again !
   Knight.   Not one were heard
Had our prince dropt.   The fiercest enemy
Had shrunk appall'd from such majestic beauty
Falling from heaven upon the earth beneath ;
And his own people with closed teeth had fought.
Not for their lives, but for his death : no such   40
Loud acclamation, lady ! had been heard,
But louder woe and wailing from the vanquisht.
   Giovanna (aside).   Praises to thee, O Virgin ! who
      concealedst
So kindly all my fondness, half my fears !
   Acciajoli.   The dust is rising nearer.   Who rides hither
In that black scarf ? with something in his hand
Where the sword should be.   'Tis a sword, I see,
In form at least.   The dust hangs dense thereon,
Adhesive, dark.
   Del Balzo.   Seneschal ! it was brighter   50
This morning, I would swear for it.
   Acciajoli.   He throws
The bridle on the mane.   He comes.
   Del Balzo.   He enters . .
We shall hear all.

ACT V.   SCENE III.

   Luigi of Taranto (throwing up his vizor).   Pardon this
      last disguise !
There was no time to take my vizor off,
Scarcely to throw my sword down in the hall.
My royal cousin ! let a worthier hand
Conduct you to the city you have won,
The city of your fathers.
   Giovanna.   O Luigi !
None worthier, none more loyal, none more brave.
Cousin ! by that dear name I do adjure you !
Let others . . these my friends and ministers . .   10

Conduct me to the city you have won,
The city of your fathers, as of mine.
Let none who carried arms against the worst
Of my own people (for the very worst
Have only been misguided) come into it
With me, or after.   Well thou governest
Thy vassals, O Luigi!   Be thy dukedom
Increast in all the wealth my gratitude
Can add thereto, in chases, castles, towns ;
But hasten, hasten thither !   There are duties   20
(Alas ! thou knowest like ourselves what duties)
I must perform.   Should ever happier days
Shine on this land, my people will remember,
With me, they shine upon it from Taranto.

FRA RUPERT.

MALE CHARACTERS.

URBAN. *Pope.* BUTELLO, *his nephew.* CHARLES II., OF DURAZZO. OTHO, *husband of Giovanna.* FRA RUPERT. MAXIMIN. STEPHEN, *a shepherd.* HERALD. PAGE. MONK. CHANCELLOR. HIGH STEWARD. LORD CHAMBERLAIN. COUNSELLORS, SECRETARIES, OFFICERS. SOLDIERS.

FEMALE CHARACTERS.

GIOVANNA, *Queen.* MARGARITA, *her niece, wife of Charles.* AGNES OF DURAZZO. AGATHA, *sister of Maximin.*

ACT I.   SCENE I.

VATICAN.

URBAN.   DURAZZO.

Urban.   Charles of Durazzo! I have found thee worthy
To wear not only ducal coronet,
But in that potent, in that faithful hand,
To wield the royal sceptre.
Durazzo.   Holy father !
I am half-ready to accept the charge,
When it befalls me, studying your content.
     Urban. So be it. The crown of Naples is now vacant.
     Durazzo. Good heavens ! is then my mother (let me
          call her
Even my mother, by whose bounteousness   10
My fortunes grew, my youth was educated)
Giovanna ! is she dead ?
     Urban.   To virtuous deeds,

Like those, she long hath been so.
   Durazzo.   His Beatitude,
The predecessor of your Holiness,
Who through her hands received his resting-place
At Avignon, when Italy rebell'd,
Absolved her from that heavy accusation
Her enemy the Hungarian brought against her.   20
   Urban.   I would not make Infallibility
Fallible, nor cross-question the absolved,
I merely would remove that stumbling-block
The kingdom from her.
   Durazzo.   Let another then
Aid such attempt.
   Urban.   Another shall.
   Durazzo.   Another
Nearer in blood is none.
   Urban.   Ere long, Durazzo,   30
I may look round and find one, if not nearer
In blood, yet fitter to perform the duties
Imposed on him by me.
   Durazzo.   None, holy father!
Is fitter.
   Urban.   Easy then are the conditions.
I would not place Butello, my own nephew,
Altho' deserving, and altho' besought
By many of the Neapolitans,
By many of the noble and the powerful   40
In every city of that realm, not him,
Durazzo! would I place, against thy interests,
So high.   But haply from thy gratitude
Accept I might in his behalf a dukedom
Or petty principality, dependent
Upon our See or (may-be) independent;
For there are some who fain would have things so.
We must content the nations of the earth,
Whom we watch over, and who look to us
For peace and quiet in the world we rule.   50
Why art thou beating time so with thy foot
At every word I speak? why look so stern

And jerk thy head and rest thy hand on hip?
Thou art determin'd on it, art not thou?

   Durazzo.   I can not, will not, move her from her seat,
So help me, God!

   Urban.   Impious young man! reflect!
I give thee time; I give thee all to-morrow.

ACT I. SCENE II.

A STREET IN NAPLES.

MAXIMIN. AGATHA.

   Agatha. (to herself). 'Twas he! 'twas father Rupert.
   Maximin (overhearing). Well! what then?
What wouldst thou with him? thou must wait his leisure:
I have some business first with father Rupert.
   Agatha (gazing anxiously). Can it be? can it be?
   Maximin.   Have not men sins
As well as women? have not we our shrivers,
Our scourers, soderers, calkers, and equippers?
   Agatha (embracing him). Forbear! O, for the love of
     God, forbear!
Heed him not, Maximin! or he will cast   10
Thy soul into perdition; he has mine.
   Maximin. And who art thou, good woman?
   Agatha.   That fair name
Is mostly given with small courtesy,
As something tost at us indifferently
Or scornfully by higher ones. Thy sister
Was what thou callest her; and Rupert knows it.
   Maximin. My sister? how! I had but Agatha.
Agatha!
   Agatha. Maximin! we have not met   20
Since that foul day whose damps fell not on thee,
But fill'd our father's house while thou wert absent.
Thou, brother! brother! couldst not save my peace,
Let me save thine. He used to call me daughter,

And he may call thee son.
    Maximin.   The very word!
He began fathering early : seven years old
At most was father Rupert.   Holy names
Are covered ways . .
    Agatha.   . . To most unholy deeds.   30
    Maximin. I see it ; say no more : my sword is reddening
With blood that runs not yet, but soon shall run.
    Agatha.   Talk not thus loud, nor thus, nor here.
    Maximin.   Cross then
Over the way to that old sycamore ;
The lads have left off playing at pallone.
I found out long ago his frauds, his treasons,
His murders ; and he meditates a worse.
Agatha ! let me look into thine eyes,
Try to be glad to see me : lift them up,   40
Nay, do not drop them, they are gems to me,
And make me very rich with only looking.
Thou must have been most fair, my Agatha !
And yet I am thy brother !   Who would think it ?
    Agatha.   Nor time nor toil deforms man's countenance,
Crime only does it : 'tis not thus with ours.
Kissing the seven nails burnt in below
Thy little breast, before they well had healed,
I thought thee still more beautiful with them.
    Maximin.   Those precious signs might have done better
    for me.   50
    Agatha.   Only the honest are the prosperous.
    Maximin.   A little too on that side hath slipt off.
    Agatha.   Recover it.
    Maximin.   How can I ?
    Agatha.   Save the innocent.
    Maximin.   But whom ?
    Agatha. Giovanna.
    Maximin.   Is the queen in danger ?
    Agatha.   Knowest thou not ?
    Maximin.   Hide we away our knowledge ;   60
It may do harm by daylight.   I stand sentry
In many places at one time, and wink,

But am not drowsy.   Trust me, she is safe.
And thou art then our Agatha!   'Twould do
Our mother good, were she alive, to find thee;
For her last words were, " Agatha, where art thou ? "
   Agatha.   Oh! when our parents sorrow for our crimes,
Then is the sin complete.
   Maximin.   She sorrows not,
And 'tis high time that thou should'st give it over.   70
   Agatha.   Alas! our marrow, sinews, veins, dry up,
But not our tears; they start with infancy,
Run on through life, and swell against the grave.
   Maximin.   I must now see Fra Rupert.   Come thou after.
He shall admit thee.   Pelt him with reproaches,
Then will I . .
   Agatha.   Brother! not for these came I,
But to avert one crime from his o'erladen
Devoted head.   He hath returned . .
   Maximin.   . . To join   80
Giovanna with Andrea?   On with me :
We may forbid the banns a second time,
Urging perhaps a few impediments.
He hath been in some convent o'er the hill,
Doing sad penance on Calabrian rye,
How then couldst thou have heard about him ? how
Find he was here in Naples ?
   Agatha.   There he should
And may have been : of late he was in Buda.
   Maximin.   You met in Buda then ?   90
   Agatha.   Not met.
   Maximin.   How know
His visit else, if he was there indeed ?
   Agatha.   While thou and Stephen Stourdza tended sheep
Together, I was in our mother's sight,
And mostly in her chamber; for ill-health
Kept her from work.   Often did Father Rupert
Pray by her, often hear her long confession,
Long, because little could be thought of for it.
" Now what a comfort would it be to you,   100
If this poor child read better," said the friar,

" To listen while she read how blessed saints
Have suffered, and how glorious their reward."
My mother claspt her hands, and " What a comfort ! "
Echoed from her sick bosom.

        " Hath she been
Confirm'd ? " he askt.   " Yea, God be prais'd," sigh'd she.
" We may begin then to infuse some salt
Into this leaven," said the friar, well-pleas'd.
" The work is righteous : we will find spare hours."   110
She wept for joy.
 Maximin.   Weep then (if weep at all)
Like her.
 Agatha.   Religious tracts soon tost aside,
Florentine stories and Sicilian song
Were buzz'd into my ears.   The songs much pleas'd me,
The stories (these he cull'd out from the book,
He told me, as the whole was not for maids)
Pleas'd me much less ; for woman's faults were there.
 Maximin.   He might have left out half the pages, still
The book had been a bible in its bulk   [120
If all were there.
 Agatha.   To me this well applies,
Not to my sex.
 Maximin.   Thou art the best in it.
Those who think ill of woman, hold the tongue
Thro' shame, or ignorance of what to say,
Or rifle the old ragbag for some shard
Spotted and stale.   On, prythee, with thy story.
 Agatha.   He taught me that soft speech, the only one
For love ; he taught me to repeat the words   [130
Most tender in it ; to observe his lips
Pronouncing them ; and his eyes scorcht my cheek
Into deep scarlet.   With his low rich voice
He sang the sadness of the laurel'd brow,
The tears that trickle on the rocks around
Valchiusa.   " None but holy men can love
As thou, Petrarca ! " sighed he at the close.
Graver the work he brought me next.   We read
The story of Francesca.   140

Maximin.   What is that?
Agatha.   Piteous, most piteous, for most guilty, passion.
Two lovers are condemn'd to one unrest
For ages.   I now first knew poetry,
I had known song and sonnet long before :
I sail'd no more amid the barren isles,
Each one small self ; the mighty continent
Rose and expanded ; I was on its shores.
Fast fell the drops upon the page : he chided :
"And is it punishment to be whirl'd on   150
With our beloved thro' eternity ?"
"Oh ! they were too unhappy, too unhappy ! "
Sobb'd I aloud : "Who could have written this ?"
"Tenderest of tender maids ! " cried he, and claspt me
To his hot breast.   Fear seiz'd me, faintness, shame.
Be calm, my brother !
    Maximin.   Tell then other tale,
And skip far on.
    Agatha.   The queen Elizabeth
Heard of me at the nunnery where I served ;   160
And the good abbess, not much loving one
Who spoke two languages and read at night,
Persuaded her that, being quick and needy,
'Twould be by far more charitable in her
To take me rather than some richer girl,
To read by her, and lace her sandals on.
I serv'd her several years, to her content.
One evening after dusk, her closet-door
Being to me at every hour unclosed,
I was just entering, when some voice like his,   170
Whispering, but deep, struck me : a glance sufficed :
'Twas he.   They neither saw me.   Now occurr'd
That lately had Elizabeth said more
And worse against Giovanna.   "She might be
Guiltless, but should not hold the throne of Naples
From the sweet child her daughter : there were some
Who had strong arms, and might again do better
In cowl than fiercer spirits could in casque."
Sleepless was I that night, afraid to meet

The wretched man, afraid to join the queen.
Early she rose, as usual ; earlier I.   180
My sunken eyes and paleness were remarkt,
And, whence ? was askt me.
                              "Those who have their brothers
At Naples," I replied, "most gracious lady,
May well be sleepless ; for rebellion shakes
A throne unsteady ever."
                              First she paus'd,
Then said, with greater blandness than before,
" Indeed they may.   But between two usurpers   190
What choice ?   Your brother may improve his fortune
By loyalty, and teaching it.   You wish
To join him I see clearly, for his good ;
It may be yours : it may be ours : go then,
Aid him with prudent counsel : the supply
Shall not be wanting, secrecy must not."
She urged my parting : the same hour we parted.

ACT I.   SCENE III.

RUPERT'S CELL.

RUPERT.   MAXIMIN.

Rupert.   Thou hast delaid some little, Maximin.
Maximin.   Frate ! I met a woman in the street,
And she might well delay me : guess now why.
Rupert.   Who in the world can guess the why of women ?
Maximin.   She said she knew us both in Hungary.
Rupert.   I now suspect the person : she is crazed.
Maximin.   Well may she be, deprived of such a friend.
Rupert.   No friend was ever mine in that false sex.
I am impatient, Maximin.
Maximin.   Impatient !   10
And so am I.
              (*Maximin throws open the door, and Agatha enters.*)
Knowest thou this woman, Frate ?

Rupert.　　Art thou crazed too?　I know her?　Not at all.
Maximin.　　And hast thou never known her? never toucht
　　her?
I only mean in giving her thy blessing.
Rupert.　　A drunken sailor in a desert isle
Would not approach her.
Maximin (indignant).　　Not my sister?
Agatha.　　　　　　　　　　　　　　　　Scorner!
Insulter!　　　　　　　　　　　　　　　　　　　　　　20
　　(*Aside.*)　He may have forgotten.　Can he?
He did not see me, would not look at me.
Maximin.　　My sword shall write her name upon thy
　　midrif.
Prepare!
Agatha.　　Hold! hold!　Spare him yet, Maximin!
How could I . . and the man who . .
Maximin.　　　　　　　　　　　　　　　Speak it out,
Worthless one!
Agatha.　　　　　　　　I am worthless.　Let him live!
Oh let him live!　　　　　　　　　　　　　　　　　30
Maximin.　　　　　　　　　Thou lovest thy betrayer.
Agatha.　　The once beloved are unestranged by falsehood;
They can not wholly leave us, tho' they leave us
And never look behind.
Maximin.　　　　　　　　Wild! wild as hawk!
Rupert (on his knees).　　Vision of light, of love, of purity!
Dost thou revisit on the verge of earth
A soul so lost, to rescue it?　Enough,
Agatha!　Do not ask him for my life;
No, bid him slay me; bid him quench the days　　　40
That have in equal darkness set and risen
Since proud superiors banisht faithful love.
I am grown old; few years are left me, few
And sorrowful: my reason comes and goes:
I am almost as capable of crimes
As virtues.
Maximin.　　By my troth, a hundred-fold
More capable.
Rupert.　　　　　　Both ('tis Heaven's will) are over.

Here let me end my hours : they should have all   50
Been thine ; he knows it ; let him take them for thee ;
And close thou here mine eyes where none behold,
Forgiving me . . no, not forgiving me,
But praying, thou pure soul ! for Heaven's forgiveness.
 Maximin. I will not strike thee on the ground : rise up,
Then, when thou risest . .
 Agatha.   Come away, my brother !
 Rupert. Never, so help me saints ! will I rise up :
I will breathe out my latest breath before her.   [60
 Maximin. It sickens a stout man to tread on toads. [*Goes.*
 Rupert (*rising slowly, and passing a dagger through his fingers*).
And the stout man might slip too, peradventure.

ACT I. SCENE IV.

PALACE NEAR NAPLES.

DURAZZO. MARGARITA.

 Durazzo. The Pope is not averse to make me king.
 Margarita. Do we not rule already ?
 Durazzo.   Rule indeed !
Yes, one small dukedom. Any shepherd-dog
Might make his voice heard farther off than mine.
 Margarita. Yet, my sweet Carlo, oftentimes I've heard you,
When people brought before you their complaints,
Swear at them for disturbing your repose,
Keeping you from your hounds, your bird, your ride
At evening, with my palfrey biting yours   10
Playfully (like two Christians) at the gate.
 Durazzo. I love to see my bird soar in the air,
My hound burst from his puzzlement, and cite
His peers around him to arraign the boar.
 Margarita. I think such semblances of high estate
Are better than the thing itself, more pleasant,
More wholesome.
 Durazzo.   And thinks too my Margarita

Of the gray palfrey? like a summer dawn
His dapper sides, his red and open nostrils,   20
And his fair rider like the sun just rising
Above it, making hill and vale look gay.
 Margarita. She would be only what Durazzo thinks her.
 Durazzo. Queenly he thinks her: queen he swears to
  make her.
 Margarita. I am contented; and should be, without
Even our rule: it brings us but few cares,
Yet some it brings us: why add more to them?
 Durazzo. I never heard you talk so seriously.
Not long ago I little heeded state,
Authority, low voice, bent knee, kist hand: 30
The Pope has proved to me that, sure as any
Of the seven sacraments, the only way
To rise above temptation, is to seize
All that can tempt.
 Margarita. There must be truth then in it.
But what will some men think when you deprive
Our aunt of her inheritance?
 Durazzo.   Men think!
Do not men always think what they should not?
 Margarita. We hear so from the pulpit: it must be.   40
But we should never take what is another's.
 Durazzo. Then you would never take another's child
To feed or clothe it.
 Margarita. That is not my meaning.
I am quite sure my aunt has loved me dearly
All her life long, and loves me still; she often
(Kissing me) said, *How like thou art Maria!*
You know, Durazzo, how she loved my mother.
 Durazzo. And she loved me no less: and we love her
And honour her.   50
 Margarita. May we not then obey her?
 Durazzo. The Pope, who teaches best, says otherwise.
Rule has been tedious to her all her reign,
And dangerous too.
 Margarita. Make it less dangerous, make it
Less tedious.

Durazzo.   She has chosen the duke Otho
To sit above thy husband, and all else.
  Margarita.   I think my husband is as brave as he.
  Durazzo.   I think so too: yet people doubt.   60
  Margarita.   Indeed!
  Durazzo.   And doubt they will, unless the truest knight
Of Margarita takes to horse, and scours
Her grandsire's realm of foreigners like Otho.
  Margarita.   If you do that, you must displease our aunt.
  Durazzo.   Perhaps so : and hast never thou displeas'd her?
  Margarita.   Never; although I sometimes did what might.
  Durazzo.   I can not disappoint the Holy Father.
  Margarita.   Nay, God forbid!   But let me no more see her,
To hear her tell me all she did for me!   70
I can bear anything but evil tongues.
  Durazzo.   Then let us slink away and live obscurely. [*Going.*
  Margarita.   Come back again . . Now! would you leave
    me so ?
I have been thinking I must think no more
About the matter . . and am quite resolved.
  Durazzo.   My sweetest! you have several female cousins ;
What are they ?
  Margarita.   Duchesses.
  Durazzo.   But are they queens ?
  Margarita.   No indeed ; and why should they be ?   They
    queens ?   80
  Durazzo.   I know but one well worthy of the title.
  Margarita.   Now, who can possibly that be, I wonder!
  Durazzo.   She on whose brow already Majesty
Hath placed a crown which no artificer
Can render brighter, or fit better, she
Upon whose lip Love pays the first obeisance.   [*Saluting her.*
  Margarita.   I know not how it is that you persuade
So easily . . not very easily
In this, however : yet, if but to tease
And plague a little bit my sweet dear cousins,   90
Writing the kindest letters, telling them
That I am still, and shall be, just the same,
Their loving cousin ; nor in form alone ;

And if I write but seldom for the future,
'Tis only that we queens have many cares
Of which my charming cousins can know nothing.
   Durazzo.   What foresight, friendliness, and delicacy!
   Margarita.   Nothing on earth but these, in the idea
Of vexing . . no, not vexing . . only plaguing
(You know, love! what I mean) my sweet dear cousins, 100
Could make me waver . . and then you, sad Carlo!
   Durazzo.   To please me . .
   Margarita.   Now, what would you have me say?

ACT I.   SCENE V.

NAPLES.

Page, Giovanna, Agnes, Maximin.

Page.   Fly, O my lady!   Troops are near the city.
Giovanna.   There always are.
Page.   But strangers.   People say
Durazzo . .
   Giovanna.   What of him?
   Agnes.   Now then confess
I knew him better.   No reports have reacht us
These several days: the roads were intercepted.
   Giovanna.   I will fear nothing: Otho watches over us.
Insects, that build their tiny habitations   10
Against sea-cliffs, become sea-cliffs themselves.
I rest on Otho, and no storm can shake me.
   Agnes.   How different this Durazzo!
   Giovanna.   All men are:
But blame not without proof, or sign of proof,
Or accusation, any man so brave.
   Page.   Lady! his soldiers on Camaldoli
Wave the green banner and march hitherward.
   Giovanna (after a pause).   It can not be! my Carlo! my
     Carlino!
What! he who said his prayers with hands comprest   20
Between my knees, and would leap off to say them?

Impossible !   He may have been deterred
From helping me : his people, his advisers,
May have been adverse . . but . . make war upon me !
O they have basely slandered thee, my Carlo !
   Agnes.   He has been with the Holy Father lately.
   Giovanna.   This would relieve me from all doubt, alone.
   Agnes.   So kind as you have been to him ! a mother !
   Giovanna.   Remind me not of any benefit
I may have done him : tell me his good deeds,   30
Speak not (if some there may have been) of mine :
'Twould but disturb the image that has never
Yet fallen from my breast, and never shall.
He was my child when my own child indeed,
My only one, was torn away from me.
   Agnes.   And you have brooded o'er a marble egg,
Poor darkling bird !
   Giovanna.   O Agnes ! Agnes ! spare me.
Let me think on . . how pleasant 'twas to follow
In that Carlino, in that lovely boy,   40
The hidings of shy love, its shame, its glee,
Demurest looks at matters we deem light,
And, well worth every lesson ever taught,
Laughter that loosens graver, and that shakes
Our solemn gauds into their proper place.
   Maximin (out of breath).   The castle-gates are open for
      one moment . .
Seize them and enter . . Crowds alone impede
Durazzo, and not arms.
   Agnes.   Do you believe
His treason now ?   50
   Giovanna.   Peace, peace ! 'tis hard, 'tis hard !

ACT II.   SCENE I.

RUPERT'S CELL.

RUPERT *and* MAXIMIN.

   Rupert (alone).   I've dogged him to the palace : there's
some treachery.
Giovanna . . and that witch, too, Agatha . .

Why not all three together? Sixty miles
From Naples there is Muro. Now, a word
Was dropt upon it. We must be humane.
But, one more trial first to make him serve
In 'stablishing the realm. I fain must laugh
To think what creatures 'stablish realms, and how.

(MAXIMIN *enters.*)

Well, Maximin! We live for better days
And happier purports. Couldst thou not devise   10
Something that might restore the sickened state,
And leave our gracious king the exercise
Of his good will, to give them companies
Who now are ensigns? Ah brave Maximin!
I do remember when thou wert but private.
Pscin, Klapwrath, Zinga, marcht, and made thee way.
Nothing in this our world would fain stand still.
The earth we tread on labours to set free
Its fires within, and shakes the mountain-heads ;
The animals, the elements, all move,   20
The sea before us, and the sky above,
And angels on their missions between both.
Fortune will on. There are whom happiness
Makes restless with close constancy ; there are
Who tire of the pure air and sunny sky,
And droop for clouds as if each hair were grass.
No wonder then should more aspiring souls
Be weary of one posture, one dull gloom
All the day through, all the long day of life.
    Maximin (gapes). Weary! ay am I. Can I soon be
      captain ?   30
    Rupert. Why not ?
    Maximin.   And then what service ?
    Rupert.   Queen Giovanna
Is blockt up in the castle, as thou knowest ;
Was not my counsel wise, to keep thee out ?
Famine had else consumed thee ; she spares none.
Charles of Durazzo, our beloved king,
Presses the siege ; and, when the queen gives up,

Thou art the man I prophesy to guard her.
There are some jewels: lightly carried in,   40
A thousand oxen cannot haul them forth ;
But they may drop at Muro, one by one,
And who should husband them save Maximin ?
   Maximin (pretending alarm).   I will not leave my sister out
     of sight :
She ne'er must fall again.
   Rupert.   Forefend it, heaven !
I might be weak !   She would indeed be safe
Where the queen is !   But who shall have the heart
To shut her up ?   What has she done ?   Her brother
Might be a comfort to her ; and the queen   50
And some few ladies trust her and caress her.
But, though the parks and groves and tofts around,
And meadows, from their first anemones
To their last saffron-crocuses, though all
Open would be, to her, if not to them,
And villagers and dances, and carousals
At vintage-time, and panes that tremble, partly
By moon-ray, partly by guitar beneath,
Yet might the hours, without street-views, be dull.
   Maximin. Don't tell her so.   Get her once there.   But
     how ?   60
Beside, the queen will never trust Hungarians.
There would be mortal hatred.   Is there fire
Upon the hearth ?
   Rupert.   None.
   Maximin.   Why then rub your hands ?

ACT II.   SCENE II.

CASTEL-NUOVO.

GIOVANNA *and* AGNES.

  Giovanna.   'Tis surely wrong that those who fight for us
So faithfully, so wretchedly should perish ;
That thriftless jewels sparkle round your temples

While theirs grow dank with famine.
  Agnes.   Now I see,
O my poor queen! the folly of refusal,
When they had brought us safety.
  Giovanna.   Not quite that,
To me at least, but sustenance and comfort
To our defenders in the castle here.   10
  Agnes.   Will you now take them?
  Giovanna.   If some miracle
Might turn a jewel to a grain of corn,
I would : my own were kneaded into bread
In the first days of our captivity.
  Agnes.   And mine were still withholden! Pardon me,
Just Heaven!
  Giovanna.   In words like those invoke not Heaven.
If we say *just*, what can we hope? but what
May we not hope if we say *merciful?*   20
  Agnes.   And yet my fault is very pardonable.
We, at our time of life, want these adornments.
  Giovanna.   We never want them. Youth has all its own ;
None can shed lustre upon closing days,
Mockers of eyes and lips and whatsoever
Was prized ; nor can they turn one grey hair brown,
But, skilfully transmuted, might prolong
The life and health and happiness of hundreds.
  Agnes.   Queens may talk so.
  Giovanna.   Not safely, but to friends.   30
  Agnes.   With power and pomp . .
  Giovanna.   Behold my pomp, my power !
These naked walls, cold pavement, grated windows.
  Agnes.   Let me share these with you. Take all my
    jewels.
  Giovanna.   Forbear, forbear, dear Agnes !
  Agnes.   Earth then, take them !
                      [*Throwing them from her.*

ACT II. SCENE III.

CASTEL-NUOVO.

DURAZZO. RUPERT. GIOVANNA. AGNES.

Durazzo. Upon my knees I do entreat of you
To hear me. In sincerity, the crown
(Now mine) was forced upon me.
Giovanna. Carlo! Carlo!
Know you what crowns are made of?
Durazzo (rising). I must wear one,
However fitly or unfitly made.
Giovanna. The ermine is outside, the metal burns
Into the brain.
Durazzo. Its duties, its conditions,   10
Are not unknown to me, nor its sad cares.
Giovanna. 'Tis well Maria my sweet sister lives not
To see this day.
Durazzo. But Margarita lives,
Her beauteous daughter, my beloved wife.
She thinks you very kind who let her go
And join me, when strange rumours flew abroad
And liars call'd me traitor.
Giovanna. With my blessing
She went, nor heard (I hope) that hateful name.   20
Durazzo (negligently). My cousin Agnes! not one word
    from you?
Agnes. Charles of Durazzo! God abandons thee
To thy own will: can any gulph lie lower!
Durazzo. 'Twas not my will.
Agnes. No!
Durazzo. What I did, I did
To satisfy the people.
Agnes. Satisfy
Ocean and Fire.
Durazzo. The Church too.   30
Agnes. Fire and Ocean
Shall lie together, and shall both pant gorged,

Before the Church be satisfied, if Church
Be that proud purple shapeless thing we see.
  Durazzo (*to Rupert*)   Show the pope's charter of in-
    vestiture.
  Rupert.   'Tis this.   May it please our lady that I read it.
  Giovanna (*to Durazzo*).   Reasons where there are wrongs
    but make them heavier.
  Durazzo (*to Agnes*).   When the whole   nation cries in
    agony
Against the sway of Germans, should I halt?
  Agnes.   No German rules this country; one defends   40
And comforts and adorns it: may he long!
The bravest of his race, the most humane.
  Durazzo.   Quell'd, fugitive, nor Germany nor France
Afford him aid against us.
  Giovanna.   Sir! he hoped
No aid from France.
  Agnes.   Does any?   What is France?
One flaring lie, reddening the face of Europe.
  Durazzo.   French is Provenza.
  Agnes.   There our arts prevail,   50
Our race: no lair of tigers is Provenza.
I call that France where mind and soul are French.
  Durazzo.   Sooner would he have graspt at German arms.
  Giovanna.   God hold them both from Italy for ever!
  Durazzo.   She shall want neither.   The religious call
Blessings upon us in long-drawn processions.
  Agnes.   Who are the men you please to call religious?
Sword-cutlers to all Majesties on earth,
Drums at the door of every theatre
Where tragedies are acted: that friar knows it.   60
  Rupert.   Such is the fruit of letters sown in courts!
Peaches with nettle leaves and thistle crowns!
Upon my faith! kings are unsafe near them.
  Durazzo (*to Agnes*).   May-be we scarcely have your
    sanction, lady?
Am I one?
  Agnes.   No.
  Durazzo.   What am I?

Agnes.   What! an ingrate.
  Durazzo (scoffingly).   Is that to be no king? You may
    rave on,
Fair cousin Agnes: she who might complain   70
Absolves me.
  Agnes.   Does the child she fed? the orphan?
The outcast? does he, can he, to himself,
And before us?
  Durazzo.   I, the king, need it not.
  Agnes.   All other blind men know that they are blind,
All other helpless feel their helplessness.

ACT II. SCENE IV.

UNDER CASTEL-NUOVO.

DURAZZO *and* RUPERT.

Rupert.   Remarkt you not how pale she turn'd?
Durazzo.   At what?
Rupert.   I said kings were unsafe.   She knew my meaning.
Durazzo.   No man alive believes it: none believed it,
Beside the vulgar, when Andrea died.
  Rupert.   Murdered he was.
Durazzo.   Mysteriously.   Some say . .
  Rupert.   What do some say?
Durazzo.   I never heeded them.
I know thee faithful: in this whole affair   10
I've proved it.   He who goes on looking back
Is apt to trip and tumble.   [*Goes.*
  Rupert (alone).   Why this hatred?
Are there no memories of her far more pleasant?
I saw her in her childish days: I saw her
When she had cast away her toys, and sate
Sighing in idleness, and wishing more
To fall into her lap; but what? and how?
I saw her in the gardens, still a child,
So young, she mockt the ladies of the court,   20

And threw the gravel at them from her slipper,
And ran without if they pursued, but stopt
And leapt to kiss the face of an old statue
Because it smiled upon her : then would she
Shudder at two wrens fighting, shout, and part them.
Next came that age (the lovely seldom pass it)
When books' lie open, or, in spite of pressing,
Will open of themselves at some one place.
Lastly, I saw her when the bridal crown
Entwined the regal.   Oh ! that ne'er these eyes   30
Had seen it ! then, Andrea ! thou had'st lived,
My comfort, my support.   Divided power
Ill could I brook ; how then, how tolerate
Its rude uprooting from the breast that rear'd it !
And must I now sweep from me the last blossoms
That lie and wither in the walk of life ?
Fancies ! . . mere fancies ! . . let me cease to waver.
Who would not do as I did ?   I am more
A man than others, therefore I dare more,
And suffer more.   Such is humanity :   40
I can not halve it.   Superficial men
Have no absorbing passions : shallow seas
Are void of whirlpools.   I must on, tho' loath.

ACT II.   SCENE V.

PALACE-GARDEN.

Maximin *and* Agatha.

Maximin.   Courage ! or start and leave me.   Sobs
    indeed !
Pack those up for young girls who want some comfits.
Nay, by my soul, to see grown women sob it,
As thou dost, even wert thou not my sister,
Smites on me here and whets my sword at once.
It maddens me with choler . . for what else
Can shake me so ?   I feel my eyes on fire.

He shall pay dear for it, the cursed Frate.
  Agatha.   Why, Maximin, O why didst thou consent
To meet the friar again ?   10
  Maximin.   To make him serve thee.
  Agatha.   Poverty rather ! want . . even infamy.
  Maximin   Did'st thou not pity, would'st not serve, the
     queen ?
  Agatha.   O might I ! might I ! she alone on earth
Is wretcheder : my soul shall ever bend
Before that sacredest supremacy.
  Maximin.   Come with me : we will talk about the means.
  Agatha.   But, be thou calm.
  Maximin.   A lamb.
                      He little thinks   [*Aside.*
To see the lamb turn round and bite the butcher.   [20

Agatha ! Agatha ! while I repeat
Thy name again, freshness breathes over me.
What is there like it ?   Why, 'tis like sweet hay
To rest upon after a twelve hours' march,
Clover, with all its flowers, an arm's length deep.

ACT II.   SCENE VI.

NAPLES.   PALACE OF BUTELLO.

BUTELLO *and* RUPERT.

  Butello (reads).   " We, Urban, by the grace of God . ."
  Rupert.   Well, well ;
That is all phrase and froth ; dip in the spoon
A little deeper ; we shall come at last
To the sweet solids and the racy wine.
  Butello.   Patience, good Frate, patience !
  Rupert.   Now, Butello,
If I cried *patience*, wouldst not thou believe
I meant *delay ?*   So do not cry it then.
Read on . . about the middle.   That will do . .   10

Pass over *love, solicitude, grief, foresight,*
Paternal or avuncular.   Push on . .
There . . thereabout.
    Butello.   Lift off thy finger, man,
And let me, in God's name, read what wants reading.
    Rupert.   Prythee be speedy . . Where thou seest my
        name . .
    Butello (reads).   " If that our well-beloved Frate Rupert
Shall, by his influence thereunto directed
By the blest saints above, and the good will
Which the said Frate Rupert ever bore us,   20
Before the expiration of one month,
So move the heart of Carlo of Durazzo
That the said Carlo do invade and seize . .
    Rupert.   What would his Holiness have next ?
    Butello.   Wait, wait.
" Naples, a kingdom held by our permission . .
    Rupert.   Ho ! is that all ?   'Tis done.
    Butello.   Hear me read on.
" From those who at this present rule the same . .
    Rupert.   This present is already past.   I've won.   30
    Butello.   " And shall consign a princely fief thereof,
Hereditary, to our foresaid nephew
Gieronimo Butello, We, by power
Wherewith we are invested, will exalt
Our trusty well-beloved Frate Rupert
Unto the highest charge our Holy Church
Bestows upon her faithful servitors."
    Rupert.   Would not one swear those words were all en-
        grossed,
And each particular letter stood bolt-upright,
Captain'd with taller at the column-head ?   40
What marshall'd files ! what goodly companies !
And, to crown all, the grand heaven-sent commission
Seal'd half-way over with green wax, and stiff
With triple crown, and crucifix below it.
Give me the paper.
    Butello.   Why ?
    Rupert (impatient).   Give me the paper.

Butello.   His Holiness hath signed it.
Rupert.   Let me see.
Butello.   Look.   50
Rupert.   Nay but give it me.
Butello.   A piece of paper!
Rupert. . . Can not be worth a principality.
Butello (giving it).   There then.
Rupert.   What dukedom has the grandest sound?
Butello.   Dukedom! the Pope says principality.
Rupert.   Thou soon shalt blazon.
Butello.   I rely on you :
Adieu, my lord!
Rupert.   My prince, adieu!   (*Alone.*) Who knows
If this will better me!   Away from court :   [60
No ; never.   Leave the people?   When he leaves it,
The giant is uplifted off the earth
And loses all his strength.   My foot must press it.
Durazzo, in things near, is shrewd and sighted :
I may not lead him.   If I rule no more
This kingdom, yet ere long my tread may sound
Loud in the conclave, and my hand at last
Turn in their golden wards the keys of heaven.

ACT II.   SCENE VII.

CASTLE OF MURO.

Giovanna *and* Agatha.

Giovanna.   Both mind and body in their soundest state
Are always on the verge of a disorder,
And fear increases it : take courage then.
Agatha.   There is an error in the labyrinth
Of woman's life whence never foot returns.
Giovanna.   Hath God said that ?
Agatha.   O lady ! man hath said it.
Giovanna.   He built that labyrinth, he led that foot
Into it, and there left it.   Shame upon him !

I take thee to my service and my trust.   10
To love the hateful with prone prudent will
Is worse than with fond unsuspiciousness
To fall upon the bosom of the lovely,
The wise who value us, the good who teach us,
The generous who forgive us when we err.
    Agatha.   Oh! I have no excuse.
    Giovanna.   She stands absolved
Before her God who says it as thou sayst it.
I have few questions for thee : go, be happier.
I owe thy brother more than I can pay,   20
And would, when thou hast leisure, hear what chance
Rais'd up a friend where the ground seem'd so rough.
    Agatha.   Leave me no leisure, I beseech of you :
I would have cares and sorrows not my own
To cover mine from me : I would be questioned,
So please you, I may else be false in part,
Not being what eyes bedim'd with weeping see me.
    Giovanna.   You come, 'tis rumour'd here, from Hungary.
My infant was torn from me by his uncle
And carried into Hungary.   30
    Agatha.   I saw it.
    Giovanna.   Saw it! my infant! to have seen my infant,
How blessed! Was it beautiful? strong? smiling?
    Agatha.   It had mild features and soft sunbright hair,
And seem'd quite happy.
    Giovanna.   No, poor thing, it was not ;
It often wanted me, I know it did,
And sprang up in the night and cried for me,
As I for it . . at the same hour, no doubt.
It soon soon wasted . . And you saw my child!   40
I wish you would remember more about him . .
The little he could say you must remember . .
Repeat it me.
    Agatha.   Ah lady! he was gone,
And angels were the first that taught him speech.
    Giovanna.   Happier than angels ever were before !
    Agatha.   He happier too !
    Giovanna.   Ah ! not without his mother !
Go, go, go . . There are graves no time can close.

ACT III.   SCENE I.

NAPLES.   PALACE.

DURAZZO.   RUPERT.   HERALD.   OFFICERS.

Durazzo.   I thought I heard a trumpet.   But we reel
After we step from shipboard, and hear trumpets
After we ride from battle.   'Twas one.   Hark !
It sounds again.   Who enters ?
Officer.   Please your Highness !
A herald claims admittance.
Durazzo.   Let him in.
Rupert.   Now for disguises ; now for masks ; steel, silk ;
Nothing in these days does but maskery.
Pages talk, sing, ride with you, sleep beside you,   10
For years : behold-ye ! some fine April-day
They spring forth into girls, with their own faces,
Tricks, tendernesses . . . ne'er a mark of saddle !

(HERALD *enters.*)

Bacco ! this is not one of them, however !
Durazzo.   Well, sir, your message.
Herald.   '   Herald from duke Otho,
I bring defiance and demand reply.
Durazzo.   I know duke Otho's courage, and applaud
His wisdom.   Tell duke Otho from king Carlo,
I would in his place do the very same :   20
But, having all I want, assure your lord
I am contented.
Rupert.   Blessed is content.
Durazzo.   Now, should duke Otho ever catch the reins
(For all things upon earth are changeable)
He can not well refuse the turn he tries,
But will permit me to contend with him
For what at present I propose to keep.
Herald.   If then your Highness should refuse the encounter,
Which never knight, and rarely king, refuses . .   30

Durazzo.   Hold, sir! All kings are knights. The al-
     ternative?
Herald.   None can there be where combat is declined.
He would not urge in words the queen's release,
But burns to win it from a recreant knight.
     Durazzo.   Did Otho say it?
     Herald.   Standing here his herald,
I have no voice but his.
     Durazzo.   You may have ears:
Hear me then, sir! You know, all know at Naples,
The wife and husband are as near at present   40
As ever, though the knight and lady not.
She, when she married him, declined his love,
And never had he hers: Taranto won it,
And, when he squandered it, 'twas unretrieved.
     Herald.   Is this, sir, for my ears or for my voice?
My voice (it is a man's) will not convey it.
     Durazzo [*to guards*].   Escort the herald back with honours
     due.   [*To Rupert.*
What think you, my lord bishop of Nocera?
     Rupert.   Troublesome times! troublesome times indeed!
My flock, my brethren at Nocera, will,   50
Must want me: but how leave my prince, a prey
To tearing factions, godless, kingless men!
     Durazzo.   Never mind me, good father!
     Rupert.   Mind not you?
I can not go; I would not for the world.
     Durazzo.   The world is of small worth to holy men.
     Rupert.   I will not hence until the storm be past.
     Durazzo.   After a storm the roads are heavier.
Courage! my good lord bishop! We must speed
And chaunt our *Veni Domine* at Nocera.   60
     Rupert.   Then would your Highness . .
     Durazzo.   Not corporeally,
But, where my bishop is, I am in spirit.   [*Goes.*
     Rupert (*alone*).   So! this is king . . and wit too! *that's*
     not kingly.
Can he be ignorant of who I am?
They will show fragments of this sturdy frock,

Whence every thread starts visible, when all
The softer nappery, in its due descent,
Drops from the women, Carlo, to the moths.

ACT III.   SCENE II.

APARTMENT IN THE CASTLE OF MURO.

MAXIMIN *and* AGATHA.

Maximin.   How fares thy lady?
Agatha.   As one fares who never
Must see the peopled earth, nor hear its voice
Nor know its sympathy; so fares Giovanna;
But, pure in spirit, rises o'er the racks
Whereof our world is only one vast chamber.
Maximin.   Dost thou enjoy the gardens, fields, and forests?
Agatha.   Perfectly.
Maximin.   Hast a palfrey?
Agatha.   Had I ever?   10
Reading and needlework employ the day.
Maximin.   Ah! our good mother little knew what pests
Those needles and those books are, to bright eyes;
Rivals should recommend them, mothers no.
We will ride out together.
Agatha.   On what horses?
Maximin.   One brought me.   Are the queen's at grass?
Agatha.   We have none.
Maximin.   Thou art hale, Agatha, but how enjoy
Perfectly, as thou sayest, these domains?   20
Agatha.   By looking out at window with the queen.
Maximin.   All the day thro'?
Agatha.   I read to her: and then,
If she suspects it tires me, she takes up
The volume, and pretends great interest
Just there, and reads it out.
Maximin.   True history?
Agatha.   History she throws by.

Maximin.   Then sweet-heart songs,
Adventures?   30
Agatha.   Some she reads, and over some
Tosses her work, rises, and shuts the cover.
Maximin.   I would not shut the song-book.   There are
      others
That show within them gold-and-purple saints,
Heads under arm, eyes upon platter, laughing
At her who carries them and lately wore them.
Agatha.   Such are not wanting.
Maximin.   Pleasant sights enough !
I would fain see them.
Agatha.   Quite impossible.   40
Maximin.   On feast-days ?
Agatha.   All are in her bedroom-closet.
Maximin.   So ! the best books then must be out of sight,
As all the best things are !   What are her pictures ?
Agatha.   Chiefly her own lost family, and those
She loved the most in it.
Maximin.   O for a glimpse !
Tell me at least who are they.
Agatha.   Good king Robert,
Whose face she often kisses.   50
Maximin.   None more worth it ?
Agatha.   There are the two Marias : one elate
With merriment, her eyes orbs wing'd with flame ;
Long deep and dark the other's, and within
Whose cooler fountains blissfully might bathe
A silenter and (haply) purer love.
Maximin.   I should be glad to look at them, but rather
At the kind queen herself.
Agatha.   That thou mayest do.
Maximin.   When ?   ·   60
Agatha.   Now ; I think ; for having heard who 'twas
That warned her of her danger when the duke
Rode in, she wisht to thank thee.   Come with me :
I must first enter and announce your name.
Maximin.   I thought you said she knew it.   Take your
      course.

ACT III. SCENE III.

CHAMBER AT MURO.

GIOVANNA. MAXIMIN. AGATHA.

Giovanna.   Accept my too few thanks, sir, for your zeal . .
Maximin.   Fine air, my lady queen, in this high tower;
Healthy as Hungary; may you enjoy it
These many days!
Giovanna (*bending*).   I fancied Hungary
Was moister, leveler, than hereabout.
Maximin.   We have a plain in Hungary on which,
Just in the middle, all of Italy's
You shall pin down nor see them from the sides.
And then what cattle! horse, ox, sheep! God's blessing 10
Upon hard-working men, like furlough soldiers,
And rare sport at the foray, when the Turk
Might seize them if we sent them not to quarters.
Here too seems nothing wanting.   [*Looking round.*
Giovanna.   A few friends
Were welcome, could they but return, whose pen
And conversation lighten'd former hours.
Maximin.   Learned ones; ay?
Giovanna.   The learned came around me.
Maximin.   Whistle, and they are at the barley-corns,   20
Wing over wing, beak against beak, I warrant.
I knew two holy friars, as holy men
As ever snored in sackcloth after sinning,
And they were learned.   What now was the upshot?
I should have said one's crucifix was white,
The other's black.   They plied mild arguments
In disputation.   *Brother*, was the term
At first, then *sir*, then nothing worse than *devil*.
But those fair words, like all fair things, soon dropt.
Fists were held up, grins in the face grew rife,   30
Teeth (tho' in these one had the better of it
By half a score) were closed like money-boxes

Against the sinner damn'd for poverty.
At last the learned and religious men
Fell to it mainly, crucifix in hand,
Until no splinter, ebony or linden,
Was left, of bulk to make a toothpick of.
    Agatha.   Brother! such speech is here irreverent.
    Giovanna.   Let him speak on: we are not queens all day.
Soldiers are rivals of the hierarchs,   40
And prone to jealousy, as less at ease,
Less wealthy, and, altho' the props of power,
Less powerful and commanding.
    Maximin.   Never queen
Spoke truer.   I bear lusty hate to them.
    Agatha.   Again?   O Maximin! before our princes
We never hate nor love.
    Maximin.   Then, lady, I
Am your worst vassal.
    Giovanna.   How?   50
    Maximin.   Being taught to hate you . .
God pardon me!   None but the frockt could teach
So false a creed.   But now the heart let loose
Swings quite the other way.   Folks say they love
Their princes: sure they must have wrong'd them first.
I turned away mine eyes from your young beauty,
And muttered to my beard, and made it quiver
With my hard breathing of hard thoughts: but now
Conspirators shall come in vain against you:
Here is the sill they tread upon who enter.   60
                                   [*Striking his breast.*

ACT III.   SCENE IV.

RUPERT'S CLOISTER.

    Rupert (alone).   Fëalty sworn, should I retract so soon?
I will live quiet . . no more crimes for me . .
When this is fairly over . . for a crime
It surely is . . albeit much holier men

Have done much worse and died in odour after.
They were spare men, and had poor appetites,
And wanted little sleep.   "Twont do with me.
Beside, I must get over this bad habit
Of talking to myself.   One day or other
Some fool may read me, mark me, and do hurt.   10
And furthermore . . when highest dignities
Invest us, what is there to think about?
What need for cleverness, wit, circumspection,
Or harm to any . . who keep still, submiss,
And brush not in attempting to pass by.

ACT III.   SCENE V.

Stephen *enters.*

So, Stephen! we Hungarians are sent off.
  Stephen.   Your Reverence is made bishop, we hear say:
As for us all . .
  Rupert.   Lupins . . when times are good.
Ah! thou hast bowels; thou canst pity others.
  Stephen.   I can myself.
  Rupert.   I all my countrymen.
I have been lately in that happy realm
Our native land.   [*Whispers.*
       Her kings should govern here.   10
  Stephen.   And everywhere.   What loyal subject doubts
His prince's right o'er all other princes?
  Rupert.   Here are sad discontents.   The prince Butello,
Nephew of His Beatitude the Pope,
Can not yet touch this principality.
Durazzo, our sharp king, snatches it back,
Altho' the kingdom was bestowed on him
Under this compact.
  Stephen.   He will bring down bull
And thunder on his crown.   The pope's own nephew!   20
  Rupert.   No less a man.
  Stephen.   If there's pope's blood in

He won't stand robbery.
 Rupert.   We owe obedience
To kings . . unless a higher authority
Dissolves it.
 Stephen.   Doubtless: but what kings? our own
Say I.
 Rupert. O Stephen! say it, say it softly.
Few ears can open and can close like mine.   30
 Stephen (aside). Ah! how good men all over are
  maligned!
 Rupert. I would not trust another soul on earth . .
But others must be trusted. Lucky they
Who first bring over to right ways the brave,
First climb the pole and strip the garland off
With all its gold about it. Then what shouts!
What hugs! what offers! dowers, in chests, in farms . .
Ah! these are worldly things too fondly prized!
But there are what lie deeper; the true praise
Of loyalty, of sanctity.   40
 Stephen (pondering). 'Tis pleasant
To look into warm chest with well-wrought hinges
That turn half-yearly. Pleasant too are farms
When harvest-moons hang over them, and wanes
Jolt in the iron-tinged rut, and the white ox
Is call'd by name, and patted ere pull'd on.
 Rupert. These are all thine. I have lived many days
And never known that man unprosperous
Who served our holy church in high emprize.
 Stephen. If so, I wish I could.   50
 Rupert.   Wish we had kings
Who keep their words like ours of Hungary.
 Stephen. Just.
 Rupert.   I have half a mind to let Elizabeth
Know what a zealous subject, what a brave,
Her daughter has at Naples.
 Stephen.   Would she give me
(For thanks in these hard times are windy) money?
Think you?
 Rupert. Don't squander all away. Few know   60

Its power, its privilege.   It dubs the noble,
It raises from the dust the man as light,
It turns frowns into smiles, it makes the breath
Of sore decrepitude breathe fresh as morn
Into maternal ear and virgin breast.
    Stephen.   Is that all it can do ?   I see much farther.
I see full twenty hens upon the perch,
I see fat cheese moist as a charnel-house,
I see hogs' snouts under the door, I see
Flitches of bacon in the rack above.   70
    Rupert.   Rational sights ! fair hopes ! unguilty wishes !
I am resolved : I can refrain no longer :
Thou art the man for prince to rest upon,
The plain, sound, sensible, straightforward man,
No courtier . . or not much of one . . but fit
To show courts what they should be.   Hide this letter.
Mind ! if thou losest it, or let'st an eye
Glance on it, I may want the power again
To serve thee : thou art ruin'd.   The new king
Might chide and chafe should Rupert ask another   80
To forward any sent he would prefer
For friend or kindred.   Since thou must return
To Hungary, thou shalt not go ill-fed.
'Tis to the queen's confessor ; look at it ;
Now put it up ; now, godson of our Saint !
Take this poor purse, and, honest soul ! this blessing.
Guides thou shalt have all the first day, and rules
How to go forward on the road : so speed thee !

ACT IV.   SCENE I.

CASTLE OF MURO.

Giovanna, Agatha.

    Giovanna.   Long have we lived in one imprisonment ;
Our tears have darkened many a thread about
Each distaff, at the whitening half-spent fire
On winter-night ; many a one when deep purple

Cloth'd yonder mountain after summer-day,
And one sole bird was singing, sad though free.
Death, like all others, hath forgotten me,
And grief, methinks, now growing old, grows lighter.
 Agatha. To see you smile amid your grief, consoles me.
 Giovanna. I never wanted confidence in you, 10
Yet never have I opened my full mind,
Keeping some thoughts secreted, altho' bent
To draw them out before you. They have lain
Like letters which, however long desired,
We cover with the hand upon the table
And dare not open.
 Agatha.   If relief there be,
Why pause? if not, why blame your diffidence?
 Giovanna. Fostered too fondly, I shot up too tall
In happiness: it wasted soon. Taranto 20
Had my first love; Andrea my first vow,
And warm affection, which shuts out sometimes
Love, rather than embraces it. To lose him
Pained me, God knows! and worse (so lost!) than all
The wild reports Hungarians spread about me.
My first admirer was my first avenger.
He, laying at my feet his conquering sword,
Withdrew. Two years elapst, he urged the dangers
That still encompast me; recall'd our walks,
Our studies, our reproofs for idling, smiled at 30
By (O kind man!) the grandfather of both.
I bade him hope. Hope springs up at that word
And disappears; Love, radiant Love, alights.
Taranto was my joy; my heart was full:
Alas! how little can the full heart spare?
I paus'd . . because I ill might utter it . .
In time he turn'd his fancies to another.
Wretchedest of the wretched was I now;
But gentle tones much comforted my anguish,
Until they ended; then loud throbs confused 40
The treasured words; then heavy sleep opprest me.
I was ashamed . . I *am* ashamed . . yet (am I
Unwomanly to own it?) when he loved

One only, I was driven to despair;
When more . . *Adieu Taranto!* cried my heart
And almost sank thro' sorrow into peace.
O that fresh crimes in him should solace me!
My life of love was over, when his spirit
Flew from my lips, and carried my forgiveness
On high, for Heaven's.   50
                  Wars burst forth again;
He who defended me from their assaults
Saw in me what to love, but whom to love
He found not in me.
                  " If my confidence,
My gratitude," said I, "suffice thee, Otho,
Here is my hand."
                  He took it, and he wept.
Brave man! and let me also weep for thee!
  Agatha.   Not beauteous youth enrobed in royal purple 60
And bright with early hope, have moved you so.
  Giovanna.   Record not either; let me dwell on Otho:
The thoughts of him sink deeper in my pillow;
His valiant heart and true one bleeds for me.

ACT IV.   SCENE II.

COURT-YARD OF MURO.

Maximin *and* Stephen.

  Stephen. Maximin! art thou close?
  Maximin.   Yea, close enough,
Altho' I have the whole court-yard to cool in.
  Stephen. I meant not that.
  Maximin.   A baton to a pike
Thou didst not; else thou hadst not spoken it.
  Stephen. Some folks think better of my understanding.
  Maximin. None of thy heart: give me thy fist then,
    Stephen.
  Stephen. That sets all right.
  Maximin.   What brought thee hither? 10

Stephen.   What ?
Maximin.   Hast secrets ?
Stephen.   None worth knowing.
Maximin.   No man has :
They never did any one good.
Stephen.   They may.
Maximin ! hast commands for Hungary ?
Maximin.   For Hungary ?
Stephen.   What ! is there no such place ?
Maximin.   No, by my soul ! nor ever will for me.   20
Were not my sister here about her duty,
I could knock out my brains against the wall
To think of Hungary.
Stephen.   Yet thou hast there
No croft, no homestead, pullet, chick.
Maximin.   Hast thou ?
Stephen.   I am a man at last.   Wert thou but one !
Maximin.   Stephen, we will not quarrel.
Stephen.   I am rich
I meant to say.   30
Maximin.   So far so well : however,
Not some bold thief who stands some ages back
(Tho' better there than nearer) nor some bolder
Who twists God's word and overturns his scales,
Nor steel, nor soil in any quantity,
Nor gold, whose chain encompasses the globe,
Nor even courage, Stephen, is sufficient
To make a man : one breath on Woman's wrongs,
Lifting the heart, does that.
Stephen.   And other things.   40
Maximin.   Chick, pullet, homestead, croft ; are these our
   makers ?
Stephen.   I have them in this lining, one and all.
Maximin (suspecting).   Stephen ! I could show thee the
   duplicate
In the same hand.   He who fixt me at Muro
Will fix thee too in some such place as firmly.
What ! hast no heart for castles ? art low-minded ?
How ! with chick, pullet, homestead, croft ? Sit down :

Thou didst not sweat so after all thy walk
As thou dost now.   What ails thee, man ?
   Stephen.   What ails me !   50
Nothing.
   Maximin.   But did Fra Rupert, did he truly
Clap thee up here ?   Cleverly done !   Don't blame him.
   Stephen.   Blame him ! if friar he were not, and moreover
The tadpole of a bishop, by the martyr !
I would run back and grapple with his weazon.
   Maximin.   He is too cunning for us simple men.
   Stephen.   For thee, it seems, he has been . . but for me,
I, man or child, was never yet out-witted.
   Maximin.   Ah ! we all think so ; yet all are, by weaker.
And now about the letter.   [60
   Stephen.   Thee he trusted ;
I know he did ; show me the duplicate.
   Maximin.   Duplicates are not written first nor shown first.
How many men art good against ?
   Stephen.   One only.
   Maximin.   Then five might overmaster thee and gag thee,
And five are ready in the Apennines ;
If I knew where exactly, I would tell thee.
   Stephen.   A fiend of hell in frock !   70
   Maximin.   No, not so bad :
He, without blame or danger on thy part,
Shall build thy fortune.
   Stephen.   He ? I scorn the thief . .
Beside . . he would not.
   Maximin.   Would or not, he shall.
                    [Stephen *hesitates.*
Am I an honest man ?
   Stephen.   Why ! as men go.
   Maximin.   Give me the letter then, and, on my life,
It shall do more and better for thee much   80
Than placed in any other hands but mine.
                    [*An* Officer *passes.*
Ho ! Captain ! see an honest man at last,
                    [*Giving him the letter.*
And you the very one he came about.

Stephen (*threatening* MAXIMIN).   Traitor !
Maximin.   A traitor, with a vengeance, is he.
Stephen.   Hangman !
Maximin.   Thou needst not call him ; he will come
Presently.   [*To the* Officer.
                   This poor hind hath saved the prince
From insurrection, from invasion. Read.   [Officer *reads.* 90
The royal favour will shine warm upon
One friend of mine.
   Officer.   Be sure : he will be made.
'Tis but our service . . We must not complain . .
Tho' there are things, of late, which soldiers' crops
Swell high against.   We captains . .
   Maximin.   Ay, we captains! . .
   Officer.   I must be gone to Naples ; so must thou
My gallant grey-coat.   [*Goes out.*
   Maximin.   Tell me how thou camest   100
To Muro, of all places in the world,
It lies so wide of any road to Hungary.
   Stephen.   Fra Rupert bade me follow at mid-day
A band of holy mendicants, due-south,
To baffle all suspicion : the next morn
To cross the mountains on my left, and turn
Northward, and then take boat by Pesaro.
While they were stretcht along the levelest tiles
In the best chamber . . being mendicants . .
Each on his sheepskin . . for they love soft lying . .   110
Of grand farm-house ; and while nighthawk and grillo
Fought for it which should sing them first to sleep ;
And while aside them, in brass pot unfathom'd,
The rich goat-whey was ripening for next breakfast,
I thought of my far sheep and my near friend ;
My near friend first ; and so, by luck, here am I.
   Maximin.   But how didst dream that thou shouldst find
      me here ?
   Stephen.   Who, in the Virgin's name, should first step up,
After I bade the mendicants good-bye,
Who but Augustin !   Much about our country,   120
Mops, wakes, fairs, may-poles, gipsy-girls, and fortunes,

When suddenly, as one that knew them all,
He whisper'd thou wert art this Muro here,
Some twenty miles, or near upon it, off.
I must fain see thee.   After three hours' walk
I ask the distance : twenty-five miles scant.
At night I supt and slept with an old shepherd :
His dog soon crope betwixt us, so genteely,
I should have never known it, but his nose
Was cold against my ear, and, when I turn'd,   130
A snag or two was at it . . without harm.
Morning blew sharp upon us from the hills.
" How far are we from Muro, my good man ? "
Said I, and dipt my olive in the salt.
" Scant thirty miles."   Let never man believe
In luck !   I overturned the salt, alert
To hurry on ; yet here thou seest me, rich . .
Sleeping six hours in winter, five in summer.
      Maximin (*pondering*).   Augustin told thee I was here!
         Augustin !
How should he know ?   One only knew beside   140
The friar : he never would have told : she told him.
                              [*Walks about impatiently.*
Augustin has smooth locks and fresh complexion,
And heels for dance and voice for dulcimer,
Rare articles at finding secrets out :
But, with thy slanting face, and arm curl'd round
The inside canework of a padded chair,
And leg oblique slid negligently under,
If thou wouldst keep them nicely in repair
Ferret no more my secrets out, Augustin !
      Officer (*returned*).   Ready ? my dapple grey ! ready for
         Naples ?   150
      Stephen.   Not without Maximin.   By his advice
I call'd you in to help us : he shall have
His share.
      Maximin.   When our blythe king sniffs up the wind,
And sees the clouds roll mainly from the north,
And finds Giovanna's enemies advance,
He may be kinder to her : so, commander,

If you believe I did my duty now,
Let me confirm the letter you convey.
  Officer.   Canst thou add aught ?   160
  Maximin.   Much, were there much required.
  Officer.   Come then along : we will drink gold to-morrow.

ACT IV.   SCENE III.

MONASTERY GARDENS.

  Rupert (alone).   I must have peace : I can not live with-
    out it :
Only few years (who knows) may yet remain.
They shall not hurt the queen : in part the harm
Would be my doing.   But then Maximin . .
He too . . yet why not let him die in battle ?
Battles there will be : kings are all tenacious
Of their king-life : Italians are astute,
Hungarians valiant : two stout swords must clash
Before one break.
             That Agatha, that Agatha   10
Troubles me most of all !   Suppose she comes
Into my very palace at Nocera,
And tells the people what the bishop did !
Never was blow cruel like this since Herod.
Giovanna must then live, if for her sake
Alone ; for such her tenderness, her truth,
She'll not abandon her while life remains.

ACT IV.   SCENE IV.

PALACE IN NAPLES.

  DURAZZO.   CHANCELLOR.   PRIVY-COUNSELLORS.

  Durazzo.   Speak, my lord chancellor : you now have read
The letter through : can doubt remain upon it ?
               [CHANCELLOR *shakes his head.*
Gentlemen ! you have heard it : what think you ?
  First Counsellor.   Traitorous, if there be treason.

Second Counsellor.   Sentence then.
Chancellor.   Powerful is Rupert: many think him saintly,
All know him wise and wary: he has friends
In every house, and most among the women.
Such men are dangerous to impeach: beside,
Being now bishop . .   10
Durazzo.   Not quite yet: appointed,
Not seated.
Chancellor.   No ?   This changes the whole aspect.
Once bearing that high dignity, once throned . .
Durazzo.   I like no thrones that narrow mine too much,
And wonder wherefore clergymen should mount them.
Chancellor.   However, sir, since such hath been the custom
From barbarous times . .
Durazzo.   Till times herein as barbarous . .
Chancellor.   We must observe the usage of the realm,   20
And keep our hands from touching things held sacred.
Few days ago, for lighter crimes the friar
Might have been punisht with severity.
First Counsellor.   Even now, although his legs begin to
    sprout
With scarlet plumage, we may crop his crest ;
But better on the beam than in the yard.
Third Counsellor.   It would put by much bickering.
Fourth Counsellor.   There are many
Expectants, holy men, who would condemn
In any court ecclesiastical   30
Appeal so manifest to foreign force,
And strip him to the skin to wash him clean.
Fifth Counsellor.   And there are civil laws which tread on
    velvet
And leave no scandal when they pass the door ;
Modest and mild and beautifully drest,
And void of all loquacity, all pomp ;
They, should you ask them what they are, reply
"We are not laws ; we are prerogatives."
Carlo.   Paoluccio ! wit may give the best advice.
Far be from me all violence.   If the criminal   40
Be strong and boisterous, the ecclesiastical

Craving and crafty, swift or slow at pleasure,
At least our civil laws are excellent,
And what you call prerogatives are civil.
    Paoluccio.   I class them so.
    Many at once.   They are the best of all.
    Carlo.   I will pursue this counsel.
                             You may rise.

ACT V.   SCENE I.

CASTLE OF MURO.

GIOVANNA.   AGATHA.   OTHO.   Officers.

    Giovanna.   What shouts are those? whose voice, above them
      all,
Above the neighing horse and trumpet's clang,
Calls to the rescue?   Can I doubt? . .
                         My Otho!
My Otho! rush not rashly into fight:
Thou canst not free me.
    Agatha.   He has beat them off . .
He enters.
    Officer.   Yes, he enters.
    Otho (wounded mortally).   Take the ransom . .   10
'Tis small . . 'tis only one worn life . . and loose her.
    Giovanna.   Not from thy neck, my Otho, while thou livest,
Or while I live.
    Otho.   Giovanna hath embraced me . .
I now have lived . . life should be over now.
    Officer.   His breath is gone: bear him away: the king
                   [*Points to the* QUEEN, *who swoons.*
May have commands for her.
    Agatha.   My queen! my queen!
My friend! my comforter!   Oh! *that* no more.   [*Falls.*

ACT V.   SCENE II.

PALACE, NAPLES.

MARGARITA.   DURAZZO.

Margarita.   I can not see what mighty things indeed
My aunt Giovanna ever did for me :
Can you ?
   Durazzo.   They long are over, if she did.
   Margarita.   Beside . .
   Durazzo.   Now what beside ?
   Margarita.   I had almost
Said such a foolish thing !
   Durazzo.   You ! Margarita !
   Margarita.   I was about to say she did no more   10
For me than you.   If she loved *me*, she loved me
Because she loved my mother, her own sister ;
Where is the wonder ? where the merit ?
   Durazzo.   None.
   Margarita.   She even loved another sister, her
Whom people called *Fiammetta ;* God knows why ;
No Christian name, nought Christian-like about it.
She was the one of Sicily, who fancied
(O shame upon her !) somebody . . a writer.
   Durazzo.   What writer ?   20
   Margarita.   Is not that enough ? a writer !
   Durazzo.   There is not much to thank her for, if all
Partake of her affection, even those
Who sink so low.
   Margarita.   She played with *you* the most ;
Perhaps because she thought you like her child.
She did show pleasure when she fondled *me ;*
But 'twas not to make *me* the happier,
Although it did so, but herself . . herself.
Yet, Carlo, would you think it ! there are times   30
When I am ready to desire of you
That you would let her out of such a den

At Muro.
   Durazzo.   Had you mentioned it before,
As wishing it . . why, then indeed . .
   Margarita.   So, then,
You would have let her out?　How very kind!
   Durazzo.   If we could have persuaded her to go.
   Margarita.   Persuaded her? what! out of prison?
   Durazzo.   Do not   40
Term it so harshly: who can bear to hear
Of prisons?
   Margarita.   Is the tower indeed not lockt
Nor bolted?
   Durazzo.   People would run into it
And trouble her devotions.　At this time
She needs them most particularly.
   Margarita.   Why?
   Durazzo.   Her health declines.
   Margarita.   Is she in danger?   50
   Durazzo.   Some.
   Margarita.   Imminent?
   Durazzo.   There are fears.
   Margarita.   About her life?
   Durazzo.   Men shake their heads.
   Margarita.   O Carlo! O my Carlo!
I have . . (will God forgive me?) been ungrateful.
And all this time! . . when, but one moment of it . .
My hand in hers, or hers upon my head . .
   Durazzo.   Hush! Margarita! thou'rt a queen: be
   calm,   60
And worthy of the station we enjoy.   [*He leads her out.*

ACT V.　SCENE III.

PALACE, NAPLES.

High Steward. Chamberlain. Chancellor. Durazzo.

   Chamberlain.   Wary and slow is this our chancellor,
Where title-deeds are fluttering in suspense;
The perill'd life and honour of his queen

He passes as he would a wretch in chains
On the road-side, saying, *So! there thou art!*
  Lord High Steward. We want such men's religion, their
    sound sense,
Coolness, deliberation, ponderous front,
Broad and dark eyebrow. Much of dignity,
Reverence and awe, build on these crags alone.
  Lord Chamberlain. Ye have them all in one. I hear his
    foot: 10
The king steps lighter: both advance.
  Lord High Steward.   Who come
Behind? · for there are many.

    (Durazzo, Chancellor, Counsellors, *enter.*)

  Durazzo.   Take your seats.
Gentlemen! ye have heard with indignation
The rash attempt against my peace and yours,
Made by the Suabian, husband of Giovanna.
  Lord Chamberlain. We hear, by Heaven's protection of
    your Highness,
It fail'd.
  Lord High Steward. And that he fell in the attempt. 20
  Durazzo. Desperate, he cut his way, tho' wounded, thro'
My bravest troops, but could not force the gate;
Horsemen are weak at walls nine fathoms high;
He had scarce twenty with him.
  Chancellor.   There he paid
His forfeit life, declared already traitor.
  Durazzo. On this we are not met, but to deliberate
On the state's safety. My lord chancellor,
Is the queen guilty?
  Chancellor (starts). We must try her first,   30
Privately; then decide.
  Durazzo.   Yea, privately;
So pleaseth me. Take then your secretaries
And question her; decorously, humanely.

ACT V. SCENE IV.

CASTLE OF MURO.

Giovanna. Chancellor. High Steward. Chamberlain.
Secretaries.

Chancellor.   Lady! we have heard all, and only ask
(For the realm's weal) your Highness will vouchsafe
To sign this parchment.
    Giovanna (taking it).   What contains it?
    Chancellor. Peace.
    Giovanna.   I then would sign it with my blood; but blood
Running from royal veins never sign'd peace.   [*Reads.*
It seems I am required to abdicate
In favour of Duke Carlo of Durazzo.
    Chancellor.   Even so.   10
    Giovanna (to the others).   To you I turn me, gentlemen!
If ever you are told that I admitted
His unjust claims, if ever you behold
Sign'd, as you fancy, by my hand the parchment
That waives our kingdom from its rightful heir,
Believe it not: only believe these tears,
Of which no false one ever fell from me
Among the many 'twas my fate to shed.
I want not yours; they come too late, my friends;
Farewell, then! You may live and serve your country; 20
These walls are mine, and nothing now beyond.

ACT V. SCENE V.

NAPLES.

Maximin. Stephen.

Maximin.   Among the idle and the fortunate
Never drops one but catafalc and canopy
Are ready for him: organ raves above,
And songsters wring their hands and push dull rhymes
Into dull ears that worse than wax hath stopt,

And cherubs puff their cheeks and cry half-split
With striding so across his monument.
Name me one honest man for whom such plays
Were ever acted.
    They will ne'er lay Otho   10
With kindred clay! no helm, no boot beside
His hurried bier! no stamp of stately soldier
Angry with grief and swearing hot revenge,
Until even the paid priest turns round and winks.
I will away: sick, weary . .

     (STEPHEN *enters.*)

Stephen.   Hast thou heard
The saddest thing?
 Maximin.   Heard it? . . committed it,
Say rather. But for thee and thy curst gold,
Which, like magician's, turns to dust, I trow, 20
I had received him in the gate, and brought
The treasure of his soul before his eyes:
He had not closed them so.
 Stephen.   Worst of it all
Is the queen's death.
 Maximin. The queen's?
 Stephen.   They stifled her
With her own pillow.
 Maximin. Who says that?
 Stephen.   The man 30
Runs wild who did it, through the streets, and howls it,
Then imitates her voice, and softly sobs
"*Lay me in Santa Chiara.*"

    ACT V. SCENE VI.

NAPLES. BEFORE THE PALACE. AMONG GUARDS.

  MAXIMIN. DURAZZO.

 Maximin.   Gallant prince!
Conqueror of more than men, of more than heroes!
What may that soldier merit who deserts

His post, and lets the enemy to the tent?
   Durazzo.   Death is the sentence.
   Maximin.   Sign that sentence then.
I shall be found beside a new-made grave
In Santa Chiara.
   Durazzo.   Art thou mad?
   Maximin.   I shall be   10
If you delay.
   Durazzo (to Guards).   See this man into Hungary.

ACT V.   SCENE VII.

NAPLES.   MONASTERY GARDEN.

   Rupert (alone).   There are some pleasures serious men sigh
       over,
And there are others maniacs hug in chains:
I wonder what they are: I would exchange
All mine for either, all that e'er were mine.
I have been sadly treated my whole life,
Cruelly slighted, shamefully maligned:
And this too will be laid upon my shoulders.
If men are witty, all the wit of others
Bespangles them; if criminal, all crimes
Are shoveled to their doors.   10
                God knows how truly
I wisht her life; not her imprisonment
More truly.   Maximin and Agatha
In the queen's life would never have come forth.
   Men of late years have handled me so roughly,
I am become less gentle than I was.
Derision, scoffs and scorns, must be rebuft,
Or we can do no good in act or counsel.
Respect is needful, is our air, our day,
'Tis in the sight of men we see ourselves,   20
Without it we are dark and halt and speechless.
Religion in respect and power hath being,
And perishes without them.   Power I hold:

Why shun men's looks? why my own thoughts . . afraid?
No, I am not afraid : but phantasies
Long dwelt on let us thro'.
　　　　　　　　　　If I do quail,
'Tis not the mind, the spirit ; 'tis the body.
　　A Monk (entering).　　Father I come from Muro, where a
　　　　woman
(Sickly before) for days refused all food,　　　　　30
And now is dead.
　　Rupert.　　　　　　What is her name?
　　Monk.　　　　　　　　　　One Agatha.
　　Rupert.　　Did she receive the holy Sacrament?
　　Monk.　　You must have known she did, else why such joy?
She would receive nought else.
　　Rupert.　　　　　　　　Then she is safe.
·　*Monk.*　　We trust in God she is : yet she herself
Had pious doubt.
　　Rupert.　　Of what was her discourse?　　　　　40
　　Monk.　　.Her mind, ere she departed, wandered from her.
　　Rupert.　　What did she talk about? dost hear?
　　Monk.　　　　　　　　　　She said,
" Rupert, if he could see me, might be " . . .
　　Rupert.　　　　　　　　What?
　　Monk.　　Her mind, observe, was wandering.
　　Rupert.　　　　　　　　Thine is too.
Tell me the very word she uttered.
　　Monk.　　　　　　　" Saved."
Blessings upon her! your uplifted hands　　　　　50
And radiant brow announce her present bliss.
　　Rupert.　　Said she no more?
　　Monk.　　　　　　" Since he's not here, take these,
And let the friar and his brotherhood
Say·masses for my soul : it may do good
To theirs no less."
　　　　　　　　I stoopt the holy taper,
And through her fingers and her palm could see
That she held something : she had given it
But it dropt out of them : this crucifix,　　　　　60
From which the square-set jewels were removed,

And this broad golden piece, with its long chain
Of soft dark hair, like our late queen Giovanna's.
   Rupert.   Her medal .. *anno primo* .. All goes right.
   Monk.   Your blessing !
   Rupert.   Take it, pr'ythee, and begone.   [Monk *goes.*
Nothing has hurt me : none have seen me. None ?
Ye saints of heaven ! hath ever prayer been miss'd ?
Penance, tho' hard, been ever unperform'd ?
Why do ye then abandon me ? like one   70
Whom in your wrath ye hurl aside ; like one
Scathed by those lightnings which God's sleepless eye
Smites earth with, and which devils underneath,
Feeling it in the abysses of the abyss,
Rejoice was not for them.
                    Repent I did . .
Even of Agatha I did repent.
I did repent the noble friends had fallen.
Could they not have been wiser, and escaped,
By curbing evil passions, pride, distrust,   80
Defiance ? It was wrong in them : in me
'Twas not quite well : 'twas harsh, 'twas merciless :
Andrea had not done it : wrong'd, betray'd,
Andrea had not done it.
                  Have my words
Sorcery in them ? do they wake the dead ?
Hide thy pale face, dear boy ! hide from my sight
Those two dark drops that stain thy scanty beard,
Hide those two eyes that start so ! Curse me, kill me ;
'Twere mercy, 'twere compassion, not revenge ;   90
Justice, the echo of God's voice, cries *More !*
I can endure all else.
             I will arise,
Push off this rack that rends me, rush before him
And ask him why he made me what I am.

        (*Enter* Officers.)
   First Officer. Traitor ! the king hath traced all thy devices.
   Rupert. Without them he had ne'er been what ye style
him.

Second Officer.   Avowest thou thy perfidy?
Rupert.   And his.
Third Officer.   Murderer! thou shalt confess.   100
Rupert.   'Twere royal bounty.
Third Officer.   And die.
Rupert.   'Twere more than royal.
First Officer.   Come thy way.
Rupert.   My way? my way? . . I've travell'd it enough,
With or without thee I will take another.
Second Officer.   Whither!
Rupert (*points to the window*).   Look yonder!
There it lies.   [*Stabs himself.*
                    Andrea!   110
First Officer (*after a pause*).   Merciful God! end thus his
    many crimes?
Third Officer (*after a pause*).   What moans and piteous
    wailings from the street!
Second Officer.   Can they arise for him so suddenly?
First Officer.   There are too many.   None hath told the
    deed
Beyond this spot, none seen it.
Third Officer.   Now you hear
Distinctly; if distinctly may be heard
The wail of thousands.
Second Officer.   Their queen's name they cry . .
Third Officer.   With blessings.   120
First Officer.   Now, at last, ye know Giovanna;
And now will Rupert too be known, tho' late.

THE SIEGE OF ANCONA.

No event in the history of Italy, including the Roman, is at once so tragical and so glorious as the siege of Ancona; nor shall we find at any period of it, two contemporary characters so admirable for disinterested valour and prompt humanity, as William degli Adelardi of Marchesella, and the Countess of Bertinoro. The names of those who sustained the siege are, for the most part, forgotten: but Muratori has inserted in his imperishable work the narratives of contemporary and nearly contemporary authors; and Sismondi has rendered many of the facts more generally known.—*Hist. des Répub. Ital.*, tome xi. ch. i.

MALE CHARACTERS.

The Consul of Ancona. The Archbishop of Mentz. The Bishop of Ancona. Antonio Stamura. Father John. Minuzzi. Costanzio. Corrado, *brother of Costanzio.* Paolucci, *formerly Consul.* Marchesella. Herald, Senators, Officers, Priests, People.

FEMALE CHARACTERS.

Erminia, *the Consul's daughter.* Nina, *her companion.* Angelica, *mother of Antonio Stamura.* Malaspina. Countess of Bertinoro. Marca, *attendant on Erminia.*

ACT I.   SCENE I.

On the steps of the cathedral, commanding a view of the country. Many of all ages are leaving the church and looking at the approach of the Archbishop, just beyond the walls, descending the hill.

   Erminia.   Nina! see what our matin prayers have brought us.

O what a sight!   The youth and maidens fly,

Some to the city, others up the hills,
With the fresh tale each for the one loved best.
   Nina. They are afraid to meet so many horses;
I would not scud away so, were I there,
Would you?
   Erminia. My dress would show the dust; or else . .
I run to tell my father: go, tell yours.

ACT I. SCENE II.

CONSUL'S HOUSE.

CONSUL *and* ERMINIA.

   Erminia. Father! why are not all the bells set ringing?
   Consul. What should the bells be ringing for to-day?
   Erminia. Such a procession comes along the road
As never was: some bishop at the head:
And what a horse is under him! and what
Beautiful boys . . they really are but boys,
Dear father . . hold the bridle on each side!
Scarlet and gold about their surplices,
And waving hair; not like church servitors,
But princes' sons. I would give all the world   10
To see their faces . . not quite all the world . .
For who would care about boys' faces, father?
Beside, they are too distant, very far.
   Consul. Art thou gone wild, Erminia?
   Erminia.   Come and see.
   Consul (*listening, and rising*). What means this tumult?

               Senators *enter.*

               Consul! we are lost.
   Consul. How so?
   First Senator.   The archbishop comes, from Barbarossa,
Against the city.   20
   Consul.   What archbishop comes?
   Second Senator. Of Mentz.
   Consul.   Then close the gates, and man the walls,

And hurl defiance on him.   Bring my robe,
Erminia ! I will question this proud prelate.
Gasparo, lift my armour from the wall
In readiness.
    Officer.   A herald, sir, claims entrance.

Herald *enters.*

    Consul.   What would your master with his perfidy ?
    Herald.   My master is the emperor and king.   30
    Consul.   The more perfidious.   Binds him not his oath
To succour Italy ?   Is slavery succour ?
Tell the false priest thou comest from, that priest
Who took the name of *Christian* at the font,
'Twere well he held not in such mockery
The blessed one he bears it from.   But wealth
And power put Wisdom's eyes out, lest she rule.
    Herald.   Sir Consul ! if the archbishop never preaches,
Pray why should you ?   It ill becomes my office
To bandy words : mine is but to repeat   40
The words of others : and their words are these :
" The people of Ancona must resign
Their lawless independence, and submit
To Frederick, our emperor and king."
    Consul.   Brief is the speech ; and brief is the reply.
The people of Ancona will maintain
Their lawful independence, and submit
No tittle, sir, to emperor or king.
    Herald.   Is this the final answer ?
    Consul.   Lead him forth.   50
    Officer (*enters*).   Sir ! ere you hasten to the walls, look
      once
Toward the harbour.
    Consul.   Gracious Heaven ! what sails
Are those ?   Venetian ?
    Officer.   Yes ; and they take soundings.
    Consul.   Venice against us ? Freedom's first-born child,
After the deluge that drowned Italy.
Alas ! the free are free but for themselves ;
They hate all others for it.   The first murderer

(Their patron) slew his brother.   Thus would they.   60
                                     [*To the Officer.*

Merluccio ! hasten, man ! call back again
Our mariners to leave the battlements
And guard their sisters and their mothers here.
  Officer.   Mothers and sisters follow'd them, to bring
Munition up the towers.
  Consul.   Bid them return :
The beach is open : thither is my road
Until more hands arrive.
  Messenger (enters).   Sir ! they weigh down
Machines for storming.   70
  Consul.   Go thou, tell Campiglio
To intercept them, if he can, before
They join the Germans on the hills above.
  Erminia.   O father ! here are none beside ourselves :
And those few people hauling in the boats
Can help us little ; they are so afraid.
  Consul.   Think not they are afraid because they pull
The oars with desperate strength and dissonance :
Who knows if they have each his loaf at home,
Or smallest fish set by from yesterday ?   80
The weather has been rough ; there is a swell
From the Adriatic.   Leave me now, Erminia !
  Erminia.   Alone, dear father ?
  Consul (placing his hand on the head of ERMINIA).
                             He who watches over
The people, never is alone, my child !
  Erminia (running back).   Here come the men who were
    debarking.
                 MINUZZI *and others.*
  Minuzzi.   Hail,
Sir Consul !   All our fears then were but vain ?
  Consul.   So ! you *did* fear ?
  Minuzzi.   Ay did we.   The Venetians 90
Ride in huge galleys ; we ply boats for trade.
But since, Sir Consul, you expected them,
We are all safe.   I did not much misgive
When one in gallant trim, a comely youth,

Outside the mole, but ready to slip in,
Beckon'd me from his boat, and gave me, smiling,
This letter, bidding me deliver it
Into no other hand beside the consul's,
And adding, " All will soon be well again."
I hope it may.   But there was cause for doubt !   100
The galleys have cast anchor.
  Consul.   Sure enough
They join our enemies.
  Minuzzi.   How !   One free state
Against another ! Slaves fight slaves, and kings
Fight kings : so let them, till the last has bled :
But shall wise men (and wise above the wise,
And free above the free are the Venetians)
Devastate our joint patrimony . . freedom ?
I fear not him who falls from such a highth   110
Before he strikes me.   At him ! my brave boys !
At him ! the recreant !   We have borne too much
In seeing his attempt.   Could not we cut
The cables ?
  Stamura.   Rare, rare sport for us !
  Consul.   Stamura !
If wise Minuzzi deems it feasible,
Ye shall enjoy the pastime, while the wind
Sits in this quarter, blowing from due-east
Hard into port : else must ye to the walls,   120
To meet full twenty thousand, well approved
In arms the most-part, all athirst for plunder.
  Minuzzi.   Where are they posted ?
  Consul.   At the battlements.
  Minuzzi.   Lads ! we must lose no time.
  Sailor.   Now let us see
Whether we too may not be mischievous
As they could wish us, this fine April morn.
  Minuzzi.   Each bring his hatchet.   Off ! and quickly
  back.   [*They go.*
    Father John *enters.*

One word, Sir Consul, ere we part, this one :   130
My wife sits nigh the old church porch, infirm

With many watchings ; thro' much love for me,
True-hearted ! should the waters wash me home,
Stiffen'd a little more than is convenient,
Let none displace her from that low stone seat.
Grant me my suit, unless I fail in duty.
    Consul (presses his hand).   And these are breasts despotic
      power would crush !
       [*Minuzzi going, meets* Father John, *who had listened.*
    Father John.   Talk ye of hatchets ?
    Consul.   Father John ! good day !
    F. John.   Yea, with God's blessing, we will make it so.
    Consul.   I want your counsel on a perilous move.   [140
Father ! you were a diver in time past.
    F. John.   And in time present may be one again.
    Minuzzi.   Ah ! could you join us in our enterprise !
    F. John.   What is it ?
    Minuzzi.   Why, to dive and cut the cables
Of yon Venetians dancing there so gaily,
And bowing in bright pennons to each other.
    F. John.   Is this the Doge's wedding-day with Adria ?
No dame in Venice ever played him falser   150
Than she will do, and haply before night.
Ye spoke of hatchet !   'Twould but do poor work
Against a cable.
    Stamura.   We can hold our breath
A good while on such business.
    Consul.   Father John,
Could you devise some fitter instrument ?
    Minuzzi.   Ah ! what inventions have not priests devised !
We all of us are what we are thro' them.
    F. John.   I love this reverence, my grey boy ! and aptly
Hast thou believed that Father John could frame   [160
What will perform the work, else difficult.
I thought of Turks and Saracens, and flags
Bearing the crescent, not the winged lion,
When I prepared my double-handed sickle
To reap the hemp-field that lies under water.
I will dive too, and teach you on the way
How ye shall manage it.   So fare you well,
Sir Consul !   [*To the* Man.

We have all the day before us   170
And not long work (tho' rather hard) to do.

ACT I.   SCENE III.

Consul *and* Erminia.

Consul.   Erminia ! read this letter.   Wait awhile . .
Repress thy curiosity . . First tell me,
Erminia ! would'st thou form some great alliance ?
   Erminia.   Yes, father ! who would not ?
   Consul.   I know that none
Hath won that little heart of thine at present.
   Erminia.   Many, many have won it, my dear father !
I never see one run across the street
To help a lame man up or guide a blind man
But *that* one wins it : never hear one speak   10
As all should speak of you, but up my arms
Fly ready to embrace him !
   Consul.   And when any
Says thou art beautiful, and says he loves thee,
What are they ready then for ?
   Erminia.   Not to beat him
Certainly : but none ever said such things.
They look at me because I am your daughter,
And I am glad they look at me for that,
And always smile, tho' some look very grave.   20
   Consul.   Well now, Erminia, should his Holiness
The Pope have sent his nephew with this letter,
Would you receive him willingly ?
   Erminia.   Most willingly.
   Consul.   Nay, that is scarcely maidenly, so soon.
   Erminia.   I would not if you disapprove of it.
   Consul.   I do suspect he came aboard the galleys.
   Erminia.   O then, the galleys are not enemies.
   Consul.   Not if thou givest him thy hand.   What say'st
      thou ?
   Erminia.   I never saw him.   30

Consul. But suppose him handsome.
Indeed I hear much of his comeliness.
   Erminia. Is that enough ?
   Consul. And virtues.
   Erminia. That alone
Is not enough, tho' very, very much.
He must be handsome too, he must be brave,
He must have seen me often, and must love me,
Before I love or think of him as lover :
For, father, you are not a king, you know,   40
Nor I a princess : so that all these qualities
(Unless you will it otherwise) are necessary.
   Consul. Thou art grown thoughtful suddenly, and prudent.
   Erminia. Do not such things require both thought and
      prudence ?
   Consul. In most they come but slowly ; and this ground
Is that where we most stumble on. The wise
Espouse the foolish ; and the fool bears off
From the top branch the guerdon of the wise :
Ay, the clear-sighted (in all other things)
Cast down their eyes and follow their own will,   50
Taking the hand of idiots. They well know
They shall repent, but find the road so pleasant
That leads into repentance.
   Erminia. Ah, poor souls !
They must have lost their fathers : then what wonder
That they have lost their way !
   Consul. Now, in few words,
Erminia, for time presses, let me tell thee,
The Pope will succour us against our foe
If I accept his nephew for a son.   60
   Erminia. O father ! does that make our cause more
      righteous ?
Or more unrighteous theirs who persecute us ?
   Consul. No, child : but wilt thou hear him ? Rank and
      riches
Will then be thine. Altho' not born a princess,
Thou wilt become one.
   Erminia. I am more already ;

I am your daughter ; yours, whom not one voice
Raised over all, but thousands.
   Consul.   I resign
My station in few days.   70
   Erminia.   O stay in it
Until the enemy is beaten back,
That I may talk of it when I am old,
And, when I weep to think of you, may dry
My tears, and say, *My father then was Consul.*
   Consul.   The power may be prolonged until my death.
   Erminia.   O no : the laws forbid it : do they not ?
   Consul.   He who can make and unmake every law,
Divine and human, will uphold my state
So long, acknowledging his power supreme ;   80
And laying the city's keys before his feet.
   Erminia.   Hath he not Peter's ? What can he want
      more ?
O father ! think again ! I am a child
Almost, and have not yet had time enough
Quite to unlearn the lessons you enforced
By precept and example.   Bear with me !
I have made you unhappy many times,
You never made me so until this hour :
Bear with me, O my father !
   Consul.   To my arms,   90
Erminia ! Thou hast read within my breast
Thy lesson backward, not suspecting guile.
Yes, I was guileful. I would try thy nature :
I find it what is rarely found in woman,
In man as rarely. The Venetian fleet
Would side with us ; their towers, their catapults
Would all be ours, and the Pope's nephew thine,
Would but thy father place the power supreme
Within his hands, becoming his vicegerent.
I turn aside from fraud, and see how force   100
May best be met, in parley with the German.

ACT I.   SCENE IV.

THE ENCAMPMENT AND TENT OF THE ARCHBISHOP UNDER THE WALLS.

Consul *and* Archbishop.

Archbishop.   I do presume from your habiliments
You are the consul of this petty state.
  Consul.   I am.
  Archbishop.   You may be seated.   Once again . .
Will you surrender unconditionally?
  Consul.   Nor unconditionally nor conditionally.
  Archbishop.   I sent for you to point where lies your duty.
  Consul.   It lies where I have left it, in the town.
  Archbishop.   You doubt my clemency.
  Consul.   Say rather ' *honour.* '   10
  Archbishop.   Doubt you a soldier's honour?
  Consul.   Not a soldier's.
But when the soldier and the priest unite,
Well may I doubt it.   Goats are harmless brutes;
Dragons may be avoided; but when goat
And dragon form one creature, we abhor
The flames and coilings of the fell chimæra.
  Archbishop.   And therefore you refused a conference
Unless I pitch my tent beneath your walls,
Within an arrow's shot, distributing   20
Ten archers on each side; ten mine, ten yours?
  Consul.   No doctor of divinity in Paris
Is cleverer at divining.   Thus it stands.
  Archbishop.   Ill brook I such affronts.
  Consul.   Ill brook, perhaps,
Florence and Pisa their ambassadors
Invited to a conference on peace,
And cast in prison.
  Archbishop.   Thus we teach the proud
Their duty.   30
  Consul.   Let the lame man teach the lame
To walk, the blind man teach the blind to see.

Archbishop.   Insolent !   Unbecoming of my station
Were it to argue with a churl so rude.
Rise : look before you thro' the tent : what see you ?
  Consul.   I see huge masses of green corn upheaved
Within a belt of palisades.
  Archbishop.   What else ?
  Consul.   Sheep, oxen, horses, trampling them.
  Archbishop.   No more?   40
  Consul.   Other huge masses farther off are smoking,
Because their juices quench the faggot-fire.
  Archbishop.   And whence come these ?
  Consul.   From yonder houseless fields,
Of crops, and even of boundaries, bereft.
  Archbishop.   Whose were they?
  Consul.   Whose? The church's, past a doubt :
It never takes what is not freely given.
  Archbishop.   Proud rebels! you have brought upon your
      heads
This signal vengeance from offended Cæsar.   50
  Consul.   And must ten thousand starve because one man
Is wounded in that part which better men
Cut from them, as ill-sorted with our nature ?
If Satan could have dropt it, he were saved.
  Archbishop.   What meanest thou ?   What cast they from
      them ?
  Consul.   Pride.
It clings round little breasts and masters them,
It drops from loftier, spurn'd and trodden down.
Is this, my lord archbishop, this your Eden ?
Is this the sacrifice of grateful herbs   60
Ye offer to your Gods?   And will the next
Be more acceptable ?   Burnt-offerings raised
In your high places, and fossed round with blood !
  Archbishop.   Blasphemer ! I am here no priest ; I come
Avenger of insulted majesty.
But, if thou mindest Holy Writ, mind this,
The plainest thing, and worthiest of remembrance : . .
Render to Cæsar what is Cæsar's, man !
  Consul.   God will do that for us.   Nought owe we Cæsar

But what he sent us when he sent you hither, 70
To cut our rising wheat, our bleeding vines,
To burn our olives for your wild carousals . .
   Archbishop. The only wood that will burn green : it blazes
Most beautifully, and no smell from it.
But you Anconites have poor olive grounds,
We shall want more by Sunday.
   Consul. May the curse
Of God be on you !
   Archbishop. We are not so impious :
It *is* on you : it were a sin to wish it. 80
   Consul. Prince and archbishop ! there are woes that fall
Far short of curses, though sore chastisements ;
Prosperities there are that hit the mark,
And the clear-sighted see God's anger there.
   Archbishop. Are *we* constrain'd to drag and vex the sea
And harrow up the barren rocks below
For noisome weeds ? Are household animals
Struck off the knee to furnish our repast ?
   Consul. Better endure than cause men this endurance.
   Archbishop. Clearly ye think so : we think otherwise. 90
'Tis better to chastise than be chastised,
To be the judge than be the criminal.
   Consul. How oft, when crimes are high enough to strike
The front of Heaven, are those two characters
Blended in one !
   Archbishop. I am not to be school'd
By insolence and audacity.
   Consul. *We* are,
It seems : but fortitude and trust in God
Will triumph yet. Our conference is closed. 100

ACT II. SCENE I.

AT THE RAMPARTS.

Angelica, Stamura, *and* Soldiers.

   Angelica. See ye those towers that stride against the walls ?
   Soldier. See you this arrow ? Few were not more fatal

That flew from them : but this arrests my arm
Perhaps beyond to-morrow.
    Angelica (to others).   Fight amain.
    Soldier.   The widow of Stamura is below,
And, slender tho' her figure, fair her face,
Brave as her husband. Few her words : beware
Of falling back, lest they increase and shame us.
    Another Soldier.   Long live Stamura ! She hath crost
    already   10
The sallyport.
    Another Soldier.   What held she in her hand ?
    Another Soldier.   A distaff.
    Soldier.   Hush ! what cries are those ?
    Another Soldier.   All German.
    Soldier.   What dust is overhead ?
    Another Soldier.   Is not it smoke ?
Hurrah ! flames mount above the battlements.
    Soldier.   It was her deed.
    Another Soldier.   But whose those cries behind us,
Along the harbour ?   [20
    Soldier.   Those all are Italian.
    Another Soldier.   Look ! How yon tower curls outward,
    red and reeling !
    Soldier.   Ay ; it leans forward as in mortal pain.
    Another Soldier.   What are those things that drop ?
    Soldier.   Men, while we speak,
Another moment, nothing.
    Another Soldier.   Some leap down ;
Others would keep their desperate grasp : the fire
Loosens it ; and they fall like shrivell'd grapes   30
Which none will gather. See it, while you can ;
It totters, parts, sinks. What a crash ! The sparks
Will blind our archers.
    Another Soldier.   What a storm of fire !

ACT II.   SCENE II.

THE CONSUL'S HOUSE.

CONSUL, ERMINIA.

Erminia.   The men you spoke with in the port have pass'd
The window, and seem entering.
   Consul.   Friends, come in.
   Minuzzi (entering with STAMURA *and others).*
Sir Consul! we are here inopportunely,
Our work is done : God prosper'd it.   Young lady!
We come no feasters at a consul's board.
   Consul.   Erminia ! coverest thou our scanty fare
Because 'tis scanty, and not over-nice?
Child ! thou hast eaten nothing.
   Erminia.   Quite enough.   10
   Consul.   No wonder thou hast lost thy appetite,
And sighest.
   Erminia.   I am sure I did not sigh ;
Nor have I lost my appetite.
   Consul.   Then eat :
Take off the napkin.
   Erminia.   Father ! you well know
What is beneath it.
   Consul.   Half a cake.
   Erminia.   Of beans,   20
Of rye, of barley, swept from off the manger :
My little horse had eaten them ere now,
But . .
   Consul.   The child weeps.   Even such flesh must serve.
Heaven grant us even this a few days hence.
   Erminia (to STAMURA).   Signor Antonio ! do not look
     at me,
I pray you, thinking of my greediness ;
Eat, eat ! I kept it . . If the sea's fresh air
Makes hungry those who sail upon it, surely
It must . . after such toil . .   30

Stamura.   Such toil 'twas not.
Erminia.   Father! could you persuade him?
Stamura.   Pray excuse me!
I want no food.
Consul.   Take what there is, and wine,
Wine we have still in plenty, old and strong.
Stamura.   Grant me this one half-beaker.
Erminia.   Let me run
And rinse it well.
Stamura.   Forbear! forbear!   40
Consul.   We have
No man or maiden in the house; they all
Fight or assist the fighting.
Erminia.   He has taken
And drank it every drop! Poor, poor Antonio!
O how he must have thirsted!

          [*To* Stamura.
       'Twas half water.

Stamura.   It was not very strong.
Minuzzi.   And yet the colour
Mounts to his eyes as 'twere sheer wine of Crete.   50
Consul.   I am impatient (you must pardon me)
To hear what you have done. Pour out the wine,
Erminia! that can cause but short delay.
    [*They drink, all but* Stamura. *Cries in the street,*
       " Long live Stamura! *"*
Stamura.   Call they me? why me?
    [*Cries again. " Long live the brave* Angelica.*"*
Stamura.   My mother!
Minuzzi.   Now for the wine! The boy will faint.
Angelica.   Help! father!
Officer.   Sir! saw you not the flames along the sky?
Has no one told you how that noble lady
Burnt down the tower with all its galleries,   60
Down to the very wheels?
Stamura.   Who minds the tower?
Sir! is she safe? unhurt?
Officer.   Sir! the ram's head,
Blacken'd with smoke, lean'd prone against the wall,

Then seem'd to shudder as 'twere half-alive.
Then fell the iron mass.   It made no sound
Among the ashes.   Had it made a loud one
There were much louder from the wretches crusht
Beneath it and its tower; some tearing off   70
Their burning armour agonised with pain,
And others pierced with red-hot nails that held
The rafters; others holding up their arms
Against the pitch and sulphur that pour'd down.
It was a sight!   Well might it have detain'd,
Those who beheld it, from their duty here.
Up flew, not sparks alone, but splinters huge,
Crackling against the battlements, and drove
More men away than all their arrows could.
   Stamura.   Sir Consul!   I must warm myself with fighting 80
After this dip.   [*Aside.*
             Nor see my mother first?
She would be first to blame me if I did.   [*Goes.*
  Consul.   God prosper thee, brave youth, God prosper thee!
  Erminia (aside).   Discourteous man!   he said no word
    to me!
He even forgot my father.

          FATHER JOHN *enters.*

  Minuzzi.   Here comes one
Who can relate to you the whole exploit
Better than we.
  Father John.   Where is Antonio?   90
  Minuzzi.   Gone
This instant.   How was it ye did not meet?
  Father John.   Ha!   I am this time caught in my own net.
I knew the knave would run away at seeing me;
He told me if I came he would be gone,
Fearing to hear my story.   So, sir Consul,
I stole in softly through the stable-door.
I can not keep my breath beneath the surface
So long as boys can.   They are slenderer,
Less buoyant too, mayhap.   Oft as I rose   100
    VOL. I.   T

My pilot-fish was with me; that Stamura
Would never leave me.
    Erminia.   Father John! your blessing.
You always used to give it me.
    Father John.   There, take it.
How the girl kisses my rough hand to-day!   [*Aside.*
Forgetful, heedless, reckless of himself
He held a shapeless shield of cork before me,
Wherefrom a silent shower of arrows fell
From every galley, amid shouts like hunters'   110
As they caught sight of us.   The bright steel points
Rebounding (for not one of them bit through)
Glistened a moment as they clove the water,
Then delved into the uneven furrow'd sands.
Surely the lustrous and unclosing eyes
Of well-poised fishes have enjoy'd to-day
A rarity; they never saw before
So many feathers sticking all upright
Under the brine so many fathoms deep.
    Consul.   Father! your gaiety will never fail you.   120
    Father John.   Not while it pleases God to use my arm
Or wits, such as they are, to serve my country.
But this I tell you: had the boy been less
Assiduous, or less brave, the fish had seen
Another sight they oftener see, and then
No Father John had blest that maiden more.
    Minuzzi.   Stamura saved our country, saving you.
    Father John.   And you too, both of you, did well your duty.
    Minuzzi.   Aground are five good galleys, and their crews
Await your mercy.   130
    Father John.   Did Stamura bring
His captive, that spruce Roman-spoken gallant?
    Consul.   He brought none hither.
    Minuzzi.   Now our tale is told,
A little fighting will assuage the toil
And cold of diving.   Brave Stamura toss'd
The net above his forehead fifty times
And drew it off and shoved it back again,
Impatient for his mother.   He will knead

(I trow) a pasty German ere he see her ; 140
We too may lend a hand.   Come, Father John !
Shrive as if we should need it.
   Consul.   Fare ye well.
Thank God ! I am not rich ; but this one day,
My friends, I would be richer, to reward you.
The ships are yours : let none else claim one plank.

ACT II.   SCENE III.

THE QUAY.

PEOPLE. STAMURA.

   Stamura.   Stand off ! The stores within the barks belong
Alike and equally to all.   Much grain
Will there be spilt unless a steady hand
Conveys it, and divides it house by house.
Horses no fewer than three score are dragged
Within the gates, from the last charge against us :
What would ye ?   Wait another charge, and take it.
   People.   Brave, brave Antonio !

ACT II.   SCENE IV.

ARCHBISHOP'S TENT.

ARCHBISHOP.   *The Brothers* COSTANZIO *and* CORRADO.

   Archbishop.   Could ye not wait for death within the walls,
But must rush out to meet it ?
   Costanzio.   We could wait
As others do.
   Corrado.   And fight we could as others.
   Archbishop.   Costanzio and Corrado ! I am grieved
That you should war against your lawful prince,
Your father being most loyal.
   Costanzio.   So are we.
   Archbishop.   What ! when he serves the emperor and king,
And you the rabble ? [10

Corrado.   Who made men the rabble ?
Archbishop.   Will not your treason and your death afflict
him ?
Costanzio.   Our treason would : God grant our death may
not.
Corrado.   We never took the oaths that he has taken,
And owe no duty but to our own land.
Archbishop.   Are ye Anconites ?   .
Corrado.   No, sir, but Italians,
And in Ancona lies the cause of Italy.
Archbishop.   Pernicious dreams !   These drive young men
astray ;   20
But when they once take their own cause, instead
Of ours who could direct them, they are lost :
So will ye find it.   As ye were not born
In this vile city, what, pray, could have urged you
To throw your fortunes into it when sinking ?
Costanzio.   Because we saw it sinking.
Corrado.   While it prosper'd
It needed no such feeble aid as ours.
Marquises, princes, kings, popes, emperors,
Courted it then : and you, my lord archbishop,   30
Would have it even in its last decay.
Archbishop.   There is a spirit in the land, a spirit
So pestilential that the fire of heaven
Alone can purify it.
Costanzio.   Things being so,
Let us return and die with those we fought for.
Archbishop.   Captious young man !   Ye die the death of
traitors.
Corrado.   Alas ! how many better men have died
That death ! alas, how many must hereafter !
Archbishop.   By following your example.   Think of that ;
Be that your torture.   [40
Costanzio.   As we never grieved
At following our betters, grant, just Heaven !
That neither may our betters ever grieve
At following us, be the time soon or late.   [*To the* Guards.
Archbishop.   Lead off these youths.   Separate them.

Corrado.   My lord !
We are too weak (you see it) for resistance ;
Let us then, we beseech you, be together
In what is left of life !   50
  Archbishop.   One hour is left:
Hope not beyond.
  Corrado.   We did hope more ; we hoped
To be together, tho' but half the time.
  Archbishop.   It shall not be.
  Costanzio.   It shall be.
  Archbishop.   Art thou mad ?
I would not smile, but such pride forces me.
  Costanzio.   God, in whose holiest cause we took up arms,
Will reconcile us.   Doubt it not, Corrado,   60
Altho' such men as that man there have said it.

ACT II.   SCENE V.

CONSUL'S HOUSE.

STAMURA.   ERMINIA.

Stamura.   Lady ! you need not turn your face from me.
I leave the town for aid.   But one perhaps
May bring it, if you listen to him.
  Erminia.   Who ?
  Stamura.   I made a captive.
  Erminia.   So I hear.
  Stamura.   I come
Seeking the consul : he expected me.
  Erminia.   And *him ?*
  Stamura.   Him also.   10
  Erminia.   Know you what he asks ?
  Stamura.   I know it.
  Erminia.   And you wish it ? *you*, Stamura ?
  Stamura.   I have no voice in it.
  Erminia.   True. Go. I know it. [STAMURA *goes.*
Shameless ! to ask him !   Never did we meet
But, if his eye caught mine, he walk'd aside :

Yet, by some strange occurrence, we meet daily.

The Consul *enters.*

Consul.   Erminia! didst thou send away Stamura?
Erminia.   He went away: no need for me to send him.
Consul.   Knowest thou whom he made his captive?   [20
Erminia.   Yes:
That insolent young Roman.
Consul.   Speak not thus
Before thou seest him.
Erminia.   I will never see him.
Consul.   Nay, I have promised scarce five minutes since
That thou shalt hear him.
Erminia.   Has he then found favour
With you so suddenly?   30
Consul.   Stamura speaks
Much in his favour.
Erminia.   Are they friends already?
Consul.   Hardly; we must suppose.   But here they come.

Stamura.   Clovio.   Consul.   Erminia.

Clovio.   Sir Consul! I am Clovio Fizzarelli.
Have you received the letter?
Consul.   I received it.
Clovio.   On bended knee permit me to salute
The lady who shall rule my destiny,
Your fair Erminia.   40
Erminia.   You are the Pope's nephew,
Sir Clovio! I have heard; and you come hither
Most strongly recommended.
Clovio.   True, sweet lady!
But I do trust, with all humility,
There may be a mere trifle in myself,
Not to engage you in the first half-hour,
But so to plead for me, that in a day
Or two, or three at farthest . .
Erminia.   Sir, your pleader   50
Stands there; you are his captive, and not mine.
Clovio.   He knows me well.   He threw my whole boat's
        crew

(Four of them) overboard, but found his match
In me.
    Erminia.   It seems so : does it not, Antonio ?
    Stamura.   More ; how much more !
    Clovio.   There !   He could not deny it.
    Erminia.   And now he has persuaded my kind father
To grant you audience.
    Clovio (to STAMURA).   She is proud : I'll tame her.   60
    Stamura (angrily).   Sir !   [*Aside.*
                    No : he is my prisoner and my guest.
    Erminia.   This gentleman, who is so confidential
With you, and whom you whisper to for counsel,
May give my hand away . . and will most gladly,
I doubt not . . for my father can refuse
Nothing to one who made so great a prize,
Beside the preservation of the city.
    Clovio.   Speak then, my worthy friend, if thus the consul
Honours your valour ; speak for me ; and let me   70
Who owe my life, owe more than life to you.
    Stamura.   The consul knows what suits his honour best,
And the young lady seems not ill disposed
To shower his favour on such high desert.
I have my duties ; but this is not one.
Let the young lady give her hand herself.
If I had any wish . . but I have none . .
It should be, Sir, that you had won it first
By a brave action or a well-tried love.
But, what is love ?   My road lies towards the walls.   80
                        [*To the* CONSUL.
With your permission, Sir !   I have yours, lady !
                        [STAMURA *goes.*
    Erminia.   Father ! I am unwell. This gentleman
Comes unexpectedly, demands abruptly . .
    Clovio.   Impatiently, but not abruptly.
    Erminia.   Sir !
I will not marry : never, never, never.
                        [ERMINIA *goes.*
    Clovio.   Ha ! ha ! all women are alike, Sir Cousul.
Leave her to me.

   Consul.   Sir Clovio Fizzarelli !
I will do more than what you ask of me.   90
I grant you freedom.   Go aboard the pinnace
Which bore you into port ; and say at Rome
That you have seen men starving in the streets,
Because his Holiness refused us help
Unless a father gave a daughter up ;
And say the daughter would not sell her heart,
Much less her country ; and then add, Sir Clovio,
(O were it true !) " All women are alike."

ACT III. SCENE I.

EPISCOPAL PALACE.

BISHOP *of* ANCONA *and* FATHER JOHN.

   Bishop.   I have been standing at my terrace-wall
And counting those who pass and cry with hunger.
Brother ! the stoutest men are grown effeminate ;
Nay, worse ; they stamp and swear, even in my presence,
And looking up at me.
   Father John.   Sad times indeed !
   Bishop.   I calculate that giving each an ounce
Only one day, scarce would a sack remain
In my whole garner ; I am so reduced.
   Father John.   I come to beg your lordship for one ounce
Of your fine flour, to save a child ; to save   [10
A mother, who loathes ordinary food . .
Not ordinary, but most bitter lupin :
She has no other in the house.
   Bishop.   No other ?
Poor soul !   This famine is a dreadful thing !
Pestilence always follows it !   God help us !
I tremble ; I start up in sleep.
   Father John.   My lord !
An ounce of meal, a single ounce, might calm   20
These tremblings, well applied.   The nurse that should be

Can be no nurse : the mother very soon
Will be no mother, and the child no child.
   Bishop.   You know not how things stand, good brother
     John !
This very morning, as I hope for grace,
I paid three golden pieces for the head,
Think you, of what ? an ass !
   Father John (aside).   The cannibal !
            [*To the* Bishop.]
Ah, my good lord ! they bear high prices now.
   Bishop.   Why, brother ! you yourself are grown much
     thinner.   30
How can you do your duty ?
   Father John.   Were I not
Much thinner, I should think I had not done it.
   Bishop.   My cook assures me that with wine and spice
Elicampane, cumin, angelica,
Garlic, and sundry savoury herbs, stored by
Most providentially, the Lord be praised !
He can make that strange head quite tolerable . .
The creature was a young one . . what think you ?
   Father John.   They are more tolerable than the old.   40
   Bishop.   The sellers take advantage of bad times,
Quite without conscience, shame, respect for persons,
Or fear of God. What can such men expect ?
You must have seen sad sights about our city :
I wonder you are what you are.
   Father John.   Sad sights
Indeed !
   Bishop.   But all will give their confessor
Part of their pittance ; and the nearer death
The readier ; knowing what the church can do.   50
Tell me now, for my entrails yearn to hear it,
Do they not take due care of you ?
   Father John.   No meals
Have now their stated hour. Unwillingly
I enter houses where the family
Sits round the table at the spare repast.
Sometimes they run and hide it.

   Bishop.   Most unmannerly !
Inhuman, I would add unchristianlike.
   Father John.   Sometimes they push toward me the un-
     tasted   60
And uninviting food, look wistfully,
Press me ; yet dread acceptance.   Yesterday
A little girl, the youngest of the five,
Was raising to her lips a mealy bean
(I saw no other on the unsoil'd plate)
And, looking at my eyes fixt hard on hers,
And thinking they were fixt upon the morsel,
Pusht it between my lips, and ran away.
   Bishop.   Brother ! I should have call'd her a good child ;
I should myself have given the benediction   70
With my own hand, and placed it on her head :
I wonder you don't praise her.   Brother John !
I have my nones to run thro' ; so, good-by.
   Father John.   Just God ! does this house stand ?   Dark
     are thy ways,
Inscrutable !   Be thy right hand our guide !

ACT III.   SCENE II.

SENATE-HOUSE.

SENATORS.   CONSUL.

   Consul.   Senators ! ye have call'd me to debate
On our condition.
   Senator.   Consul ! we are lost.
   Consul.   All are who think so.
   Second Senator.   Even the best want food.
   Consul.   The bravest do.
   Third Senator.   How shall men fight without it ?
   Fourth Senator.   Concord and peace might have return'd.
   Consul.   By yielding,
Think ye ?   Not they : contempt and sorrow might.   10
Can there be ever concord (peace there may be)

Between the German and Italian ?   None.
Remember how that ancient city fell,
Milano.   Seven whole years resisted she
The imperial sword : she listened to conditions
And fell.   The soldiers of His Majesty . .
His soldiers, ay, his very court . . shed tears
At such affliction, at such utter ruin,
At such wide wails, such universal woe.
They all were equal then ; for all were slaves,   20
Scatter'd, the poor, the rich, the brave, the coward,
Thro' Bergamo, Pavia, Lodi, Como,
The cities of the enemy.   There stood
No vestige of the walls, no church to pray in . .
And what was left to pray for ?   What but Cæsar ?
Throw rather all your wealth into the sea
Than let the robber priest lay hold upon it,
And, if ye die of famine, die at least
In your own houses while they *are* your own.
But there are many yet whose hearts and arms   30
Will save you all : to-day you all can fight,
The enemy shall feed you all to-morrow.
Were it no shame a priest should seize the prey
That kings and emperors dropt with broken talon ?
The eagle flew before your shouts ; and now
A vulture must swoop down ! but vultures keep
From living men and from warm blood ; they revel
(And most the Roman vulture) in corruption.
Have ye forgotten how your fathers fought,
When Totila with Goths invincible   40
Besieged you ; not with priests and choristers ;
When twenty-seven ships assail'd your port
And when eleven only ever left it ?
Rome fell before him twice ; not once Ancona.
Your fathers saved the city . . ye shall save her.
  Senator.   Weapons are insufficient ; courage, vows,
Avail not.   We are unprepared for war :
Scanty was our last harvest : and these winds
Are adverse.   They know that who now defy us,
Blockading us alike by sea and land.   50

Consul.   We some are poor, we some are prosperous,
We all alike owe all we have : the air
Is life alike to all, the sun is warmth,
The earth, its fruits and flocks, are nutriment,
Children and wives are comforts ; all partake
(Or may partake) in these.   Shall hoarded grain
Or gold be less in common, when the arms
That guard it are not those that piled it up,
But those that shrink without it ?   Come, ye rich,
Be richer still : strengthen your brave defenders,   60
And make all yours that was not yours before.
Dares one be affluent where ten thousand starve ?
Open your treasuries, your granaries,
But throw mine open first.   Another year
Will roughen this equality again,
The rich be what they were ; the poor . . alas !
What they were too perhaps . . but every man
More happy, each one having done his duty.
    Senator (to another).   Hark ! the young fools applaud !
      they rise around ;
They hem him in ; they seize and kiss his hand ;   70
He shakes our best supporters.
    Another.   Give the sign.
To those without.

[PEOPLE enter.]

    Consul.   Who called you hither ?   [*Various voices.*
    First.   Want.
    Second.   Famine.
    Third.   Our families.
    Fourth.   I had three sons ;
One hath been slain, one wounded.
    Fifth.   Only one   80
Had I : my loss is greatest.
    Sixth.   Grant us peace.
Sir Consul, peace we plead for, only peace.
    Consul.   Will peace bring back the dead ? will peace restore
Lost honour ? will peace heal the wounds your sons
And brothers writhe with ?   They who gave those wounds

Shall carry home severer, if they live,
And never in my consulate shall laugh
At those brave men whom men less brave desert.
True, some have fallen : but before they fell　　　90
They won the field ; nor now can earthly power
Take from their cold clencht hands the spoil they grasp ;
No mortal spoil, but glory.　Life, my sons,
Life may lose all : the seal that none can break
Hath stampt their names, all registered above.
　　Senator (*to a* Man *near*).　Speak ; you poor fool ! speak
　　　loudly, or expect
From me no favour . . and tell that man next.
　　Man.　Oh ! we are starving.
　　Consul.　　　　　　　　Better starve than serve.
　　Another.　He has no pity.　　　　　　　100
　　Consul.　　　　　　　What is that I hear ?
I have no pity.　Have I not a daughter ?
　　Another.　O what a daughter !　How compassionate !
How charitable !　Had she been born poor
She could not more have pitied poverty.
　　Consul.　Two ounces of coarse bread, wine, which she
　　　loathes,
And nothing more, sustain her.
　　Another.　　　　　　God sustains her ;
He will not leave his fairest work to perish.
　　Consul.　Fight then, fight bravely, while ye can, my
　　　friends !　　　　　　　　　110
In God have confidence, if none in me.
[*Shouts of applause.　Part of the* People *leave the* Senators.]
　　Senator (*to another*).　Seducer of the people ! shall it end
Thus vilely ?　　　　　[*To the* Consul.]
　　　　　　You have stores at home, Sir Consul !
You have wide lands.
　　Another Senator.　You should support your order.
　　Consul.　My order ! God made one ; of that am I.
Stores, it appears, I have at home ; wide lands ;
Are those at home too ? or within my reach ?
Paternal lands I do inherit ; wide
They are enough, but stony, mountainous,　　　120

The greater part unprofitable.
   Senator.   Some
The richest in rich wine.
   Consul.   Few days ago
Nearly a hundred barrels were unbroached.
   Another Senator.   A hundred loaves, tho' small indeed and
      dry,
Would they be worth in such distress as ours.
We could raise half among us.
   Consul.   Shame upon you !
Had not your unwise laws and unfair thrift   130
Prohibited the entrance of supplies
While they *could* enter, never had this famine
Stalked through the people.
   Senator.   But the laws are laws.
   Consul.   Yours ; never theirs.
   Another Senator.   Why thus inflame the people ?
   Consul.   Who brought the people hither ? for what end ?
To serve you in your avarice ; to cry *peace !*
Not knowing peace from servitude.
   Senator.   For quiet,   140
Spare them at least a portion of the wine.
   Consul.   Nor them nor you ; nor price nor force shall gain it.
   People.   Are we to perish ?   Hunger if we must,
Let us be strengthen'd by a draught of wine
To bear it on.
   Senator.   Wine is the oil of life,
And the lamp burns with it which else were spent.
   People.   Sir Consul ! we forbear ; we honour you,
But tell us, ere we sink, where one flask lies.
   Consul.   Go ask the women labouring of child,   150
Ask those who nurse their infants, ask the old,
Who can not fight, ask those who fought the best,
The wounded, maim'd, disabled, the Anconites.
Sirs ! if ye find one flask within our cellar,
Crack it, and throw the fragments in my face.
   People.   Let us away.   [*Shouts of applause.*
   Consul.   Follow me to the walls ;
And you, too, senators, learn there your duty.

People.   We swear to do our best.
Consul.   Sworn wisely ! Life   160
Is now more surely to be won by arms
Than death is, and the sword alone can win it.
I lead the way ; let who will lag behind.

ACT III.   SCENE III.

THE CITY.

PAOLUCCI, Officers, Citizens.

Officer.   The Consul has been wounded.   Who is left
To lead us ? and what leader would suffice ?
The strongest sink with famine, lying down
Along the battlements, and only raised
When sounds the trumpet.
    First Citizen.   And most fall again.
    Second Citizen.   Our day is come, the day of our disgrace.
    Paolucci.   Ours never was that day, and never shall be.
Ye may have lost your consul (let us hope
He is not lost to us) but we are sure   10
His memory and example yet remain
With all their life in them.
        [*To the* People.]
                                Young men ! perhaps
Ye know me not : your fathers knew me well ;
Their fathers better.   Three-score years ago
I was your consul : none then preached surrender ;
And let none now : yet there were those around
Who would have pinfolded the quiet flock
As gladly as yon shepherd at the gate.
    People.   We can resist no longer.   Who can count   20
The slain ?
    Paolucci.   Say, rather, who can praise the slain ?
Glorified souls ! happy your sleep ! ye hear
No shameful speech from brethren !
    People.   Arms alone
Should not subdue us : famine has : we starve.

Paolucci.   While life remains life's sufferings will arise,
Whether from famine or from sharper sting
Than famine : upon every hearth almost
There creeps some scorpion never seen till felt.   30
But until every arm that guards our walls
Drop helpless at the starting ribs, until
That hour, stand all united.   Ye despair
Untimely.   He who rules us rules us well,
Exciting no false hope, as bad men do
When they have led where none can extricate.
I was your consul while the king Lothaire
Besieged the city, proud as any prelate,
Swearing he would reduce it.   Other kings
Have sworn the same . . and kept their word like kings . . 40
Cursing and flying.   We have met brave foes ;
But they met braver.   Fly ; and let the crook
Drag a vile flock back from its flight to slaughter.
    All.   We scorn the thought.   But where lies human help ?
    Paolucci.   I may be spared to seek it, spared to try
If one brave man breathes yet among the powerful.
Who knows not Marchesella ?
    Officer.   Brave he is,
But mindful of the emperor.   He saw
Milano, which had stood two thousand years,   50
Sink ; * every tree, on hill or vale, cut down,
The vine, the olive, ripe and unripe corn
Burnt by this minister of God.   Throughout
There was no shade for sick men to die under,
There was no branch to strew upon the bier.
    Another Officer.   His father was courageous, why not he ?
    A third Officer.   Above all living men is Marchesella
Courageous : but pray what are our deserts
With him, that he should hazard for our sake
His lordly castles and his wide domains ?   60
Perhaps his fame in arms !   'Twere mad to hope it.
Prudence, we know, for ever guides his courage.
    Paolucci.   If generous pity dwells not in his house,

* Ancona was besieged 1162. 1174.

As once it did, with every other virtue,
Seek it, where brave men never seek in vain,
In woman's breast: away to Bertinoro:
Take heart: the countess is a Frangipani:
There are a thousand trumpets in that name:
Methinks I hear them blowing toward Ancona.
Old men talk long: but be not ye so idle: 70
Hie to the walls: I will sue her.   To arms!
To arms! the consul of past years commands you.

ACT III.   SCENE IV.

CONSUL'S HOUSE.

PAOLUCCI. CONSUL. ERMINIA.

Paolucci.   Consul! how fare you?
Consul.   Not amiss.
Paolucci.   But wounded?
Consul.   There was more blood than wound, they say who
    saw it.
Erminia.   My father, sir, slept well all night.
Paolucci.   All night
An angel watched him; he must needs sleep well.
  Consul.   I drove away that little fly in vain,
It flutter'd round the fruit whose skin was broken.
  Erminia.   Sweet father! talk not so; nor much at all. 10
  Paolucci.   Consul! I have not many days of life,
As you may see; and old men are in want
Of many little things which those in power
Can give: and 'twere amiss to hold them back
Because unclaim'd before.
  Consul.   I well remember,
Though then a child, how all this city praised
Your wisdom, zeal, and probity, when consul.
Ancona then was flourishing; but never
Were those compensated who served their country,   20
Except by serving her; 'twas thought enough;
We think so still. Beside, the treasury

Is emptied, that it may procure us food
And troops.   Be sure the very first that eats
The strangers' corn (if any reach our port)
Shall be no other than yourself: your age
And virtue merit from us this distinction.
   Paolucci.   Sir Consul! I want more than that.
   Consul.   Receive it
And welcome from the father and the man,   30
Not from the consul.   Now would you yourself
Act differently (I ask) on this occasion ?
   Paolucci.   More kindly, no ; but differently, yes.
   Consul.   What would you from me ?
   Paolucci.   High distinction, consul !
   Consul.   I will propose it, as I justly may,
And do regret it has been so deferred.
   Paolucci.   May I speak plainly what ambition prompts ?
   Consul.   I hear all claims.
   Paolucci.   Those sacks hold heavy sums.   40
   Consul.   Avarice was never yet imputed to you.
   Paolucci.   'Tis said you can not move them from the
     town.
   Consul.   Difficult, dangerous, doubtful, such attempt.
The young Stamura loves bold enterprises,
And may succeed where others would despair :
But, such the lack of all that life requires
Even for a day, I dare not send one loaf
Aboard his bark.   Hunger would urge the many
To rush and seize it.
   Paolucci.   They would not seize *me*.   50
One loaf there is at home : that boy shall share it.
   Erminia.   He would not, though he pined.
   Consul.   A youth so abstinent
I never knew.
   Paolucci.   But when we are afloat . .
   Consul.   We shall not be :
We think not of escape.
   Paolucci.   No : God forbid !
We will meet safety in the path of honour.
   Consul.   Why say *afloat* then ?   60

Paolucci.   Only he and I.
This is the guerdon I demand, the crown
Of my grey hairs.
    Erminia.   Alas! what aid could either
Afford the other?   O sir! do not go!
You are too old; he much too rash . . Dear father!
If you have power, if you have love, forbid it!
    Paolucci.   It was advised that younger ones should go:
Some were too daring, some were too despondent:
I am between these two extremes.   70
    Consul.   But think
Again!
    Paolucci.   I have no time for many thoughts,
And I have chosen out of them the best.
    Erminia.   He never will return! he goes to die!
I knew he would!
    Consul.   His days have been prolonged
Beyond the days of man: and there goes with him
One who sees every danger but his own.

ACT III.   SCENE V.

SEASIDE.   NIGHT.

PAOLUCCI, STAMURA.

Paolucci.   I feel the spray upon my face already.
Is the wind fair?
    Stamura.   'Tis fiercely fair.
    Paolucci.   The weather
Can not be foul then.
    Stamura (lifting him aboard).   Sit down here.   Don't
        tremble.
    Paolucci.   Then tell the breeze to wax a trifle warmer,
And lay thy hand upon those hissing waves.
She grates the gravel . . We are off at last.

ACT IV.   SCENE I.

CASTLE OF BERTINORO.

COUNTESS OF BERTINORO, MARCHESELLA, PAOLUCCI,
and STAMURA.

Page.   My lady! here are two such men as never
Enter'd a palace-gate.
   Countess.   Who are they?
   Page.   One
Older than anything I ever saw,
Alive or dead; the other a stout youth,
Guiding him, and commanding all around
To stand aside, and give that elder way;
At first with gentle words, and then with stern.
Coarse their habiliments, their beards unshorn,   10
Yet they insist on entrance to my lady.
   Countess.   Admit the elder, but exclude the other.
Wait.   [*To* MARCHESELLA.
       If the younger be his son, what little
Of service I may render to the father
Will scarce atone for keeping him apart.   [*To the* Page.
Go; bid them enter; both.
       [STAMURA, *having led* PAOLUCCI *in, retires.*
   Paolucci.   I come, O countess!
Imploring of your gentleness and pity,
To save from fire and sword, and, worse than either,   20
Worse, and more imminent, to save from famine
The few brave left, the many virtuous,
Virgins and mothers (save them!) in Ancona.
   Countess.   Nay, fall not at my knee. Age must not that . .
Raise him, good Marchesella!
   Paolucci.   You too, here,
Illustrious lord?
   Marchesella.   What! and art thou still living,
Paolucci? faithful, hospitable soul!
We have not met since childhood . . mine, I mean. .   30

Paolucci.   Smile not, my gentle lord! too gracious then,
Be now more gracious; not in looks or speech,
But in such deeds as you can best perform.
Friendship another time might plead for us;
Now bear we what our enemy would else
Seize from us, all the treasures of our city,
To throw them at your feet for instant aid.
Help, or we perish.   Famine has begun . .
Begun? has almost ended . . with Ancona.
    Countess.   Already?   We have been too dilatory.   40
    Marchesella.   I could not raise the money on my lands
Earlier; it now is come.   I want not yours:
Place it for safety in this castle-keep,
If such our lady's pleasure.
    Countess.   Until peace.
    Marchesella.   My troops are on the march.
    Countess.   And mine not yet?
Repose you, sir! they shall arrive with you,
Or sooner.   Is that modest youth your son?
    Paolucci.   Where is he? gone again?   50
    Countess.   When you first enter'd.
    Paolucci.   Some angel whisper'd your benign intent
Into his ear, else had he never left me.
My son?   Who would not proudly call him so?
Soon shall you hear what mother bore the boy,
And where he dash'd the galleys, while that mother
Fired their pine towers, already wheel'd against
Our walls, and gave us time . . for what? to perish.
    Marchesella.   No, by the saints above! not yet, not yet.
                            [*Trumpet sounds.*

    Countess.   Merenda is announced.   Sir, I entreat you 60
To lead me!   Grant one favour more; and hint not
To our young friend that we have learnt his prowess.
                            [*To a* Page.
Conduct the noble youth who waits without.

ACT IV.   SCENE II.

COUNTESS, MARCHESELLA, PAOLUCCI, STAMURA, *at Table.*

Countess (to Stamura).   Sir, there are seasons when 'tis incivility
To ask a name; 'twould now be more uncivil
To hesitate.
Stamura.   Antonio is my name.
Countess.   Baptismal.   Pray, the family?
Stamura.   Stamura;
But *that* my honour'd father gave in marriage
To her who wears it brighter day by day:
She calls me rather by the name he bore.
Countess.   It must be known and cherisht.   10
Stamura.   By the bravest
And most enduring in my native place;
It goes no farther: we are but just noble.
Countess.   He who could heed the tempest, and make serve
Unruly ocean, not for wealth, nor harm
To any but the spoiler, high above
That ocean, high above that tempest's wing,
He needs no turret to abut his name,
He needs no crescent to stream light on it,
Nor castellan, nor seneschal, nor herald.   20
Paolucci.   Ha! boy, those words make thy breast rise and fall,
Haply as much as did the waves.   The town
Could ill repay thee; Beauty overpays.
Countess.   Talk what the young should hear; nor see the meed
Of glorious deeds in transitory tints,
Fainter or brighter.
Paolucci.   I was wrong.
Countess.   Not quite:
For beauty, in thy native town, young man,
May feel her worth in recompensing thine.   30

Stamura (aside).   Alas! alas! she perishes! while here
We tarry.
  Paolucci (overhearing).   She?   Who perishes?
Stamura.   The town.
  Paolucci.   How the boy blushes at that noble praise!
  Countess.   They blush at glory who deserve it most.
. . Blushes soon go : the dawn alone is red.
  Stamura.   We know what duty, not what glory is.
The very best among us are not rich
Nor powerful.   40
  Countess.   Are they anywhere ?
  Paolucci.   His deeds,
If glorious in themselves, require no glory.
Even this siege, those sufferings, who shall heed ?
  Countess.   He gives most light by being not too high.
Remember by what weapon fell the chief
Of Philistines.   Did brazen chariots, driven
By giants, roll against him ?   From the brook,
Striking another such, another day,
A little pebble stretcht the enormous bulk   50
That would have fill'd it and have turn'd its course.
And in the great deliverers of mankind
Whom find ye ?   Those whom varlet pipers praise.
The greatest of them all, by all adored,
Did Babylon from brazen-belted gate,
Not humble straw-rooft Bethlehem, send forth ?
We must not be too serious.   Let us hear
How were the cables cut.
  Paolucci.   I saw the shears
That clipt them.   Father John, before he went,   60
Show'd me them, how they workt.   He himself held
The double crescent of sharp steel, in form
Like that swart insect's which you shake from fruit
About the kernel.   This enclaspt the cable ;
And too long handles (a stout youth, at each
Extremity, pushing with all his strength
Right forward) sunder'd it.   Then swiftly flew
One vessel to the shore ; and then another :
And hardly had the youths or Father John

Time to take breath upon the upper wave,　　　70
When down they sank again and there swang round
Another prow, and dasht upon the mole.
Then many blithe Venetians fell transfixt
With arrows, many sprang into the sea
And cried for mercy.　Upon deck appeared
The pope's own nephew, who ('tis said) had come
To arbitrate.　He leapt into a boat
Which swam aside, most gorgeously array'd,
And this young man leapt after him and seized him.
He, when he saw a dagger at his throat,　　　80
Bade all his crew, four well-built men, surrender.
　　Stamura.　They could not have feared *me* : they saw our
　　　archers.
　　Countess.　And where is now your prisoner ?
　　Stamura.　　　　　　　　　　　He desired
An audience of the consul.
　　Countess.　　　　　　　To what end ?
　　Stamura.　I know not : I believe to court his daughter.
　　Countess.　Is the girl handsome ?　Is that question harder
Than what I askt before ?　Will he succeed ?
　　Stamura.　Could he but save from famine our poor city,
And . . could he make her happy . .　　　　　[90
　　Countess.　　　　　　　　　　Pray go on.
It would delight you then to see him win her ?
　　Stamura.　O that I had not saved him ! or myself !
　　Countess.　She loves him then ?　And you hate foreigners.
I do believe you like the fair Erminia
Yourself.
　　Stamura.　She hates me.　Who likes those that hate him ?
　　Countess.　I never saw such hatred as you bear her :
If she bears you the like . .　　　　　　　100
　　Stamura.　　　　　　　　She can do now
No worse than what she has done.
　　Countess.　　　　　　　　　　Who knows that ?
I am resolved to see.
　　Stamura.　　　　　　O lady Countess !
How have I made an enemy of you ?
Place me the lowest of your band, but never

Affront her with the mention of my name.
When the great work which you have undertaken
Is done, admit me in your castle-walls,   110
And never let me see our own again.
   Countess.   I think I may accomplish what you wish;
But, recollect, I make no promises.

ACT IV.   SCENE III.

OPEN SPACE NEAR THE BALISTA GATE IN ANCONA.

The LADY MALASPINA, *her* Infant, *and a* Soldier.

   Soldier.   I am worn down with famine, and can live
But few hours more.
   L. Malaspina.   I have no food.
   Soldier.   Nor food
Could I now swallow. Bring me water, water!
   L. Malaspina.   Alas! I can not. Strive to gain the
     fountain.
   Soldier.   I have been nigh.
   L. Malaspina.   And could not reach it?
   Soldier.   Crowds
I might pierce through, but how thrust back their cries? 10
They madden'd me to flight ere half-way in.
Some upright . . no, none that . . but some unfallen,
Yet pressing down with their light weight the weaker.
The brows of some were bent down to their knees,
Others (the hair seized fast by those behind)
Lifted for the last time their eyes to heaven;
And there were waves of heads one moment's space
Seen, then unseen forever. Wails rose up
Half stifled underfoot, from children some,
And some from those who bore them.   20
   L. Malaspina.   Mercy! mercy!
O blessed Virgin! thou wert mother too!
How didst *thou* suffer! how did *He!* Save, save
At least the infants, if all else must perish.
Soldier! brave soldier! dost thou weep? then hope.

Soldier.   I suffer'd for myself; deserve I mercy?
L. Malaspina.   He who speaks thus shall find it. Try to
   rise.
Soldier.   No: could I reach the fountain in my thirst,
I would not.
L. Malaspina.   Life is sweet.   30
Soldier.   To brides, to mothers.
L. Malaspina.   Alas! how soon may those names pass
   away!
I would support thee partly, wert thou willing,
But my babe sleeps.
Soldier.   Sleep, little one, sleep on!
I shall sleep too as soundly, by and by.
L. Malaspina.   Courage, one effort more.
Soldier.   And tread on children!
On children clinging to my knees for strength
To help them on, and with enough yet left   40
To pull me down, but others pull down them.
God! let me bear this thirst, but never more
Bear this sad sight!   Tread on those tiny hands
Clasping the dust!   See those dim eyes upturn'd,
Those rigid lips reproachless!   Man may stir,
Woman may shake, my soul; but children, children!
O God! those are thine own! make haste to help them!
Happy that babe!
L. Malaspina.   Thou art humane.
Soldier.   'Tis said   50
That hunger is almost as bad as wealth
To make men selfish; but such feebleness
Comes over me, all things look dim around,
And life most dim, and least worth looking after.
L. Malaspina.   I pity thee.   Day after day myself
Have lived on things unmeet for sustenance.
My milk is failing . . Rise . .
               (*To the* Child) My little one!
God will feed *thee!*   Be sleep thy nourisher
Until his mercies strengthen me afresh!   60
Sink not: take heart: advance: Here, where from heaven
The Virgin-mother can alone behold us,

Draw some few drops.   [*The tocsin sounds.*
 Soldier.   Ha! my ears boom thro' faintness.
What sounds?
 L. Malaspina.   The bell.
 Soldier.   Then they are at the gate . .
I can but thank you . . Give me force, O Heaven!
For this last fight! . . and keep from harm these twain!

MALASPINA *and* Child *alone.*

 L. Malaspina.   And still thou sleepest, my sweet babe!
   Is death   70
Like sleep?   Ah, who then, who would fear to die?
How beautiful is all serenity!
Sleep, a child's sleep, O how far more serene,
And O, how far more beautiful than any!
Whether we breathe so gently or breathe not,
Slight is the difference.   But the pangs, the rage
Of famine who can bear? . . unless to raise
Her child above it!

(*Two* Priests *are passing.*)

 First Priest.   Who sits yonder? bent
O'er her dead babe? as many do within   80
Their houses!
 Second Priest.   Surely, surely, it must be
She who, not many days ago, was praised
For beauty, purity, humility,
Above the noblest of Anconite dames.
 First Priest.   The Lady Malaspina?
 Second Priest   But methinks
The babe is not dead yet.
 First Priest.   Why think you so?
 Second Priest.   Because she weeps not over it.   90
 First Priest.   For *that*
I think it dead.   It then could pierce no more
Her tender heart with its sad sobs and cries.
But let us hasten from the place to give
The dying their last bread, the only bread
Yet unconsumed, the blessed eucharist.
Even this little, now so many die,

May soon be wanting.
 Second Priest.   God will never let
That greater woe befall us.   *[The* Priests *go.*
 Malaspina.   Who runs hither? [100
        [The Soldier *falls before her.*
Art thou come back? So! thou couldst run, O vile!
 Soldier. Lady! your gentleness kept life within me
Until four fell.
 L. Malaspina. Thyself unwounded?
 Soldier.   No;
If arms alone can wound the soldier's breast,
They toucht me not this time; nor needed they;
Famine had done what your few words achieved.
 L. Malaspina. They were too harsh. Forgive me! 110
 Soldier.   Not the last.
Those were not harsh! Enter my bosom, enter,
Kind pitying words! untie there life's hard knot,
And let it drop off easily! How blest!
I have not robb'd the child, nor shamed the mother! *[He dies.*
 L. Malaspina. Poor soul! and the last voice he heard on
  earth
Was bitter blame, unmerited! And whose?
Mine, mine! Should they who suffer sting the sufferer?
O saints above! avenge not this misdeed!
What doth his hand hold out? A little crate, 120
With german letters round its inner rim . .
And . . full of wine! Yet did his lips burn white!
He tasted not what might have saved his life,
But brought it hither, to be scorn'd and die.
 [Singers are heard in the same open space before an image.]
Singers! where are they? My sight swims; my strength
Fails me; I can not rise, nor turn to look;
But only I can pray, and never voice
Prays like the sad and silent heart its last.

OLD MEN.
The village of the laurel grove*
Hath seen thee hovering high above,
Whether pure innocence was there,
Or helpless grief, or ardent prayer.

* The *House of Loreto* was not yet brought thither by the angels.

O Virgin! hither turn thy view,
For these are in Ancona too.
Not for ourselves implore we aid,
But thou art mother, thou art maid;
Behold these suppliants, and secure
Their humbled heads from touch impure!

MAIDENS.

Hear, maid and mother! hear our prayer!
Be brave and aged men thy care!
And, if they bleed, O may it be
In honour of thy Son and thee!
When innocence is wrong'd, we know
Thy bosom ever felt the blow.
Yes, pure One! there are tears above,
But tears of pity, tears of love,
And only from thine eyes they fall,
Those eyes that watch and weep for all.

[*They prostrate themselves.*

L. Malaspina.   How faintly sound those voices! altho'
    many;
At every stave they cease, and rest upon   130
That slender reed which only one can blow.
But *she* has heard them!   Me too *she* has heard.
Heaviness, sleep comes over me, deep sleep:
Can it, so imperturbable, be death?
And do I for the last time place thy lip
Where it may yet draw life from me, my child!
Thou, who alone canst save him, thou wilt save.

[*She dies: the child on her bosom still sleeping.*

ACT IV.   SCENE IV.

NIGHT: THE MOLE OF ANCONA.

CONSUL.   SENATOR.

Senator.   Sir Consul, you have heard (no doubt) that fires
Have been seen northward all along the sky,
And angels with their flaming swords have sprung
From hill to hill.   With your own eyes behold

No mortal power advancing.   Host so numerous
No king or emperor or soldan led.
   Consul.   A host, a mighty host, is there indeed?
   Senator.   It covers the whole range of Falcognara.
   Consul.   Methinks some fainter lights flit scatter'dly
Along the coast, more southward.   10
   Senator.   The archbishop
Hath seen the sign, and leads away his troops.
   Consul.   We are too weak to follow.   Can then aid
Have come so soon?   'Tis but the second night
Since we besought it.
   Senator.   In one hour, one moment,
Such aid can come, and *has* come.   Think not, Consul,
That force so mighty and so sudden springs
From earth.   And what Italian dares confront
The German?   20
   Consul.   What Italian!   All, sir; all.

ACT V.   SCENE I.

TENT OF MARCHESELLA, NEAR ANCONA.   EARLY MORNING.

MARCHESELLA.   OFFICERS.   PAOLUCCI.

   Officer.   My general! easily I executed
Your orders.
   Marchesella.   Have they fled, then?
   Officer.   Altogether.
   Marchesella.   And could you reach the gate?
   Officer.   And enter too.
Paolucci's seal unbarr'd it; not until
I held two loaves above my head, and threw
My sword before me.
   Marchesella.   And what saw you then?   10
   Officer.   There is a civil war within the city,
And insolence and drunkenness are rife.
Children and old and middle-aged were reeling,
And some were slipping over, some devouring
Long-podded weeds with jagged edges, cast

Upon the shore.
   Paolucci.   Famine had gone thus far
(Altho' with fewer) ere we left the mole.
The ancient garden-wall was overthrown
To get the twisted roots of fennel out ;   20
The fruit-tree that could give no fruit gave buds ;
The almond's bloom was withering, but whoe'er
Possest that treasure pierced the bark for gum ;
The mulberry sent her tardy shoot, the cane
Her tenderer one ; the pouting vine untied
Her trellised gems ; the apple-tree threw down
Her load of viscous mistletoe : they all
(Little it was !) did all they could for us.
   Marchesella. The Germans (look !) have left their tents
      behind :
We will explore them ; for your wary soldiers   30
Suspect, and well they may, some stratagem.

ACT V. SCENE II.

ERMINIA'S CHAMBER.

ERMINIA. MARIA.

   [MARIA *is going.* ERMINIA *calls her back.*
Erminia. Maria, is the countess very fair ?
Maria. Most beautiful. But you yourself must judge.
She sent me for you in the gentlest tone,
And far more anxious to see *you*, than you
(It seems) are to see *her*.
   Erminia.   I am afraid
To see her.
   Maria. *You* afraid ! Whom should *you* fear ?
Beautiful as she is, are not you more so ?
   Erminia. So you may think ; others think otherwise. 10
   Maria. She is so affable ! When many lords
Stood round about her, and the noblest of them
And bravest, Marchesella, who would give
His lands, his castles, even his knighthood for her . .

Whom do you think she call'd to her? . . the youth
Who cut the cables, and then hid himself
That none might praise him . . him who brought in safety
Your lover to the shore.
  Erminia (*angrily*). Whom?
  Maria.   Whom? Stamura. 20
  Erminia. What heart could he not win . . not scorn . .
   not break?
  Maria. I do not hear those shy ones ever break
A woman's heart, or win one. They may scorn;
But who minds that?
  Erminia.   Leave me.
  Maria.   And tell the countess
You hasten to her presence?
  Erminia.   Is *he* there?
  Maria. Who?
  Erminia.   Dull, dull creature!   30
  Maria.   The brave Marchesella?
  Erminia. Are there none brave but he?
  Maria.   O! then, Stamura.
No: when he led her from the mole again,
And she had enter'd the hall-door, he left her.
  Erminia. I fear'd he might be with her. Were he with her,
What matter! I could wait until . . Wait! why?
He would not look at me, nor I at him.
  Maria. No; I can answer for him. Were he born
Under the waves, and never saw the sun, 40
He could not have been colder. But you might
Have lookt at him, perhaps.
  Erminia.   Not I indeed.
  Maria. Few men are like him. How you hug me!
  Erminia.   Go . .
I will run first . . Go . . I am now quite ready.

ACT V. SCENE III.

CHAMBER IN THE CONSUL'S HOUSE.

COUNTESS *and* ERMINIA.

Countess.   The depths of love are warmer than the shallows,
Purer, and much more silent.
    Erminia (aside).   Ah! how true!
    Countess.   He loves you, my sweet girl ; I know he does.
    Erminia.   He says not so.
    Countess.   Child! all men are dissemblers
The generous man dissembles his best thoughts,
His worst the ungenerous.
    Erminia.   If, indeed, he loves me . .
    Countess.   He told me so.   10
    Erminia.   Ah! then he loves me not.
Who, who that loves, can tell it?
    Countess.   Who can hide it?
His voice betray'd him ; half his words were traitors . .
To him, my sweet Erminia! not to you.
What! still unhappy!   [ERMINIA *weeps*
    Erminia.   Let me weep away
A part of too much happiness.
    Countess.   I wish
One more could see it.   From these early showers   20
What sweets, that never spring but once, arise!

ACT V.   SCENE IV.

CONSUL *enters.*

Consul.   Before you leave us, since you part to-day,
From our full hearts take what lies deepest there,
And what God wills beyond all sacrifice . .
Our praises, our thanksgivings.   Thee we hail,
Protectress!   But can words, can deeds, requite

The debt of our deliverance?
   Countess.   What I ask
Should not infringe your freedom.   Power is sweet,
And victory claims something.   I am fain
To exercise a brief authority   10
Within the walls, appointing you my colleague.
   Consul.   Lady! this very night my power expires.
   Countess.   And mine, with your connivance, shall begin.
   Consul.   Lady! all power within the walls is yours.

ACT V.   SCENE V.

ARCH OF TRAJAN ON THE MOLE.

CONSUL, MARCHESELLA, COUNTESS, SENATORS, &c.

   Consul.   We have no flowers to decorate the arch
Whence the most glorious ruler of mankind
Smiles on you, lady! and on you, who rival
His valour, his humanity, his bounty.
Nor are there many voices that can sing
Your praises.   For, alas! our poor frail nature
(May it be seldom!) hears one call above
The call of gratitude.   The famishing
Devour your bread.   But, though we hear no praises,
There are who sing them to their harps on high,   10
And he who can alone reward you both
Listens in all his brightness to the song.
I do entreat you, blemish not your glory.
No exercise of might or sovranty
Can ever bring you such content again
As this day's victory, these altar-prayers
From rescued men, men perishing; from child
And parent: every parent, every child,
Who hears your name, should bless you evermore.
   Countess.   I find, sir, I must win you through your daughter.
   Consul.   The girl is grateful: urge her not too far: [20
I could not, without much compunction, thwart her.
Erminia! go: we meet again to-morrow.

Countess.   Come hither, my sweet girl !   Coy as thou art,
I have seen one, once in my life, as coy.
Stand forth thou skulking youth !   Here is no sea
To cover thee ; no ships to scatter.   Take
This maiden's hand . . unless her sire forbid . .
Holdest thou back ? after confession too !
I will reveal it.   [*To* ERMINIA.   30
                And art thou ashamed ?
Erminia.   I am ashamed.
Countess.   Of what ? thou simpleton !
Erminia.   I know not what . . of having *been* ashamed.
Consul.   Antonio ! if thou truly lovedst her,
What, after deeds so valiant, kept thee silent ?
Stamura.   Inferior rank, deep reverence, due fear.
I know who rules our country.
Consul.   *I, who* saved her.
                                    [FATHER JOHN *enters.*
F. John.   What ! and am I to be without reward ?   40
Consul.   Father ! be sure it will be voted you.
Marchesella.   And may not we too make our pious offerings,
For such they are, when such men will receive them.
F. John.   I claim the hand of the affianced.   Girl !
Shrink not from me ! Give it to God !
Erminia.   'Tis given :
I can not, would not, will not, take it back.
F. John.   Refractory ! hast thou not dedicated
To God thy heart and soul ?
Erminia.   I might have done it   50
Had never this day shone.
F. John.   And that youth's deeds
Outshone this day, or any day before.
When thou didst give thy hand to the deliverer
Whom God had chosen for us, then didst thou
Accomplish his great work, else incomplete.
I claim to pour his benediction on you
And yours for ever.   Much, much misery,
Have I inflicted on the young and brave,
And can not so repent me as I should ;   60
But 'twas in one day only my device

Ever wrought woe on any man alive.

[PAOLUCCI enters.

Consul.   Who enters?
Paolucci.   Who? The bridesman.
Marchesella (embracing him).   My brave friend!
My father's!
Paolucci.   Ay, thy grandfather's to boot.
And there was one, about my age, before him,
Sir Stefano, who wore a certain rose,
Radiant with pearls and rubies and pure gold,   70
Above the horse-tail grappled from the Turk.
Marchesella.   We have not in the house that ornament.
Paolucci.   I do believe he wears it in the grave.
Countess.   There is a sword here bright enough to throw
A lustre on Stamura.   Marchesella!
Marchesella.   Kneel, sir!

[He kneels to ERMINIA.

Countess.   Not there.
Marchesella.   Yes, there; what fitter place?
We know but one high title in the world,
One only set apart for deeds of valour,   80
And palsied be the hand that ill confers it.
Here is the field of battle; here I knight thee.

[Knights him.

Rise, my compeer! Teach him his duties, lady,
Toward the poor, the proud, the faith, the sex.
Countess (smiling).   Stamura! would you enter now my
    service?
Stamura.   Yes, lady, were you wrong'd, this very hour;
Then might I better earn the bliss I seek.

ANTONY AND OCTAVIUS.

Few have obtained the privilege of entering Shakespeare's garden, and of seeing him take turn after turn, quite alone, now nimbly, now gravely, on his broad and lofty terrace.

Let us never venture where he is walking, whether in deep meditation or in buoyant spirits. Enough is it for us to ramble and loiter in the narrower paths below, and to look up at the various images, which, in the prodigality of his wealth, he has placed in every quarter.

Before you, reader, are some scattered leaves gathered from under them: carefuller hands may arrange and compress them in a book of their own, and thus for a while preserve them, if rude children do not finger them first and tamper with their fragility.   W. S. L.

SCENE THE FIRST.

Soothsayer *and* Antony.

Soothsayer. Speak it I must. Ill are the auguries.

Antony. Ill ever are the auguries, O priest,
To those who fear them : at one hearty stroke
The blackest of them scud and disappear.

Now, not a word of any less than good
To Cleopatra.
    Soothsayer.   'Twas at her command
I hasten'd to consult them.
    Antony.   Rightly done
To follow her commands ; not rightly comes   10
Whate'er would grieve her ; this thou must withhold.
    Soothsayer.   Not this, not this : her very life may hang
Upon the event foretold her.
    Antony.   What is that ?
Announced then is the cursed augury
So soon ?
    Soothsayer.   She waited at the temple-door
With only one attendant, meanly drest,
That none might know her ; or perhaps the cause
Was holier ; to appease the offended Gods.   20
    Antony.   Which of them can she ever have offended ?
She who hath lavisht upon all of them
Such gifts, and burnt more incense in one hour
Before her Isis, than would wrap in smoke
A city at mid-day !   The keenest eye
Of earth or heaven could find in her no guile,
No cruelty, no lack of duty.
    Soothsayer.   True ;
Yet fears she one of them, nor knows she which,
But Isis is the one she most suspects.   30
    Antony.   Isis ! her patroness, her favourite ?
    Soothsayer.   Even so ! but they who patronise may frown
At times, and draw some precious boon away.
    Antony.   I deem not thus unworthily of Gods ;
Indeed I know but Jupiter and Mars ;
Each hath been ever on my side, and each
Alike will prosper me, I trust, to-morrow.
    Soothsayer.   But there are others, guardian Gods of Egypt ;
Prayers may propitiate them, with offerings due.
    Antony.   I have forgotten all my prayers.   40
    Soothsayer.   No need,
When holier lips pronounce them.
    Antony.   As for offerings,

There shall be plenty on the day's success.
  Soothsayer.   Merit it.
  Antony.   Do your Gods or ours mind that?
Merit! and where lies merit?
  Soothsayer.   In true faith
On auguries.
  Antony.   Birds hither thither fly,   50
And heard there have been from behind the veil
Voices not varying much from yours and mine.

SCENE THE SECOND.

Soothsayer *and* Cleopatra.

  Soothsayer.   Our lord Antonius wafts away all doubt
Of his success.
  Cleopatra.   What! against signs and tokens?
  Soothsayer.   Even so!
  Cleopatra.   Perhaps he trusts himself to Hercules,
Become of late progenitor to him.
  Soothsayer.   Ah! that sweet smile might bring him back;
    he once
Was flexible to the bland warmth of smiles.
  Cleopatra.   If Hercules is hail'd by men below
For strength and goodness, why not Antony?   . 10
Why not succeed as lawful heir? why not
Exchange the myrtle for the poplar crown?
            Antony *enters.* Soothsayer *goes.*
  Cleopatra.   Antony! is not Cæsar now a god?
  Antony.   We hear so.
  Cleopatra.   Nay, we know it.   Why not thou?
Men would not venture then to strike a blow
At thee: the laws declare it sacrilege.
  Antony.   Julius, if I knew Julius, had been rather
First among men and last among the Gods.
  Cleopatra.   At least put on thy head a kingly crown. 20
  Antony.   I have put on a laurel one already;
As many kingly crowns as should half cover

The Lybian desert are not worth this one.
 Cleopatra. But all would bend before thee.
 Antony.   'Twas the fault
Of Cæsar to adopt it ; 'twas his death.
 Cleopatra. Be then what Cæsar is.
                O Antony !
To laugh so loud becomes not state so high.
 Antony. He is a star, we see ; so is the hair   30
Of Berenice : stars and Gods are rife.
What worth, my love, are crowns ?   Thou givest pearls,
I give the circlet that encloses them.
Handmaidens don such gear, and valets snatch it
Sportively off, and toss it back again.
 Cleopatra. But graver men gaze up with awful eyes.
 Antony. And never gaze at that artificer,
Who turns his heel and fashions out his vase
From the Nile clay !   'Tis easy work for him ;
Easy was mine to turn forth kings from stuff   40
As vile and ductile : he still plies his trade,
But mine, with all my customers, is gone.
Ever by me let enemies be awed,
None else : bring round me many, near me few,
Keeping afar those shaven knaves obscene
Who lord it with humility, who press
Men's shoulders down, glue their two hands together,
And cut a cubit off, and tuck their heels
Against the cushion mother Nature gave.
 Cleopatra. Incomprehensible ! incorrigible !   50
O wretch ! if queens were ever taught to blush,
I should at such unseemly phrase as thine.
I think I must forgive it.
          What ! and take
Before I grant ?   Again !   You violent man !
Will you for ever drive me thus away ?

SCENE THE THIRD.

ANTONY *and* CLEOPATRA.

Antony.   What demon urged thy flight ?
Cleopatra.   The demon Love.
I am a woman, with a woman's fears,
A mother's, and, alas O Antony !
More fears than these.
   Antony.   Of whom ?
   Cleopatra.   Ask not *of* whom
But ask *for* whom, if thou must ask at all,
Nor knowest nor hast known.   Yes, I did fear
For my own life . . ah ! lies it not in thine ?   10
How many perils compast thee around !
   Antony. What are the perils that are strange to me ?
   Cleopatra.   Mine thou couldst not have seen when swiftest
    oars,
Attracted by the throne and canopy,
Pounced at me only, numerous as the waves ;
Couldst not have seen my maidens throwing down
Their fans and posies (piteous to behold !)
That they might wring their hands more readily.
I was too faint myself to still their cries.
   Antony (aside).   I almost thought her blameable.   20
   (*To* CLEOPATRA.)   The Gods
So will'd it.   Thou despondest . . too aware
The day is lost.
   Cleopatra.   The day may have been lost,
But other days, and happier ones, will come.
   Antony.   Never : when those so high once fall, their
    weight
Keeps them for ever down.
   Cleopatra.   Talk reasonably,
And love me as . . till now . . it should be more,
For love and sorrow mingle where they meet.   30
   Antony. It shall be more.   Are these last kisses cold ?

Cleopatra.   Nor cold are they nor shall they be the last.
Antony.   Promise me, Cleopatra, one thing more.
Cleopatra.   'Tis promist, and now tell me what it is.
Antony.   Rememberest thou this ring ?
Cleopatra.   Dost thou remember
The day, my Antony, when it was given ?
Antony.   Day happiest in a life of many happy,
And all thy gift.
Cleopatra.   'Tis call'd the richest ruby,   40
The heaviest, and the deepest, in the world.
Antony.   The richest certainly.
Cleopatra.   And not the deepest
And broadest ?   Look ! it hides all this large nail,
And mine are long ones if not very wide ;
Now let me see if it don't cover yours
As wide again ! there ! it would cover two.
Why smile you so ?
Antony.   Because I know its story.   [50
Cleopatra.   Ha ! then you have not lost all memory quite.
I told it you.   The king of Pontus sent it
When dying to my father, warning him
By letter that there was a charm in it
Not to be trifled with.
Antony.   It shall not be.
Cleopatra.   But tell me now the promise I must make ;
What has the ring to do with it ?
Antony.   All, all.
Know, Cleopatra, this is not one ruby.
Cleopatra.   The value then is smaller.   60
Antony.   Say not so,
Remark the rim.
Cleopatra.   The gold is thin, I see.
Antony.   And seest thou it will open ?   It contains
Another jewel, richer than itself.
Cleopatra.   Impossible ! my Antony ! for rubies
Are richer than all other gems on earth.
Antony.   Now, my sweet trifler, for thy promise.
Cleopatra.   Speak.
By all the Powers above and all below,   70

I will perform thy bidding, even to death.
   Antony.   To death it goes; not until after mine.
   Cleopatra.   I kiss the precious charm.   Methinks an odour
Of almond comes from it.   How sweet the flower
Of death!
   Antony.   'Tis painless death, 'tis sudden too.
   Cleopatra.   Who could wish more, even were there more
     to wish?
With us there is not.
   Antony.   Generous, pious girl!
Daughter of Ptolemies! thou hast not won   80
A lower man than they.   Thy name shall rise
Above the pyramids, above the stars,
Nations yet wild shall that name civilize,
And glorious poets shake their theatres,
And stagger kings and emperors with applause.
   Cleopatra.   I was not born to die; but I was born
To leave the world with Antony, and will.
   Antony.   The greatest of all eastern kings died thus,
The greater than all eastern kings thus died.
O glorious forgeman who couldst rivet down   90
Refractory crowds by thousands, and make quake
Sceptres like reeds! we want not here thy voice
Or thy example.   Antony alone
And queenly pride, tho' Love were dumb, would do.

SCENE THE FOURTH.

CLEOPATRA.   CHARMIAN.   IRAS.

   Cleopatra.   At the first entrance of your lord, before
He ordered you, before he spake a word,
Why did ye run away?
   Charmian.   I was afraid,
Never so in my life; he lookt so fierce
He fear'd his own wild eyes, he placed one hand
(His right) across them on lowered brow, his left
Waved us away as would a hurricane

A palm-tree on the desert.
   Cleopatra (*to* Iras).   And wert thou,   10
Iras, so terrified?
   Iras.   Not I indeed ;
My lady, never man shall frighten *me*.
   Cleopatra.   Thou silly creature! I have seen a mouse
Do it.
   Iras.   A mouse is quite another thing.
   Charmian (*hesitating*).   Our lord and master . .
   Cleopatra.   What of Antony ?
   Charmian.   Octavius . .
   Cleopatra.   Who? Our lord and master
   he?   20
He never shall be mine . . that is to say . .
   Charmian.   What! lady?
   Cleopatra.   I forget . . 'twas not worth saying.
Charmian! where hast thou been this last half-hour?
   Charmian.   In my own room.
   Cleopatra.   So fearful ?
   Charmian.   Far more sad.
   Cleopatra.   Where, Iras, thou ?
   Iras.   I wanted to report
To my sweet lady what I might espy.   30
   Cleopatra.   And what have those long narrow eyes espied ?
   Iras.   All.
   Cleopatra.   'Twas done speedily ; but what is all ?
Army and fleet from any terrace roof
Are quite discernible, the separate men
Nowhere.
   Iras.   My heart had told me what delight
Its queen would feel to hear exactly how
The leaders look.
   Cleopatra.   And how then did they look ?   40
Tell me: some might have ridden near enough
To town to judge by, where the sight is sharp.
   Iras.   Merciful Isis! ridden! and so close !
Horses are frightful, horses kick and rear
And whinny, full of wickedness; 'twere rash
To venture nigh them.

Cleopatra.   There are things more rash.
Iras.   Quieter creatures than those generals are
Never were seen.
Cleopatra.   Barbarians ! not a word   50
About them, Iras, if thou lovest me ;
They would destroy my city, seize my realm,
And ruin him we live for.
Iras.   Surely no ;
It were a pity ; none are so unkind ;
Cæsar the least of all. -
Cleopatra.   Ah simple child !
Thou knowest not his heart.
Iras.   I do indeed.
Cleopatra.   No, nor thy own.   60
Iras.   His better ; for of mine
I never askt a question.   He himself
Told me how good he would be.
Cleopatra.   He told *thee ?*
What ! hast thou seen him ?
Iras.   Aye, and face to face,
Close as our lord's to yours.
Cleopatra.   O impudence !
Iras.   But he would have it so ; just like our lord.
Cleopatra.   Impudent girl ! thou shalt be whipt for this. 70
Iras.   I am too old ; but lotuses don't hurt
Like other things ; they cool the strokes they give.
Cleopatra.   I have no patience with thee.   How I hate
That boy Octavius !
                    Dared he touch thy cheek ?
Iras.   He could ; he only whispered in my ear,
Holding it by the ring.
Cleopatra.   Whispered ? what words ?
Iras.   The kindest.
Cleopatra.   Ah ! no doubt ! but what were they ?
Iras.   He said, The loveliest creature in the world . . [80
Cleopatra.   The vulgar brute !   Our ferrymen talk so :
And couldst thou listen, Iras, to such speech ?
Iras.   Only when people praise our gracious queen.
Cleopatra.   Me ? this of me ? Thou didst thy duty, child :

He might have fail'd in what he would express.
The birds have different voices, yet we bear
To hear those sing which do not sing the best.
Iras! I never thought thee half so wise.
And so, he said those gentle words of *me?*   90
   Iras.   All, and forgot to kiss me when I vow'd
I would report them faithfully.
   Cleopatra.   Is there
Resemblance in him to that marble image
I would have broken, but my Antony
Seiz'd both my hands?
   Iras.   Alas! that image wants
The radiant eyes, and hair more radiant still,
Such as Apollo's may have been if myrrh
Were sprinkled into its redundant waves.   100
   Cleopatra.   He must be tenderer than I fanced him
If this be true.
   Iras.   He spoke those very words.
   Cleopatra.   Iras! 'tis vain to mind the words of men ;
But if he lookt as thou hast said he lookt,
I think I may put trust in him.
   Iras.   And see him?
   Cleopatra.   I am not hasty.
   Iras.   If you could but see him !
   Cleopatra.   Call Charmian : I am weary : I must rest 110
Awhile.
   Iras.   My sweetest lady! could not I,
Who have been used to it almost a year,
Help you as well as Charmian?   While you sleep
Could I not go again and bid him haste
To comfort you?
   Cleopatra.   Is the girl mad?   Call Charmian.
                                             (*To* CHARMIAN.)
Charmian! hath Iras tickled thee away
From moping in thy chamber? thou hast sped.
   Charmian.   Iras is growing bold.   120
   Cleopatra.   I was bold too
While I was innocent as Iras is.
   Charmian.   Our lady looks more flurried than deprest.

Cleopatra.   I am not flurried, I am not deprest.
                                        [*After a pause.*
Believest thou in Cæsar's generosity?
    Charmian.   I know it.
    Cleopatra.   In what matter?
    Charmian.   Half the guards
And half the ministers of state have shown
Signs of his bounty to the other half.   130
    Cleopatra.   Gifts are poor signs of bounty.   Do not slaves
Slip off the gold-black pouches from their necks
Untied but to buy other slaves therewith?
Do not tame creatures lure into the trap
Their wilder brethren with some filthy bait?
All want companions, and the worst the most.
I am much troubled : even hope troubles me.
    Charmian.   I dare not ask our lady why she weeps.
    Cleopatra.   Cæsarion, my first-born, my dearest one,
Is safely shielded by his father's name :   140
He loves his brothers, he may save them both,
He only can : I would fain take the advice
Of Dolabella, fain would venture him
In Cæsar's camp : the father's voice and look
Must melt him, for his heart is not so hard
That he could hurt so beautiful a child ;
Nay, what man's is?
    Charmian.   But trust not the two younger ;
Their father will not help them in their need.
    Cleopatra.   Cæsarion in fit hour will plead for them.   150
Charmian, what ponderest thou? what doubtest thou?
    Charmian.   Cæsar I doubt, and Dolabella more ;
And what I pondered were your words : *It may be*
That givers are not always benefactors.
    Cleopatra.   I have one secret, but keep none from thee :
He loves me !
    Charmian.   All do.
    Cleopatra.   Yes, but some have power.
    Charmian.   Power, as most power is, gain'd by treachery.
    Cleopatra.   Whom,   160

In Egypt, Europe, Asia, can I trust?
   Charmian.   Few, nor those few too far, nor without watch.
   Cleopatra.   Not Charmian?
   Charmian.   Bid her die; here; now; and judge.

SCENE THE FIFTH.

Octavius. Mecænas. Gallus.

   Octavius.   Is Dolabella to be trusted?
   Mecænas.   Youth
There is on Dolabella's side; with youth
Comes always eloquence where women are.
   Octavius.   Gallus is honester and prudenter.
   Mecænas.   But Gallus is the older by some years.
   Octavius.   A poet says, Love at odd hours hath smiled,
And covered with his pinions sportively,
Where he espied some hairs that seem'd like Time's
Rather than his.   10
   Mecænas.   There must have been but few,
Or else the poet dreamt it.
   Octavius.   Who comes hither?
   Mecænas.   Not Dolabella, but the better man.
   Octavius.   Welcome, brave Gallus, opportunely met.
We were debating how to lure that dove
Of Antony's, now in her cote, a tower,
From which we would not frighten her away,
But tempt her down.
   Gallus.   It might be difficult.   20
   Octavius.   Unless thou aidest us, indeed it might.
   Mecænas.   What sport 'twould be to see her mate descend
And catch him too!
   Gallus.   Nor this more easily.
   Octavius.   To Gallus all is easy.
   Mecænas.   Pleasant too
Would such task be.
   Gallus.   No better judge of pleasures
Than Cilnius here? but ours are not alike.   30
   Octavius.   Gallus! one word apart. We need thee much.

Gallus.   What! after Egypt won?
Octavius.   Antony lives!
Gallus.   Beaten, disgraced, imprisoned, his own jailer.
Mecænas.   Defying us, however, by the power
The queen his mistress gives him with her name . .
Gallus.   Worthless as his.
Mecænas.   Were she within our reach
We soon might bring him down.
Gallus.   What! lower?
Octavius.   Even yet?   40
Gallus.   She might succumb, and must, by promising
That Cæsar's son, after her death, shall reign.
Mecænas.   A prudent thought.   But will she give up Antony
Unless she hear it from the giver's mouth?
There is one anxious to deserve the grace
Of princes.   Dolabella could persuade
The queen to trust herself to him for Cæsar.
Gallus.   I doubt it.
Mecænas.   Doubt his honour, not his skill.
He could not keep the secret that he loves,   50
And that he often in times past hath seen her.
Gallus.   He loves her? then, by all the Gods! he never
Will win her for another than himself.
Beside, he was the friend of Antony,
And shared with him the toils at Mutina.
Altho' no eagle, he would soar aloft
Rather than bow for others, like an owl,
The smallest of the species, hooded for it.
Who knows not Dolabella?
Mecænas.   Thou hast sense,   60
Comeliness, courage, frankness.   Antony
Tore from thy couch the fairest girl in Rome.
Gallus.   And let him have her, let him have her, man.
What then?
Mecænas.   There are who would retaliate.
Gallus.   The girl hath left no mark upon my memory . .
Mecænas.   Or mine, beside a few soft lines; but mine
Retains them, mindful of a friend who sang,
Unless my singing mars the harmony,

I thought it once an idle tale   70
That lovely woman's faith could fail ;
At last I said, It may be true,
Lycoris, of them all but you.
And now you leave me ! and you go
O'er pinnacles of Alpine snow.
Another leads you (woe is me !)
Across that grim and ghastly sea !
Let him protect those eyes from sleet,
And guide and chafe those tender feet,
And fear for every step you tread,   80
Then hardly will I wish him dead.
If ice-barb'd shafts that ring around
By his neglect my false one wound,
O may the avenging Gods for this
Freeze him to death in the abyss !

    Gallus.   They have reserved him for a sadder fate.
Sleep, without painful dreams that crush the breast,
Sleep, without any joyous ones that come
Only to mock the awaken'd, comes unfelt
And unsolicited among those cliffs   90
Of ice perennial.

           Antony hath dreamt
His broken dream, and wakened to despair :
I never wisht him that ; the harm I wisht him
Was when my youth was madder than his age.
He stood a prouder and a better man
At Mutina, when Famine walkt the camp,
When I beheld him climb up painfully
A low and crumbling crag, where servises
Hung out above his head their unripe fruit :   100
That was my day.   Some grains of sodden maize
I brought and offered him : he struck them down.

    Octavius.   Rejoice at pride so humbled.

    Gallus.   I rejoice
At humbled pride, at humbled valour no.

    Octavius.   But those offending Gods whom thou invokedst
Stand now before thee and demand why call'd.

    Gallus.   They know : they pardon such irresolution

As pity, and not cowardice, persuades.
One woman has betraid me ; not one woman   110
Will I betray.
    Mecænas.   O that poetic mind !
    Gallus.   Where others sneer, Mecænas only smiles.
    Mecænas.   Such is my nature, and I widely err,
Gallus, if such be not thy nature too.
    Octavius.   Did then Lycoris, that wild girl, prefer
The unworthy to the worthy, the most rude
To the most gentle, scampering beyond reach ?
Let her repair her fault : no danger here
That angry skies turn coral lips to slate   120
Or icicles make limp the runaway.
    Gallus.   Those days are over.   He, who won the prize
May say as much and add a little more.
    Octavius.   Laughest thou not to see the tables turn'd ?
The little queen who fascinates her fool
Is now as lovely as Lycoris was,
And never ran away from any man :
Fain would I see that roysterer's spirit broken,
And she alone can do it : help her on.
    Gallus.   In any such attempt, in such a place   130
Fortune would baffle me.
    Octavius.   Then baffle *her ;*
She baffles only those who hesitate.
    Gallus.   The queen, we hear, takes refuge in the depths
Below the palace, where but reptiles lie.
    Octavius.   Indeed ! what ! scorpions, serpents ?
    Gallus.   Haply these.
    Octavius.   Poor woman ! they may bite her ! let my fears
Prove not prophetic !
                  Now, my friend, adieu !   140
Reflect upon our project ; turn it over.
                        [*Gallus goes.*

These poets look into futurity
And bring us glimpses from it more than dreams.
Asps !   But the triumph then without the queen !
Alas ! was ever mortal so perplext !
I doubt if your friend Gallus can be won.

Mecænas.   All may be won, well handled ; but the ear
Is not the thing to hold by.   Show men gold,
Entangle them in Gallic torquises,
Tie stubborn necks with ropes of blushing pearls,   150
Seat them on ivory from the realms of Ind,
Augur them consulates, proconsulates,
Make their eyes widen into provinces,
And, gleaming further onward, tetrarchies.
    Octavius.   It strikes me now that we may offer Gallus
The prefecture of Egypt.
    Mecænas.   Some time hence :
Better consult Agrippa.
    Octavius.   None more trusty.
Yet our Agrippa hath strange whims ; he dotes   160
Upon old Rome, the Rome of matted beards
And of curt tunics ; of old Rome's old laws,
Worm-eaten long, now broken and swept off.   [*Pausing.*
He stands forth high in station and esteem.
    Mecænas.   So should the man who won the world for thee.
    Octavius.   I must not play with him who won so much
From others ; he might win as much from me :
I fear his fortunes.
    Mecænas.   Bind them with your own.
Becoming are thy frowns, my dear Octavius,   170
Thy smiles alone become thee better : trust
Thy earliest friend and fondest : take not ill
My praises of Agrippa, tried in war
And friendship.
    Octavius.   And for this wouldst thou, my Cilnius,
Send him away from me ?
    Mecænas.   Thyself did fear
His popularity : all Rome applauds
His valour, justice, moderation, mercy.
    Octavius.   Not one word more.   180
    Mecænas.   One word I have to speak,
And speak it I will now.   He must away.
    Octavius.   Can Cilnius then be jealous of Agrippa ?
    Mecænas.   No ; crown him king and give him provinces,
But give him not to clench the heart of Rome.

Octavius.   I could make kings and unmake kings by scores,
But could not make nor unmake one Agrippa.
   Mecænas.   Well spoken! wisely! worthily! No praise
Can equipoise his virtues, kings may lay
Their tributes on the carpet of his throne   190
And cities hope to honour whom they serve,
The royal mantle would obscure Agrippa.
   Octavius.   I would be generous, but be cautious too.
   Mecænas.   Then grant him all beyond the sight of Rome;
Men's eyes would draw him thither tho' his will
Hung back: thus urged the steadiest might give way.
   Octavius.   I hate suspicion and suspicious men.
Gallus I fancied was the bitterest foe
Of Antony, his rival, and successful,
Then he should hate him worse than I.   200
   Mecænas.   But empire
Is more worth hatred than a silly girl,
Every day to be won and lost again.
   Octavius.   Our Gallus is weak-minded to forgive
So easily.
   Mecænas.   I find that on the hearth
Where lie love's embers there lie hatred's too,
Equally cold and not to be stir'd up.
   Octavius.   I do not think, my Cilnius, thou hast felt
Love but for me; I never knew thee hate.   210
   Mecænas.   It is too troublesome; it rumples sleep,
It settles on the dishes of the feast,
It bites the fruit, it dips into the wine;
Then rather let my enemy hate *me*
Than I hate him.
   Octavius.   We must look round.   What think you?
Is Dolabella to be trusted?
   Mecænas.   Try.
   Octavius.   I wish this country settled, us return'd.
Resolved am I to do what none hath done,   220
And only Julius ever purposed doing;
Resolved to render Rome, beneath my rule,
A second Alexandria.   Corinth, Carthage,
One autumn saw in stubble; not a wreath

Enough to crown a capital was left,
Nor capital to crown its pillar, none ;
But here behold what glorious edifices !
What palaces ! what temples ! what august
Kings ! how unmoved is every countenance
Above the crowd ! And so it was in life.   230
No other city in the world, from west
To east, seems built for rich and poor alike.
In Athens, Antioch, Miletus, Rhodes,
The richest Roman could not shelter him
Against the dogstar ; here the poorest slave
Finds refuge under granite, here he sleeps
Noiseless, and, when he wakens, dips his hand
Into the treasured waters of the Nile.

   Mecænas.   I wish, Octavius, thou wouldst carry hence
For thy own worship one of those mild Gods,   240
Both arms upon the knees : 'tis time that all
Should imitate this posture.

   Octavius.   We will close
The gates of Janus.

   Mecænas.   Janus looks both ways ;
He may like best the breezy air abroad
And knock too hard against the bolted brass.

   Octavius (*to a* Guard). Call Gallus hither.

   Gallus.   Cæsar ! what commands ?

   Octavius.   I would entrust a legion, more than one,   250
To our friend Gallus : I would fix him here
In Egypt : none is abler to coerce
The turbulent.

   Gallus.   Let others flap their limbs
With lotus-leaves when Sirius flames above,
Give me the banks of Anio, where young Spring,
Who knows not half the names of her own flowers,
Looks into Summer's eyes and wakes him up
Alert, and laughs at him until he lifts
His rod of roses and she runs away.   260

   Octavius.   And has that lovely queen no charms for thee ?

   Gallus.   If truth be spoken of her, and it may,
Since she is powerless and deserted now,

Tho' more than thrice seven* years have come and stolen
Day after day a leaf or two of bloom,
She has but changed her beauty ; the soft tears
Fall, one would think, to make it spring afresh.
  Octavius.   And not for Gallus ? Let one brave man more
Ascend the footstool of the regal bed.
  Gallus.   As the Gods will ! but may they not· will
    me !   270

SCENE THE SIXTH.

ANTONY *and* DOLABELLA·

  Antony.   Welcome, my Dolabella !   There is none
From yonder camp I would embrace beside.
My little queen hath given at last an audience
To thy persuasive tongue ?
  Dolabella.   Most graciously.
  Antony.   I never thought she would permit Cæsarion
To leave her side ; hardly can I myself
Bear separation from that brave young boy ;
I love him as my own.
  Dolabella.   Your own thus stand   10
Safe from all peril.
  Antony.   Is not it disgrace ?
A boy save *me* ? for to save them is *me.*
  Dolabella.   Create a generosity of soul
In one whom conquest now hath made secure ;
Bid him put forth his power, it now is greater
Than any man's : consider what a friend
Cæsarion hath in Julius, all whose wounds
Will bleed afresh before the assembled tribes

---

  * History and poetry do not always well agree. Julius Cæsar had
left Egypt before the birth of Cæsarion, at which time Cleopatra was
about fourteen.   That she retained her freshness seven or eight years
longer, may be attributed in part to the care she took of it, and in a
greater to her pure Macedonian blood. Beside, Alexandria is not
sultry ; and the architects of antiquity knew how to keep up an
equable and healthy temperature.

On the imperial robe thy hands outsprad   20
With its wide rents for every God above
And every Roman upon earth to number.
    Antony.   Ah! those were days worth living o'er again.
    Dolabella.   Live them again then.
    Antony.   Never, stript of power,
Of dignity, of Rome's respect, of theirs
Who compass me, who fix before these eyes
The very eagles which adorn'd my tent.
    Dolabella.   Brave thoughts! but are none weaker inter-
       mixt?
    Antony.   Smile, Dolabella!   Oh, could but that smile   30
Kill as it pierces me!   But tread the ground
Softly and lightly where her feet have moved.
My Cleopatra! never will we part,
Thy son shall reign in Egypt.
    Dolabella.   Much I fear'd,
O Antony, thy rancour might prevail
Against thy prudence.   Cæsar bears no rancour.
    Antony.   Too little is that heart for honest hatred.
The serpent the most venomous hath just
Enough of venom for one deadly wound,   40
He strikes but once, and then he glides away.
    Dolabella.   Octavius strikes not Antony.
    Antony.   One man
Alone dares strike the man whom thou hast named.
But let me hear the phrase of fraudulence.
    Dolabella.   Cæsar's, I trust, will not deserve that name,
He says his reign shall be the reign of peace.
    Antony.   Peace! what is that? a pleasant room to sit
Or walk about in, nor could heart desire
A cooler place wherein to spread the cates: 50
First, bring these cates; bring liberty, the salt
That seasons with true relish all things else.
    Dolabella.   We sometimes leave but little, when we rise
From its enjoyment, for those servitors
Who toil'd for us throughout the heat of day:
Reckless we riot: never can spilt wine
Enter the golden cup it sparkled in:

Harpies above defile the half-eaten fruit.
Rome now would rest awhile.
   Antony.   Yea, long will be   60
Her rest: the scourge of Earth will be the scorn.
   Dolabella. We must submit.
   Antony. Thou must; thou hast submitted;
But never I; what I have been I am.
   Dolabella.   Less prosperous than once, thy fortunes may
Be yet restored.
   Antony.   I would not take them back,
By any man, least by that man, bestow'd;
I would not have my portion of the world,
No, nor the whole of it, if that glib tongue   70
Call'd every God to ratify the gift.
Show me the foe he ever fairly met,
The friend he hath embraced, and not betray'd,
And tell me, Dolabella, for thou canst,
Who murder'd Hirtius; by whose agency
Poison was dropt into the wound of Pansa.
   Dolabella. Of this ask Glyco, ask Aquilius Niger
Of that.
   Antony. Both know the secret, both have told it:
And now I will tell thee one.   80
                   At the noon
Of yesterday, when fruit is most refreshing,
A countryman who brings the yellow figs
His queen is fond of, brought a basketful,
Saying to Iras:
               " These my little daughter,
Whom once you used to play with in the garden,
Bids me to give into your hands; she thinks
The queen requires some frolic; you alone
Can venture so far with her. Place within   90
The smooth cool linen of her bed this basket
Of cane-leaves and of rushes intertwined,
With all the fruit below, the leaves a-top;
You see it is but shallow, scarce a palm,
Mind it lie flat; yet she will find it out
Tho' it be always dusky in that room."

What is there in the tale that thou shouldst stare?
  Dolabella.   Enough.   An idle rumour reacht the camp
That Cleopatra stung herself to death,
Vexing two asps held close against her bosom.   100
  Antony.   Are Romans all so ignorant of the asp
That two are wanted? that he must be vext?
That, like domestic animals, he bites?
He bites not, but he strikes with upper jaw
As other vipers do, and the black lid
Drops, and he crawls away; one pang, one shriek,
Death hears it, nor delays: the hind knows that.
An earlier story now.   So exquisite
In luxury, my queen dissolved a pearl
Above all price, and drank it in her wine.   110
Bid thou the tatler of the tale expound
How that same acid which dissolved the pearl
Darken'd no tooth, abbreviated no smile,
But gave her spirits for the festive song.
Ah! had she done so, Medicine had run up
In vain to help her; Death had interposed.
  Dolabella.   Another tale, alike incredible.
'Tis said she shook from off her coronal
Poison into your cup, dashing it down
Just at the lip, and proving its effect   120
On household beast before you, thus to show
How easy were the deed to one who will'd.
  Antony.   Is such a fiction workt by homespun yarn?
I doubt it: surely some Greek needle wrought
The quaint device, for poet to adorn
By metaphor, and sage by apologue.
Thou hast among thy friends one capable,
In man's attire, fresh-blooming from Hymettus,
Handmaid of Cilnius the rich Aretine.
O Romans! are your ears to falsities   130
Wide open, and your mouths agape for them
As are the callow sparrows for their food,
Hour after hour?   Ye little know that asps
Are not mere worms of one span-length, one cubit,
But longer than the vipers in your fields,

So hideous that no woman, young or old,
Or rustic, or well train'd to monkey-gods,
But must abhor them.   Your credulity
Will urge the whisper in each other's ear
That she, the daintiest of all womankind,   140
Would handle them, now plague them, now caress
And hug them as she might a tender babe . .
Yet even the serious may believe the tale,
For what in Rome is not believed . . but truth ?
    Dolabella.   To me the queen said nothing of this snare.
    Antony.   Nothing she knows of it.

                                        I heard a scream
From Iras, and rusht in.   She threw herself
Before my feet, prayed me to strike her dead,
And ran toward the corner, where I saw   150
The beasts coil'd up, and cut them thro' and thro'.
Then told she all ; but not until her prayer
For death was fruitless, not until I warn'd her
How life and death, while yet we live, are ours.
    Dolabella.   Might I advise . .
    Antony.   Not me : I never took
Any advice, in battle or debate :
    Dolabella.   Cæsar hath urged thee sorely, and may worse ;
What wouldst thou do with him were he the vanquisht ?
    Antony.   Do with him ? throw him to the fishermen   160
To bait their hooks with and catch crocodiles,
If crocodile feeds upon crocodile.
Take him these words : we keep no secrets here.
    Dolabella.   Cæsar is lenient.
    Antony.   Never let that word
Glide o'er thy lips, no word is it for me.
Tell him no friend of mine shall ask my life,
No enemy shall give it.   I am lord
Of my own honour ; he has none to lose :
The money-changer's grandson calculates   170
But badly here.   He waits for thee : depart.

SCENE THE SEVENTH.

ANTONY *and* AGRIPPA.

Antony.　　And so, the victor comes to taunt the vanquisht!
Is this well done, Agrippa?
Agrippa.　　　　　　　　　'Twere ill done,
And never done by me.
　　　　　　　　　　　There have been some
Who carried to the forum and there cast
The tags and rags of mimes, and tarnisht spangles
Bag'd from the dusthole corner; gravity
Becomes me better and plain Roman garb
In action and in speech; no taunt is mine.　　　　　　10
　Antony.　　What then demands the vanquisher?
　Agrippa.　　　　　　　　　　　I come
To ask a favour, ask a gift, of thee.
Give me thy children.
　Antony.　　　　　　To adopt?
　Agrippa.　　　　　　　　　　To save:
They may have enemies; they shall have friends
If thou accedest to my last request:
Lose we no time; we shall be soon at Rome.
　Antony.　　Ventidius may prevent it.　　　　　　20
　Agrippa.　　　　　　　　　　He hath serv'd thee
Faithfully, and is steady to thy cause:
The sea is closed to him, the river closed,
Wide as the desert is, it is not open,
And half his army, more than half, is ours.
　Antony.　　But many yet are left me, brave and true.
　Agrippa.　　When Fortune hath deserted us, too late
Comes Valour, standing us in little stead.
They who would die for us are just the men
We should not push on death or throw away.　　　　30
　Antony.　　Too true! Octavius with his golden wand
Hath reacht from far some who defied his sword.
How little fire within warps loosen'd staves
Together, for the hoop to hold them tight!

I have too long stood balancing the world
Not to know well its weight : of that frail crust
Friends are the lightest atoms.
   Agrippa.   Not so all.
   Antony.   I thought of Dolabella and the rest.
Ventidius and Agrippa, these are men   40
Romulus might have wrestled with nor thrown.
I have proved both.
   Agrippa.   One thou shalt prove again,
In guise more friendly than when last we met.
   Antony.   To me well spoken hast thou for Ventidius,
Speak for him in that manner to another,
Tell him that he has done against the Parthian
What Julius might, perhaps might not, have done.
Triumph must follow.   I shall never see it,
Nor shall I see, nor shalt thou either, one   50
On which cold eyes, dim even in youth to beauty,
Look forward.
                Are there not kings left enow
To drag, by brace or leash, and back to back,
Along the *Sacred Way ?*
                    Vile wretch ! his steeds
Shall never at the cries of Cleopatra
Prance up against their trappings stiff with gold.
   Agrippa.   Sad were the sight.
   Antony.   Too far hath Dolabella 60
Prevail'd with her.
   Agrippa.   Hath Dolabella come
Within these walls ?
   Antony.   Hast thou not seen him then
Leave them within the hour ?
   Agrippa.   Indeed not I.
My station is the harbour where the ships
Are riding, his lies nearer to the town.
Thou musest, Antony !
   Antony.   And well may muse.   70
He was my friend . . *is* he.   Away with doubt !
   Agrippa.   He was the friend of Tullius, friend of Brutus,
Friend too of Lepidus, akin to each,

And yet betraid he them.
                        Give me the boys ;
With me they enter Rome.
   Antony.   'Take, take them ; both ?
Yes ; both are safer, both are happier so.
I love them ; but I might have loved them more ;
Now is too late.   80
              Take them ; be kind to them . .
Nay, look not back.   Tears scorch the father's eyes,
The Roman should extinguish them . . and shall.
Farewell ! Farewell !
                But turn thy face aside . .
No . . one word more.
   Agrippa.   Thy gladness gladdens me,
Bursting so suddenly.   What happy change !
   Antony.   Thou hast a little daughter, my old friend,
And I two little sons . . I had at least . .   90
Give her the better and the braver one,
When by thy care he comes to riper age.
   Agrippa.   O Antony ! the changes of our earth
Are suddener and oftener than the moon's.
On hers we calculate, not so on ours,
But leave them in the hands of wilful Gods,
Inflexible, yet sometimes not malign.
   Antony.   They have done much for me, nor shall reproach
Against them pass my lips : I might have askt,
But never thought of asking, what desert   100
Was mine for half the blessings they bestow'd.
I will not question them why they have cast
My greatness and my happiness so low ;
They have not taken from me their best gift,
A heart for ever open to my friends :
It will be cold ere long, and one will grieve.

SCENE THE EIGHTH.

OCTAVIUS, AGRIPPA, CÆSARION, MECÆNAS.

   Octavius.   What said that obstinate and proud old thief?
Couldst thou not draw him from his den, Agrippa ?

Agrippa.　　I tried not.
Octavius.　　　　　　　Nor perhaps desired.
Agrippa.　　　　　　　　　　　'Tis true,
I entered not by stealth, and broke no confidence ;
Tatius, who knew and once fought under me . .
Octavius.　　And would not he who knows thy power, and who
Admitted thee within the royal hold,
Do more ?　　　　　　　　　　　　　　10
Agrippa.　　Not even this would he have done
For any other, nor for me without
Permission from his general ; this obtain'd,
I enter'd.
Octavius.　　His audacity, no doubt,
Abated with his fortunes, and he droopt
As droops a lotus when the water fails.
Agrippa.　　Neither in life nor death will that man droop ;
He holds down Fortune, still too strong for her.
Octavius.　　We must then starve him out, or slay his sons,
Before his eyes.　　　　　　　　　　[20
Agrippa.　　　　　Thus nothing will remain
For him to fear, and every honest sword
Will skulk within its scabbard for mere shame.
This may not be the worst . . when brave men fall
By treachery, men like them avenge the blow ;
Antonius did it . . was Antonius blamed ?
Octavius.　　But who will answer for our own dear lives
If these boys live ?
Agrippa.　　　　　　I will . . the boys are mine.　　30
Octavius.　　Cæsarion is secure.
Agrippa.　　　　　　　　I do rejoice
At this.
Octavius.　　I wonder he hath not arrived.
Agrippa.　　Rescued from Egypt is the Roman lad ?
I long to see him.
Octavius.　　　　　Wait then, and thou shalt.
Agrippa.　　Women and eunuchs and Greek parasites
Educate ill those who may one day rule.
Octavius.　　True, very true . . we will bear this in mind.
Agrippa.　　He must learn better soon.　　　　[40

Octavius.   Be sure he shall.

Agrippa.   What are those sistrums and those tamborines
That trifle with the trumpet and intrude?

Octavius.   The very things that thou wouldst provide
     against.
Heigh! who commanded such obstreperous shouts?

Agrippa.   The man who gave us Egypt, sir, and thee.
The sound bursts louder from his hollow tomb:
Such are the honours which attend his child.

Octavius.   Hark! the arms strike the ground!   50

Agrippa.   Soldiers, well done!
Already do they know whom they salute.

Cæsarion.   Hail! hail! my cousin!
            Let me kiss that hand
So soft and white.   Why hold it back from me?
I am your cousin, boy Cæsarion.

Octavius.   Who taught you all this courtesy?

Cæsarion.   My heart.
Beside, my mother bade me wish you joy.

Octavius.   I would myself receive it from her.   60

Cæsarion.   Come,
Come then with me; none see her and are sad.

Octavius.   Then she herself is not so?

Cæsarion.   Not a whit,
Grave as she looks, but should be merrier still.

Octavius.   She may expect all bounty at our hands.

Cæsarion.   Bounty! she wants no bounty.
            Look around;
Those palaces, those temples, and their gods
And myriad priests within them, all are hers;   70
And people bring her ships, and gems, and gold.
    O cousin! do you know what some men say,
(If they do say it) that your sails ere long
Will waft all these away?
            I wish 'twere true
What else they talk.

Octavius.   What is it?

Cæsarion.   That you come

To carry off her also.

She is grown 80
Paler, and I have seen her bite her lip
At hearing this. Ha! well I know my mother;
She thinks it may look redder for the bite.
But will you really carry us to Rome
In triumph? thro' the streets, and up the hill,
And over arches . . foolish folks say under . .
With flowers all round them? O! what joy to see
The people that once loved my father so!
Octavius. We will do all that may oblige the queen.
Cæsarion. And yet she shudders at the very thought 90
Of those fresh honours which delight my heart.
Octavius. For her, or for yourself?
Cæsarion. We boys, you know,
Think of ourselves the first; and yet, and yet,
If my sweet mother is averse to change,
And weary of it, I would pass my days
With her; yes, even in that lonely tower
(Which to my eyes looks like a sepulchre)
Whence she protests the Gods alone shall take her.
Octavius (to a Guard). See due attention paid this royal
guest. 100
Cæsarion. Unwillingly I part from one so kind.
Octavius (to AGRIPPA). Agrippa, didst thou mark that
comely boy.
Agrippa. I did indeed.
Octavius. There is methinks in him
A somewhat not unlike our common friend.
Agrippa. Unlike? There never was such similar
Expression. I remember Caius Julius
In youth, altho' my elder by some years;
Well I remember that high-vaulted brow,
Those eyes of eagle under it, those lips 110
At which the senate and the people stood
Expectant for their portals to unclose;
Then speech, not womanly but manly sweet,
Came from them, and shed pleasure as the morn
Sheds light.

Octavius.   The boy has too much confidence.
Agrippa.   Not for his prototype.   When he threw back
That hair in hue like cinnamon, I thought
I saw great Julius tossing his, and warn
The pirates he would give them their desert.   120
     My boy, thou gazest at those arms hung round.
Cæsarion.   I am not strong enough for sword and shield,
Nor even so old as my sweet mother was
When I first rioted upon her knee
And seiz'd whatever sparkled in her hair.
Ah! you had been delighted had you seen
The pranks she pardon'd me.   What gentleness!
What playfulness!
Octavius.   Go now, Cæsarion.
Cæsarion.   And had you ever seen my father too!   130
He was as fond of her as she of me,
And often bent his thoughtful brow o'er mine
To kiss what she had kist, then held me out
To show how he could manage the refractory,
Then one long smile, one pressure to the breast.
Octavius.   How tedious that boy grows!
                                        Lead him away,
Aufidius!
               There is mischief in his mind,
He looks so guileless.   140
Agrippa.   He has lived apart
From evil counsellors, with grey-hair'd men
Averse to strife, and maidens of the queen.
Octavius.   This makes me think . .
                                   We will another time
Consider what is best.
                         Here comes Mecænas.
(*To* MECÆNAS.)   Cilnius! you met upon the stairs that boy?
Mecænas.   I did.
Octavius.   What think you of him?   150
Mecænas.   At one glance
'Twere rashness to decide.
Octavius.   Seems he not proud?
Mecænas.   He smiled and past me by.

Octavius.   What insolence! quite insupportable!
Mecænas.   Perhaps he knew me not; and, if he knew me,
I have no claim on affability
From Cæsar's enemies.
    Agrippa (to himself).   By Jove! the man
At first so calm begins at last to chafe.   160
O, the vain Tuscan of protuberant purse!
    Octavius.   What said Agrippa?
    Agrippa.   That our friend here chafes,
Altho' the mildest of all mortal men.
    Octavius.   Excepting one; one whom no wrongs can
        ruffle.
I must give orders for some small affairs,
And will rejoin you soon.
    Agrippa.   My gentle Cilnius!
Do save this lad! Octavius is so calm,
I doubt he hath some evil in his breast   170
Against the only scion of the house,
The orphan child of Julius.
    Mecænas.   Think, Agrippa,
If there be safety where such scion is,
Safety for you and me.
    Agrippa.   The mother must
Adorn the triumph, but that boy would push
Rome, universal Rome, against the steeds
That should in ignominy bear along
The image of her Julius.   Think; when Antony   180
Show'd but his vesture, sprang there not tears, swords,
Curses? and swept they not before them all
Who shared the parricide?   If such result
Sprang from torn garment, what must from the sight
Of that fresh image which calls back again
The latest of the Gods, and not the least,
Who nurtured every child within those walls,
And emptied into every mother's lap
Africa, Sicily, Sardinia, Gaul,
And this inheritance of mighty kings.   190
No such disgrace must fall on Cæsar's son.
Spare but the boy, and we are friends for ever.

Mecænas.   Friends are we, but Octavius is our master.
  Agrippa.   Let him brush kings away and blow off queens,
But there are some of us who never struck
At boys, nor trampled on a prostrate head ;
Some of us are there too who fain would see
Rome better than they left her, with high blood
Bounding along her veins ; enough hath flowed.
  Mecænas.   Here comes Octavius. We attend his will.   200
  Octavius.   Enough that I know yours, my truest friends !
I look into your hearts and find my own.
Thy wishes, O Agrippa, I divine.
Antony was thy comrade in the wars
Of Julius ; Fulvia was thy enemy
And mine : her children to the Infernal Gods
Devote I, but the born of Cleopatra
Thou shalt have saved : Cæsarion shall rest here.

SCENE THE NINTH.

Dolabella.   Cæsarion.   Scopas.

Dolabella.   Where hast thou put Cæsarion ?
Scopas.   Nigh at hand.
Dolabella.   What is he doing ?
Scopas.   Just what lads like most ;
Munching a water-melon.
                                    There is good,
At least good-nature, in that simple soul.
While most were sleeping in the night of noon
I brought him hither.   Thirsty were we both,
And wine I offer'd him : he pusht it by   10
And said, " I drink no wine ; bring water-melons."
I brought him one : he cut it fairly thro',
And gave me half before he toucht the other,
Saying, " but keep the seeds, the round and black,
That I may plant them, when we get to Rome,
With my own hands in garden all my own."

Dolabella.   Poor innocent!
Scopas.   I could not help but smile.
Dolabella.   For once I envy thee.
                                    But call him in.   20
Scopas.   Ho! youngster! here!
Cæsarion.   What means that loud rude speech?
This mah seems civiler; I may converse
With him, but never more, thou churl, with thee.
    Dolabella.   I would, my fair young friend, his voice less
        rough,
But honest Romans are sometimes abrupt.
Scopas is sorry.
    Cæsarion.   Honest! sorry too!
I then was wrong, and am more vext than he.
    Scopas.   Boy! I could wish I never saw thy face   30
Nor heard thy tongue.
    Cæsarion.   What can he mean?
    Dolabella.   He feels
The offence he gave.
    Cæsarion.   Good man, be comforted,
And let my hand atone for face and tongue.
    Scopas (to DOLABELLA).   That smile disarms me.
    Dolabella.   My sweet prince, observe
How he repents.
                    I have some words to speak   40
In private to him: but I first would hear
How fare your little brothers.
    Cæsarion.   They are gone,
Both gone: two maidens carried them away
Before a noble-looking man they call
Agrippa.
    Dolabella.   Gone? say you? and with Agrippa?
O that I could have seen them ere they went!
    Cæsarion.   No matter; I will tell you all about them,
It is not much, if you desire to know.   50
One can not talk, the other talks all day,
One smiles at me, the other pulls my hair,
But he smiles too, and then runs off as fleet
As my gazelle, yet easier to be caught.

You have heard all, and now will I return
And leave you, as you wish: I know my way.
   Dolabella.   The duty must be done; 'tis Cæsar's will.
   Scopas.   Then done it shall be.
   Dolabella.   Take this token: here;
Take this too; ninety golden of like weight   60
Lie in the leather.
   Scopas.   Thanks; the deed is done.
[*Alone.*]   What do these letters, bright and sharp, denote?
Cæsar Dictator; and what else beneath?
Perpetuo.
         Gods above!   *Perpetuo* too!
Ashes may be perpetual: nothing more
Remains of our dictator.   Take the urn,
Empty it, weigh it inwards: poise the two,
This inch-broad coin with it; and what I toss
On my forefinger is the solider   70
   I must go in.
   Cæsarion.   'Tis very kind in you
To visit me again: you bear no malice.
I know at once who loves me.
   Scopas.   And do I?
   Cæsarion.   One moment yes, one moment no.   My hand-
      some
And gentle cousin does not love me quite;
I wish he did, I want so to love *him.*
How cool and quiet is this small dim room!
It wants no cushion: I begin to think   80
The hard stone-seat refreshes more the limbs.
Will you not try?
   Scopas.   Not yet; but presently.
   Cæsarion.   My mother is not here; you need not mind.
People must not sit down before a queen;
But before boys, whatever boys they are,
Men may, and should.
             Oh! what can I have done?
And did you strike me?   Would you strike again?
What runs into my sandals from my breast?   90
Oh! it begins to pain me . . sadly, sadly!

Scopas.   By all the Gods and Goddesses above!
I have no strength to strike the boy again.
   Cæsarion.   O father! father! where is now that face
So gravely fond that bent o'er your Cæsarion?
And, mother! thou too gone!   In all this gloom
Where shall I find thee?   Scopas! Scopas! help!
   Scopas.   Away with me!   Where is the door?   Against
      it
Stands he? or follows he?   Crazed!   I am crazed!
O had but he been furious! had he struck me!   100
Struggled, or striven, or lookt despitefully!
Anything, anything but call my name
So tenderly.   O had that mild reproach
Of his been keener when his sense return'd,
Only to leave him ever-lastingly,
I might not have been, what I now am, frantic.
Upturn'd to me those wandering orbs, outspred
Those quivering arms, falling the last of him,
And striking once, and only once, the floor,
It shook my dagger to the very hilt,   110
And ran like lightning up into my brain.

SCENE THE TENTH.

Eros *and* Antony.

Antony.   Eros! I speak thee welcome.
Eros.   Hail, our lord!
Antony.   Thou hast been ever faithful to thy trust,
And spoken freely, but decorously,
On what concern'd the household and the state.
My glory is gone down, and life is cold
Without it.   I have known two honest men
Among the senators and consulars . .
   Eros.   None among humbler?
   Antony.   By the Powers above!   10
I thought but of the powerful, men of birth.
   Eros.   All men are that.   Some sink below their cradle,

Others rise higher than parental roof,
And want no sceptre to support their steps.
  Antony.   Such there may be whom we have all past by.
  Eros.   Men cast long shadows when their life declines,
Which we cross over without noticing;
We met them in the street and gave not way,
When they were gone we lifted up both hands,
And said to neighbours *These were men indeed!*   20
  Antony.   Reflections such as thine had wearied me
Erewhile, and from another even now;
But what is that thou bringest me wrapt up,
Tardy in offering it as worth too little?
  Eros.   I bring a ruby and a hollow ring
Whereon it fitted.
  Antony.   Gods of Rome! at last
Ye make me grateful.   Thanks, and thanks alone,
Have I to give, and one small sacrifice;
I vow it you before this hour is past.   30
My heart may beat against its bars awhile,
But shall not leave me yet.
                    Go, Eros, go,
I must lie down and rest, feeble and faint.
But come back presently.
  Eros (after some absence).   How fares our lord?
  Antony.   Recovered, sound again, more sound than ever.
  Eros.   And yet our lord looks more like other men.
  Antony (smiling).   We can not always swagger, always act
A character the wise will never learn: 40
When Night goes down, and the young Day resumes
His pointed shafts, and chill air breathes around,
Then we put on our own habiliments
And leave the dusty stage we proudly trod.
I have been sitting longer at life's feast
Than does me good; I will arise and go.
Philosophy would flatten her thin palm
Outspread upon my sleeve; away with her!
Cuff off, cuff out, that chattering toothless jade!
The brain she puzzles, and she blunts the sword: 50
Even she knows better words than that word *live.*

Cold Cato, colder Brutus, guide not me;
No, nor brave Cassius.
                    Thou hast brought me balm.
    Eros.   Our lord may have some message for the giver,
Which will console her.
    Antony.   She expected none:
I did; and it is come.
                    Say, lookt she pale?
Spake she no word?   60
    Eros.   Alas, most noble sir,
She would not see me.   Charmian said her face
Was indeed pale, yet grew less pale than usual
After she gave the ring, and then she spake
Amid some sighs (some spasms too interposed)
More cheerfully, and said she fain would sleep.
    Antony.   The fondest heart, the truest, beats no more.
She listened to me, she hath answered me,
She wanted no entreaty, she obeyed,
She now commands: but no command want I.   70
Queen of my soul! I follow in thy train,
Thine is the triumph.
                    Eros, up! rejoice!
Tears, man! do tears become us at this hour?
I never had too many; thou hast seen
(If thou didst see) the last of them.
                    My sword!
I will march out becomingly.
    Eros.   O sir!
Enemies watch all round, and famine waits   80
Within.
    Antony.   Thou knowest not the prudent sons
Of Egypt; corn and wine have been supplied
Enough for many years, piled underground.
Tho' stiffened by the sludge of barbarism,
Or indolent and overgorged at home,
Briton or German would take heed that none
Who fought for him should perish for the lack
Of sustenance: the timid bird herself
Will hover round and round until she bring   90

The grain cried out for in the helpless nest.
Give me my sword ! Is the point sharp ?
  Eros.   In vain
To trust it now !
  Antony.   Come, bring it ; let me try it.
  Eros. O heavens and earth ! Help ! help ! no help is
    nigh,
No duty left but one : less worthily
Than willingly this duty I perform.   [*Stabs himself.*
It pains not : for that blood I see no more.

SCENE THE ELEVENTH.

OFFICER. OCTAVIUS. MECÆNAS. GALLUS.

Officer. News ! glorious news ! news certain ! Dead as
  Death !
Octavius. Who dead ?
Officer.   The master of the horse to Julius,
Master too, but this morning, of this realm,
The great . .
  Mecænas. Halt there ! and know, where Cæsar is
There is none great but Cæsar !
  Officer.   Pardon ! true !
  Octavius. And nought about his paramour ?
  Officer.   The queen ? 10
  Octavius. Yes, fellow, yes.
  Officer.   Surely our emperor knows
Of her ; the story now is some days old.
The queen was poisoned by two little worms
Which people here call asps, most venomous things,
Coil'd in a yellow fig around the seeds.
Her maidens wail'd her loudly ; men and maidens
Alike mourn'd over . . I had nearly slipt.
  Octavius. Many have done the same.
                    Art thou a Roman ? 20
  Officer. I have the honour, sir, to be a Gaul,

A native of Massilia, that famed city
Inhabited by heroes, built by Gods,
Who entered it again with Caius Julius.
   Mecænas.   And didst thou see them enter?
Officer.   Not distinctly,
There were a few between : one told it me
Who saw them ; which, ye know, is just the same.
   Octavius.   Retire, my brave ! go sure of a reward.
Lucretia hath escaped us after all !   30
But there is wax in Egypt, there are Greeks
Who model it, and who can bear to look
On queen or asp ; this model'd to the life,
The other more like what they work upon.
No trouble in thus carrying her to Rome.
Gallus ! thou lookest grave : thou art the man
Exactly to compose an epitaph.
No matter which died first : I think the asps
Rather have had the start : I may be wrong,
A bad chronologist, a worse astrologer.   40
   Mecænas.   Where Cæsar smiles, all others smile but Gallus,
   Gallus.   Not even Cæsar's smiles awaken mine
When every enemy has dropt away,
And he who made so many safe, is safe.
   Mecænas.   I wish thou wert more joyous.
   Gallus.   Kind the wish,
Almost enough to make me so.
   Mecænas.   Come ! Come !
I know you poets : any wager now
Thou hast already forced the weeping Muse   50
To thy embraces.   Tell us honestly ;
Hast thou not turn'd the egg upon the nest
Ready for hatching ?
   Octavius.   Guilty ; look at him,
He blushes, blushes from cheekbone to beard.
Now, Gallus, for the epitaph.
   Mecænas.   Recite it.
   Gallus.   Epitaphs are but cold and chisel'd words,
Or mostly false if warmer : quite unfit
Are mine for marble or for memory.   60

I thought of her . . another would have said
He wept: I wept not, but I know I sigh'd.
 Mecænas. And wrote? For poet is half sigh half flame:
Sigh out thy sigh.
 Gallus.   Would Cæsar hear it?
 Octavius.   Yea.
 Gallus. I have not ventured to pronounce the name
Of her I meditated on.
 Cæsar.   My friend
Is here judicious as in all things else.   70
 Gallus. "Thou hast been floating on the o'erswollen
  stream
Of life these many summers; is thy last
Now over? hast thou dreamt out every dream?
 Hath horn funereal blown the pageant past?
Cæsar! thou too must follow: all the rods
 Of sternest lictor cannot scare off Death;
She claims the earth for heritage; our Gods
 Themselves have seen their children yield their breath."
 Cæsar. Gallus! I always thought thee a brave soldier,
Never a first-rate poet: I am right.   80
 Gallus. Cæsar! I never heard of one who gain'd
A battle and a kingdom who was not.
 Cæsar. If there be anything on earth I know
Better than other things, 'tis poetry.
 Mecænas. My sweet Octavius! draw not under nose
The knuckle of forefinger. Gallus aim'd
A harmless arrow: Love in sport hath done it
Often and often.
     Gallus, seize his hand.
Now sing a pæan; sing a prophet's; sing   90
Egypt! thy pyramid of power is closed.
 Gallus. I would; but want the breath: I have but
  strength
For elegy: here is the last of mine.
   "The mighty of the earth are earth,
    A passing gleam the brightest smile,
   In golden beds have sorrows birth,
    Alas! these live the longer while."

Octavius.   Unless we haste to supper, we shall soon
Forfeit our appetites.   Come, my two friends!

SCENE THE TWELFTH.

OCTAVIUS *and* OCTAVIA.

Octavius.   Embrace me, sister ; we have won ; thy wrongs
Are now avenged.
    Octavia.   Speak not of wrong, but right,
And bring Rome peace and happiness once more.
'Tis kind in thee (but thou wert always kind)
To come so soon to greet me, while the altar
Is warm and damp with incense for thy safety.
    Octavius.   Octavia ! I have brought thee from the Nile
Two pretty little serpents.
    Octavia.   Of all beasts   10
The serpent is the beast I most abhor.
Take them away.
    Octavius.   I have not brought them here,
Be not afraid ; beside, they are so young
They can not bite.
    Octavia.   But send them off.
    Octavius.   I will.
What thinkest thou are these two reptiles call'd ?
    Octavia.   I know not, nor can guess.
    Octavius.   *Lucius and Marcus,* 20
The brood of Antony.
                O Heaven ! she faints !
Rise, sister ! let me help thee up ; be sure
They shall not hurt thee.   Grasp not thus my wrist,
And shoot not up those leaden bolts at me,
For such are thy stiff eyes.   I said, and swear,
The little monsters never shall hurt *thee.*
I do not like those tears ; but better they
Than the cold flint they fall from, and now melt.
    Octavia.   Brother, I know thy purpose.   On my
      knees . .   30

Octavius.   Arise! There wants not this to seal their
doom.
Octavia.   This is my fault, not theirs, if fault there be.
Octavius.   I want, and I will have, security.
Octavia.   What is there now on earth to apprehend?
Octavius.   I dread lest he who guards them should adopt.
Octavia.   Let him! O let him! if an honest man.
Frown not, debate not, struggle not against
Thy better Genius; argue with him thus,
" *Octavius! has there not been blood enough*
Without the blood of children?"   40
Octavius.   Is my safety
Not dear to thee?
Octavia.   Thy glory, thy content,
Are . . no, not dearer, but almost as dear.
Hast thou not suffer'd pangs at every head
That fell?
Octavius.   They fell that mine might not.
Octavia.   But children
Strike not so high.
Octavius.   Are children always children?   50
Octavia.   O brother, brother! are men always men?
They are full-grown then only when grown up
Above their fears.   Power never yet stood safe;
Compass it round with friends and kindnesses,
And not with moats of blood.   Remember Thebes:
The towers of Cadmus toppled, split asunder,
Crasht: in the shadow of her oleanders
The pure and placid Dirce still flows by.
What shatter'd to its base but cruelty,
(Mother of crimes, all lesser than herself)   60
The house of Agamemnon king of kings?
Octavius.   Thou art not yet, Octavia, an old woman;
Tell not, I do beseech thee, such old tales.
Octavia.   Hear later; hear what our own parents saw.
Where lies the seed of Sulla?   Could the walls
Of his Præneste shelter the young Marius,
Or subterranean passages provide
Escape? he stumbled through the gore his father

Had left in swamps on our Italian plains.
We have been taught these histories together, 70
Neither untrue nor profitless ; few years
Have since gone by, can memory too have gone ?
Ay, smile, Octavius ! only let the smile
Be somewhat less disdainful.
   Octavius.   'Tis unwise
To plant thy foot where Fortune's wheel runs on.
   Octavia.   I lack not wisdom utterly ; my soul
Assures me wisdom is humanity,
And they who want it, wise as they may seem,
And confident in their own sight and strength, 80
Reach not the scope they aim at.
                        Worst of war
Is war of passion ; best of peace is peace
Of mind, reposing on the watchful care
Daily and nightly of the household Gods.

APPENDIX.

CONTENTS, NOTES, AND BIBLIOGRAPHY.

[Count Julian, a tragedy, 1812 ; Gebir, Count Julian, and Other Poems, 1831 ; Works, ii., 1846. The best account of the events which led to the Moorish Invasion of Spain is to be found in Mariana, " De Rebus Hispaniæ," Vol. i. From this source Landor has evidently derived his materials, though in his hands Count Julian has ceased to be the renegade at whose name "each good Spaniard spits," and has turned to the tragic figure who, to punish an evil King, has brought on his country worse ills than those from which he would have freed her. The Gothic kings of Spain held their thrones by election ; but at the date of these events, two families seemed to divide the right to the throne between them, that of Chindasuinthus and that of Wamba. Chindasuinthus, who succeeded Wamba, was followed by his son, but on that king's death his two brothers Theodofred and Favila were passed over in favour of Witiza, the son of Wamba. Witiza proved a bad and cruel king. He put Favila to death, and some declared that an unholy love for Favila's wife was the motive of the deed. He put out the eyes of Theodofred and thereby prepared his own doom. Roderick, the son of Theodofred, rebelled against Witiza, deposed and blinded him, and was elected to the throne in his place. But Witiza's brother Opas retained his position as Archbishop of Seville, his sister was the wife of Count Julian, and his two sons Eba and Sisabert still remained to represent the family of Wamba. Roderick proved little better than Witiza, and his insult to Count Julian's daughter drew down on him the vengeance of the Count and brought the Moors into Spain. It is at this point that Landor takes up the story. It is only necessary to add that the love of Sisabert for Corilla is not mentioned by Mariana.]

IPPOLITO DI ESTE   .   .   .   70

[Gebir, Count Julian, and Other Poems, 1831; Works, ii., 1846. *See* Sismondi's Italian Republics, xiii. p. 326. Landor has altered many of the incidents of the tragedy. The Cardinal caused Giulio to be seized at a hunting party, and endeavoured to have his eyes put out. Sismondi says the sight was only injured, not destroyed. The Duke Alfonso took no steps to punish this outrage; and the two brothers Ferdinand and Giulio formed a conspiracy to assassinate both Alfonso and Ippolito. The plot was discovered; both were thrown into prison. Ferdinand died there, but Giulio lived to be released in 1559. It will be noticed that Landor has interchanged the names of the two brothers.]

THE SHADES OF AGAMEMNON AND IPHIGENEIA   78

[Pericles and Aspasia, 1836. Pericles and Aspasia, Works, 1846; The Hellenics of Walter Savage Landor, 1859.
Landor's own criticism on this is well deserved. In the Satire on Satirists, he writes—

    " From eve to morn, from morn to parting night
    Father and daughter stood within my sight.
    I felt the looks they gave, the words they said,
    And reconducted each serener shade,
    Even shall these to me be well spent days,
    Sweet fell the tears upon them, sweet the praise,
    Far from the footstool of the tragic throne,
    I am tragedian in that scene alone."]

THE DEATH OF CLYTEMNESTRA   .   .   .   85

[Friendly Contributions for the Benefit of Three Infant Schools in the Parish of Kensington. Printed solely for the Right Honourable the Lady Mary Fox, 1836; The Pentameron and Pentalogia, 1837; Works, ii., 1846; The Hellenics of Walter Savage Landor, 1859.]

THE MADNESS OF ORESTES   .   .   87

[Ablett's Literary Hours, 1837; The Pentameron and Pentalogia. 1837; Pericles and Aspasia, Works, 1846; The Hellenics of Walter Savage Landor, 1859; Ablett's Literary Hours does not contain I. 53 and II. 76 to 80.]

[Andrea of Hungary and Giovanna of Naples, 1839; Fra Rupert, 1841; Andrea of Hungary, Giovanna of Naples, and Fra Rupert, a trilogy, in Works, ii., 1846.

The events which form the subject of this series of plays can be found in Sismondi's History of the Italian Republics. Landor has altered history so much in his attempt to exculpate Giovanna, that it is necessary to place here a more accurate and more complete account of the events which he describes.

Charles of Anjou, the brother of St Louis, left to his heirs claims to the kingdoms of Hungary and Naples. His great-grandson, Charles Robert, or Caribert, secured the throne of Hungary but was deprived of that of Naples by his uncle Robert. That king, after a long reign, died in 1343, leaving his grand-daughter Giovanna heir to the throne. Charles Robert of Hungary left two sons. The elder, Louis of Hungary, succeeded to the crown of Hungary. The younger, Andrea of Hungary, had been brought up at Naples under the care of Fra Rupert, a monk of whom Boccaccio in his letters gives an account which Landor has clearly copied. Before his death, King Robert tried to conciliate the Hungarian party by marrying Andrea to his daughter. But Giovanna was already closely bound by affection to Louis of Tarentum, her cousin. Andrea was a rough, uneducated lad, who could not forget that he was the rightful heir to the throne of Naples. He was jealous—and that with good cause—of Louis of Tarentum ; and the corrupt courtiers who surrounded the queen had not much difficulty in persuading her to consent to his death. On the 18th of September 1845, at Aversa, Andrea was summoned from the Queen's room on some pretext, a silk rope was thrown round his neck, and after a short struggle he was thrown out of the window and strangled. Isolda, his nurse, alarmed by the struggle, ran into the Queen's room just as the crime had been accomplished. The Pope Clement VI. determined to have the plot investigated, and charged Bertrand de Baux, justiciar of Naples, with this task. Filippa the Catanian, who had planned the conspiracy, was arrested with other suspected servants of the Queen; Filippa died under torture, and the other prisoners were secretly executed. Giovanna then wrote to Louis of Hungary to defend herself against the suspicions which had been aroused against her. Louis of Hungary answered briefly: "Giovanna, your former misconduct, the ambition you displayed in clinging to the crown, your neglect to exact the punishment of the criminals, the excuses you now offer, all these show that you were an accomplice in your husband's murder." Not content with this he sent an embassy to the Pope to demand the deposition of Giovanna and prepared to make war upon her. He even indicted her before Rienzi, then Tribune of Rome ; ambassadors from both sides pleaded the cause, but Rienzi never gave judgment. In 1347 Giovanna married Louis of Tarentum, and thereby confirmed the general opinion of her guilt. The following year Louis of Hungary led his army into Naples, and Giovanna fled to Provence. The victory was stained by one deed of blood. Charles of Durazzo, one of King Robert's nephews, had married Maria, the sister of Giovanna. But he had taken no part in the murder of Andrea and he had aided Louis of Hungary in his invasion of Naples. Nevertheless, in an access of passion, Louis of Hungary had him put to death at Aversa, in the very place where Andrea had been murdered. All the other princes of the blood royal of Naples were carried into Hungary, and among them the young son of Giovanna and Andrea.

The Black Death, however, compelled the Hungarian King to leave Naples, and at the end of the year Giovanna and Louis of Tarentum returned there. They succeeded in gaining back most of the kingdom which had been left under the care of Conrad Guilford, a captain of mercenaries, who grievously oppressed the country. In 1351, the intervention of the Pope was invoked, and after some negotiations a peace was effected between Louis of Hungary and Giovanna. The Queen was pronounced innocent, or if guilty, her guilt was attributed to witchcraft. Louis of Tarentum was recognised as King of Naples, and matters were settled for a time. Landor has made no use of Giovanna's story from this date until the year 1379, when the third part of the trilogy may be supposed to begin. Of the house of Anjou there now remained only Louis of Hungary, Giovanna, and Charles of Durazzo, nephew of the Charles whose death has already been described, and the husband of Margarita his daughter. Charles of Durazzo was thus heir to the crowns of Naples and Hungary, for Giovanna had no children living. He had been brought up in Hungary, and was thus by education no friend to Giovanna. Moreover, the Pope Urban VI. had found in the Queen a determined enemy. She had allowed an Antipope to be elected in her dominions, and he was quite ready to avenge the insult by helping Charles to drive her from the throne. Giovanna herself supplied Charles with a reason for action. She endeavoured to exclude him from the throne by adopting Louis, Count of Anjou, the brother of Charles V., king of France, as her heir. In 1380, Charles of Durazzo appeared in Rome. Urban IV. crowned him King of Naples, and received in return the promise that Francis Prignano, his nephew, should receive large fiefs in Naples. The only forces at Giovanna's disposal were the few men whom Otho of Brunswick, her fourth husband, had collected. Otho was afraid to risk a battle, and on the 16th July 1381. Charles took possession of Naples and laid siege to the Castle in which Giovanna had taken refuge. The siege only lasted a few weeks, and on the 20th August famine compelled the Queen to promise to surrender the fortress and all her possessions to Charles, unless Otho should relieve her within four days. Otho did his best; he attacked Charles with all the forces he could collect, he himself was taken prisoner, and his men utterly defeated. Giovanna was seized and imprisoned in the castle of Muro. A few months afterwards she died, smothered, it was believed, under a feather-bed. The above sketch will show how far Landor's view of Giovanna differs from that usually given by historians. In his article on " Petrarca " he tells the story in prose. The passage will do to conclude a note already too long.

" But his [Petrarca's] justice, his humanity, his gratitude, were called into action elsewhere.

" Ten years had elapsed since his mission to the court of Naples. The King Andreas had been assassinated, and the Queen Giovanna was accused of the crime. Andreas had alienated from him all the Neapolitans, excepting the servile, which in every court form a party, and in most a majority. Luigi of Taranto, the Queen's cousin, loved her from her childhood, but left her at that age. Graceful and gallant as he was, there is no evidence that she placed too implicit and intimate a confidence in him. Never has any great cause been judged with less discretion by posterity. The Pope, to whom she appealed in person, and who was deeply interested in her condemnation, with all the cardinals and all the judges, unanimously and unreservedly acquitted her of participation. or connivance, or knowledge. Giannone, the most impartial and temperate of historians, who neglected no sources of information, bears testimony in her behalf. Petrarca and Boccaccio, men abhorrent from every atrocity, never mention her but with gentleness and compassion. The writers of the country. who were nearest to her person and her times, acquit her of all complicity. Nevertheless, she has been placed in the dock by the side of Mary Stuart. It is as certain that Giovanna was *not* guilty as that Mary *was*. She acknowledged before the whole Pontifical Court her hatred of her husband; and, in the simplicity of her heart, attributed it to magic. How different was the magic of Othello on Desdemona! and this too was believed."

THE SIEGE OF ANCONA   .   .   .   274

[Works, ii., 1846. Landor has followed his authorities closely in this play. Erminia and Stamura are not mentioned by Master Buoncompagno Florentino, the author of the "Liber de obsidione Anconae," printed in Muratori, vi. 925. But in its main lines the play is historical. The date of the siege is 1174.]

ANTONY AND OCTAVIUS   325

[Antony and Octavius, Scenes for the Study, 1856.]